PSYCHOLOGICAL FOUNDATIONS OF ECONOMIC BEHAVIOR

PSYCHOLOGICAL FOUNDATIONS OF ECONOMIC BEHAVIOR _____

Edited by Paul J. Albanese

With a Foreword by Tibor Scitovsky

PRAEGER

New York
Westport, Connecticut
London

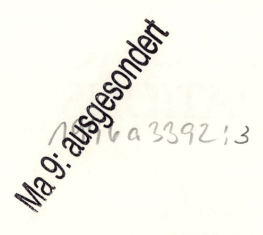

Library of Congress Cataloging-in-Publication Data

Psychological foundations of economic behavior.

Based on papers presented at an international
conference held in the fall of 1985 at the Bread Loaf
campus of Middlebury College.
Includes bibliographies and index.
1. Economics—Psychological aspects—Congresses.
I. Albanese, Paul J.
HB74.P8P698   1988   330′.01′9   87-38476
ISBN 0-275-92742-3 (alk. paper)

Library of Congress Catalog Card Number: 87-38476

ISBN: 0-275-92742-3

First published in 1988

Praeger Publishers, One Madison Avenue, New York, NY 10010
A division of Greenwood Press, Inc.

Printed in the United States of America

The paper used in this book complies with the
Permanent Paper Standard issued by the National
Information Standards Organization (Z39.48-1984).

10 9 8 7 6 5 4 3 2 1

CONTENTS

FOREWORD

Tibor Scitovsky

For the past fifteen years, I have been one of a handful of people who have tried to introduce psychology into economics. In one sense, we have been quite successful. Economists and psychologists are both now aware of the affinity between their two disciplines; and economic psychology as well as psychological or behavioral economics have become new fields, each with its own specialists, association, journal, and conferences (such as the one whose papers are reprinted in this volume).

In another sense, however, our success has been very limited. I had hoped not so much to create a special, psychological branch of economics as to infuse some psychology into the general framework of the discipline. This has happened, thanks to Herbert Simon, in the theory of the firm. It has not yet happened in the economic theory of the individual consumer or worker. One reason for this is the much greater variety and complexity of individuals' satisfactions, their many forms and sources, and the varied nature of their possible conflicts. This variety makes it very difficult to create a unified framework of individual economic behavior.

Psychologists have dealt with many of the varieties and complexities of human behavior motivation; but, as is usual in psychology, each has adopted the framework most appropriate to his own investigation; few have tried to relate their own research to other psychologists' findings. The voluminous literature of psychology lacks a common framework. If economists can be faulted for making overly simplistic assumptions about human motivations in the interest of a unified theoretical framework, psychologists can be criticized for erring in the opposite direction.

The difference between the two disciplines' approaches may be one reason why each can learn from the other; but it also explains why it is so hard to transplant psychologists' findings into the economist's framework. Economists are justly proud of the great advantages they enjoy as a result of having a common theoretical language, despite their very different ideological judgments and policy recommendations. The profession's reluctance to sacrifice this is understandable; and in this reluctance is the source of the difficulty in introducing psychologists' insights about human motivations and conflicts into the economist's world (especially since psychologists themselves have not yet managed to sort out and integrate them into an orderly framework).

More by my economist's instinct than by conscious design, I focused my attention on one of the few examples of psychologists' trying to bring order into chaos: the work of that small group of physiological psychologists who tried to explain behavior by people's (and animals') desire for the pleasurable arousal or activation of their central nervous system. This approach integrates people's desire to avoid pain and satisfy biological needs, not only with their social needs, such as the desire to emulate or outshine others, but also with the seeking of stimulation and excitement. Indeed, this approach can even explain and accommodate the conflict between the individual's desire for comfort and his desire for pleasure. This, however, is only one of psychologists' many findings that economists should become aware of and integrate, if possible, into their own discipline.

All these papers, along with my and other people's previous work in this field, constitute building blocks for the construction of a better economics. I hope they will be found useful by other workers in the field, for the difficult task of putting these building blocks together remains to be done.

INTRODUCTION

Paul J. Albanese

The exploration of the relationship between economics and psychology has been a steadily growing area of research. This volume represents the depth of interest in this area, and the progress that has been made in bridging the fields of economics and psychology. The papers collected in this volume represent a broad range of economic issues that are now being addressed by economists and psychologists, and it is hoped that this volume will serve as an indispensable resource for further research on the psychological foundations of economic behavior.

The two principal objectives for bringing psychology into economics are broadening the behavioral basis of economic analysis and expanding the limits of applicability of economic theory. Broadening the behavioral foundations of economic analysis calls for placing increased emphasis in economics on the observation of behavior. Expanding the limits of applicability of economic theory calls for the elevation of taste considerations to a position equal to that of prices and income.

To achieve these objectives, the first task is to establish a theoretical relationship between psychology and economics. This requires that two fundamental methodological issues be resolved: First, what is the common ground of analysis that bridges the disciplines of psychology and economics? Second, what is the integrative framework that brings the contributions of psychology into economics in a systematic way?

A common ground of analysis and an integrative framework are established by using a variety of approaches borrowed from psychology. Particular emphasis is placed on psychological theories of the individual personality, using primarily physiological, psychoanalytic, and interpersonal approaches to the personality. An ultimate objective for establishing a relationship between psychology and economics is to overcome the individual orientation of economic theory to form a broader social basis for economic analysis.

Once a theoretical relationship has been established, the contributions from psychology can be considered. In other words, we must ask of any contribution from psychology, "What does it have to do with economics?" The combined approach, embracing the disciplines of economics and psychology, is applied to an investigation of the economic implications of the behavior of the individual consumer, executive, and entrepreneur.

Much of the first part of this volume on the behavior of the consumer was inspired by the pioneering work of Tibor Scitovsky. In *The Joyless Economy: An Inquiry into Human Satisfaction and Consumer Dissatisfaction* (1976), Scitovsky borrowed primarily from physiological psychology. He is a central figure in the movement to bring psychology into economics, and his work represents a turning point in establishing the field of psychology and economics. Scitovsky's work, and physiological psychology, is strongly represented in this volume.

In the first paper in this volume, "Novelty, Comfort, and Pleasure: Inside the Utility-Function Black Box," Shlomo Maital attempts to model mathematically the basic theory Scitovsky presented in *The Joyless Economy*. This represents an effort to address the question of why greater wealth does not seem to have brought greater well-being. Maital's contributions to the field of psychology and economics are well known from *Minds, Markets, and Money: The Psychological Foundations of Economic Behavior* (1982). It is Maital's contention that, unless a psychological contribution can be incorporated into a mathematical model, it will not be acceptable or accessible to economists and, therefore, will not have an impact on mainstream economics. An objective for each economic application in this volume is to explore the potential for providing a mathematical model of behavior in an optimization framework.

Richard L. Solomon's little piece, "How the Opponent-Process Theory of Acquired Motivation Came Into Economics," is a masterpiece of wit and wisdom that describes how his work became known to economists. Opponent-process theory makes a very fundamental contribution to the economic analysis of consumer behavior—every act of consumption has both a positive and negative aspect. This contribution is the basis for repairing the misconception in economics that utility represents only pleasure or satisfaction from consumption behavior, which makes the analysis of consumption behavior more realistic. It also opens the way for a consideration of addictive and compulsive behavior, along with the pattern of normal consumption behavior, and thus expands the behavioral basis of economic analysis.

Lester D. Taylor's contribution to the volume, "A Model of Consumption and Demand Based on Psychological Opponent Processes," is based on Richard Solomon's opponent-process theory of motivation, which was brought to the attention of economists by Scitovsky in *The Joyless Economy*. This theory is based on extensive evidence from experimental psychology, and Taylor has succeeded in bringing a credible theory from psychology into the economic theory of the consumer, and reformulating the mathematical model of the consumer to incorporate this contribution in a systematic way. This is an important contribution to economic analysis that covers all of the issues from relating psychology and economics, elaborating the economic implications, and providing an economic application in a mathematical optimization model. It strengthens the appeal of the contributions that psychology can make to economics by demonstrating that they can be made useful to mainstream economic analysis.

In my own paper, "The Intimate Relations of the Consistent Consumer: Psychoanalytic Object Relations Theory Applied to Economics," the analysis of consumer behavior is carried even further and again builds on Scitovsky's work. This paper draws heavily on psychoanalytic theory to explore the behavior of the individual consumer. It emphasizes the relationship between the personality of the individual consumer and the pattern of consumption behavior which is a reflection of that personality. In *The Joyless Economy,* Scitovsky suggested that differences in tastes actually represent different personality types, and argued that differences in individual personality could be arranged along a continuum. This approach is elaborated in this paper; variations of consumption behavior with the personality of the individual consumer are arrayed along a personality continuum. An important finding of this study is that ordinal utility theory is strikingly supported by some ranges along the personality continuum, but not by other ranges which represent commonly observed patterns of consumption behavior. In particular, compulsive and addictive behavior cannot be modeled using a mainstream mathematical framework, and an alternative optimization model is offered. The use of psychoanalytic theory brings into economics yet another branch of psychology and, along with it, a wealth of findings which draw heavily on the contributions from clinical analysis.

The paper by Manfred F. R. Kets de Vries and Danny Miller, "Personality, Culture, and Organization," brings the analysis around to the theory of the firm, while continuing the use of psychoanalytic theory. This work represents a sophisticated combination of two distinct bodies of theory—Miller's work on classifying types of organizations and Kets de Vries' work using psychoanalytic categories to classify the personality types of executives. The collaboration has resulted in an exploration of the impact of the executive's personality on the functioning of the organization. This paper is an extension of this fruitful collaboration which links the personality of the executive to the strategy of the organization by using the concept of organizational culture.

Abraham Zaleznik pioneered the use of psychoanalytic theory in economics, and his paper, "Decisions, Coalitions, and the Economy of the Self," is perhaps the deepest and most penetrating in the volume. This paper is a thoughtful and careful consideration of various uses of psychology in economics and, although a long and difficult paper, it is a thorough critique of the uses of psychoanalytic theory in economics. A fundamental contribution to the volume, it represents an attempt to consider the efficacy of using psychological theory to overcome the individual orientation of economic theory and provide a social basis for analysis.

The limitations of the use of game theory for this purpose are intensively explored, and the later parts of the paper focus on the central role of personality by drawing on the extensive literature on leadership from political psychology.

Joshua Ronen's paper, "The Entrepreneur and Society," carries the exploration into the realm of entrepreneurial behavior. Entrepreneurial studies are very much in vogue now, and this study is distinguished by drawing on the wealth of approaches that have been developing in economics since Joseph Schumpeter's important contributions. Ronen's approach is distinctly social in orientation, and contributes directly to a major objective of the volume—to overcome the individual orientation of economic theory—and opens the way to an even broader consideration of social behavior. While this approach can accommodate individual differences in personality, it implicitly questions the usefulness of doing so in the case of entrepreneurial activity.

In Amitai Etzioni's paper, "Toward a New Paradigm," a distinguished sociologist considers the essential question, "Where do we go from here?" The consideration of the social implications of economic analysis is a constant reminder of the need to transcend the individual orientation of economic theory. He has laid out a clear research agenda for broadening the behavioral foundations of economic analysis and expanding the limits of applicability of economic theory. Primary emphasis is placed on the factors that shape preferences, a reconsideration of the postulates of rationality, the recognition that all economic activity is embedded in the society, and on enhancing the empirical study of economic behavior. This paper is a forward-looking statement of the goals that future research on the psychological foundations of economic behavior must strive to attain. The difficult issue of whether these objectives can be achieved without establishing a new discipline is raised, and this harks back to Scitovsky's concerns expressed in the Foreword.

The papers in this volume grew out of an international conference on psychology and economics that took place in the fall of 1985 at the Bread Loaf Campus of Middlebury College, Middlebury, Vermont. It was attended by many more scholars than are represented in the papers presented here, and it is hoped that the contributions, as well as the spirit, of all those who attended the conference are reflected in the pages of this volume.

PSYCHOLOGICAL
FOUNDATIONS
OF
ECONOMIC
BEHAVIOR

1

NOVELTY, COMFORT, AND PLEASURE: INSIDE THE UTILITY-FUNCTION BLACK BOX

Shlomo Maital

> . . . we have a dilemma: we must choose between pleasure at some sacrifice of comfort and more complete comfort at the sacrifice of pleasure. . . . The gain in comfort is obvious and instantaneous; the loss of pleasure is almost certain to dawn upon us gradually, only later. . . . What is more natural than that the first should outweigh the second more often than will seem rational afterwards? . . . It is reasonable to assume that the greater immediacy and clearer perception of the gain in comfort establish a bias in its favor with many people.
> —Tibor Scitovsky, *The Joyless Economy*

INTRODUCTION

Have we economists lost the art of asking good questions? Smith, Mill, Marshall, Pigou, and Keynes all mastered the art. Their questions pierced to the core of human existence, even though, as Scitovsky (1985) observes, their answers were often vague. Modern economics has become, in Richard Cyert's phrase, a branch of applied mathematics, preoccupied with building precise, rigorous answers to often banal questions. Historians of science claim this is the way science progresses—incrementally, assembling small slivers of knowledge into a large woodpile. This is certainly what scientists do, for the most part. Yet there is another type of scientific progress, one that resembles the Grand National steeplechase at Ascot—a series of great hazardous leaps, at which many competitors stumble and fall, interspersed with normal strides. Winning the race requires skill at both leaps and steps. In science, as in horse races, it is the leaps that arouse the crowd. In economics, attempted leaps are overly scarce. Tibor Scitovsky's book, *The Joyless Economy,* is one of the most interesting, significant, and original of such attempts.

In *The Wealth of Nations* (1776), Adam Smith pondered why some nations (and individuals) are rich and others are poor. In *The Joyless Economy* (1976), two centuries later, Scitovsky asked why, in Western society, unprecedented material wealth has not made us happy.[1] Surely this is the King Kong of social science questions, and perhaps the inevitable successor to Adam Smith's key question. It is a question both positive and normative in nature; positive, because happiness can be measured and its antecedents observed,[2] and normative, because welfare economics is built on the implicit value judgment that more is better than less. If well-being is more or less equal in the presence of "more" and "less," then most of what we know about positive economics must be scrapped, because it is irrelevant, and most of what we know about normative economics must be discarded, because it is wrong. Others have nibbled at pieces of this question [Galbraith (1957), Linder (1970)] but Tibor Scitovsky tackled it whole. His contribution in restoring dash and sparkle to our research agenda cannot be overestimated.

The utility-function black box that pervades microeconomic theory is a continuing scandal, as incongruous as a kerosene lamp in the space shuttle. Scitovsky pried it open. He had the vision to see, not a twice-differentiable function convex in goods and income with positive first derivative and negative second derivative, but a complex mechanism in which novelty, comfort, and pleasure warred and competed with one another.

The objective of this paper is to explore further the inner workings of the utility function, in order to better understand the causal link between wealth and well-being. I propose to reinterpret and reinforce Scitovsky's theory, by focusing on the key role played by *time*—*when* we consume, and not solely how much—a link stated explicitly in the passage from *The Joyless Economy* cited earlier.

The next section presents empirical evidence showing that people do not in fact believe that material well-being is the most important, or even *one* of the most important, determinants of personal happiness. Next, a general social-psychological model of behavior is proposed, followed by a graphic portrayal of the comfort-pleasure trade-off on which *The Joyless Economy* focuses. The next section discusses "novelty" as a component of utility, and the trade-off between comfort and novelty. Then the welfare-impairing aspects of freely available credit are discussed, followed by an examination of how, in general, welfare-improving constraints should be modeled theoretically. The next section explores and expands on some of Scitovsky's ideas concerning our diminished pleasure from work, and the last section summarizes and concludes.

WEALTH AND WELL-BEING

Before attempting to elucidate Scitovsky's hypothesis about why material prosperity has not made us happy, it is important to observe that most people clearly know that this is the case. Empirical evidence on values—what things are important in life, what makes us happy—indicates that money and wealth rank far down the list.

A study published by the Bureau of the Census (see Table 1.1) places "money" tenth in the list of things that determine "the qualities of a happy life," though a smaller proportion of respondents were "satisfied" with the amount they had than of any other variable (except education).

A study by Shlomit Levy (1986) in Israel uses a technique known as multidimensional scaling to "map" twenty-eight different values, with distances between values proportional to their correlations. "Be rich" is far distant from the

Table 1.1
"Which of the following things are important to a person's happiness?"

While economists and utility theory seem to associate happiness with wealth, ordinary people do not. An empirical evaluation of what people think are the "qualities of a happy life" revealed the following result:

QUALITY	% who felt it is very important	% who said they were "very satisfied" with current level
GOOD HEALTH	97 %	53 %
FAMILY LIFE	92	67
PEACE OF MIND	91	51
RESPECT FROM OTHERS	85	60
FRIENDS	81	63
EDUCATION	79	25
WORK	60	42
RELIGION	57	57
MONEY	47	25
SEX	38	52
ROMANTIC LOVE	33	40

Source: Bureau of the Census, 1980: Statistical Indicators.

Note: Money is notably far down the list, though the ratio of percent who felt the current level was satisfactory and the percent who felt it was important was the second lowest of all items (education was the lowest, with only a quarter of respondents satisfied with their current level, even though 79 percent felt education was very important to happiness).

centroid ("Happy life"), more distant than any other variable except possibly "Travel abroad." (See Figure 1.1.)

A passage from *Sylvia Porter's Money Book* (1975) provides a possible explanation. In a box titled "Scraping by on $40,000 a Year" (in 1974 dollars), she shows how a family income perhaps two or three times the national average can be quite inadequate—in the familiar life-cycle race between the hare of wants and needs, and the greyhound of means and income, somehow the hare stays just ahead. (In Table 1.2 Porter's passage is paraphrased and the numbers updated to 1982.)

What follows is an attempt to construct a general model of behavior followed by a specific model of the comfort-pleasure trade-off able to elucidate *The Joyless Economy* and the anomie caused by excess affluence and comfort. A mathematical version of the model is given in the Appendix.

GENERAL MODEL OF BEHAVIOR

The expected-utility theory of von Neumann and Morgenstern (1944) and the axioms that underlie it remain the cornerstone of the economic theory of choice under uncertainty. According to this theory, individuals make decisions in order to maximize the probability of an outcome multiplied by the utility value of that outcome, summed over all possible outcomes, subject to constraints on their income or wealth and on the nature and range of uncertain choices available to them. Knowledge of the probability distribution of the outcomes, the individual's utility function, and the constraints permits calculation of the optimal decision.

Work by Tversky and Kahneman (1977, 1979) and others has revealed that none of the key axioms underlying expected-utility theory—completeness, transitivity, independence, substitution—describe how people really behave. In this sense, expected-utility theory is too shallow to provide a useful empirical model of behavior.

Perhaps a more serious problem is that expected-utility theory is also too narrow; its two-dimensional view of behavior (probability times utility) ignores three other important dimensions of behavior. Walter Mischel (1977, p. 345), a leading theorist about personality, has argued that "individual differences in behavior may be caused by differences in [five] . . . person variables":

— construction competencies: how people perceive their competence or ability to carry out chosen behaviors and response patterns;

— encoding: how people categorize (group and label events and how they construe themselves and others);

— expectancies: the subjective probabilities people attach to various outcomes;

— subjective values: the perceived utility of those outcomes;

— self-regulatory systems and plans: self-imposed standards, consequences, contingency rules and plans, that specify performance levels the person must achieve and the consequences of attaining (or failing to attain) those standards.

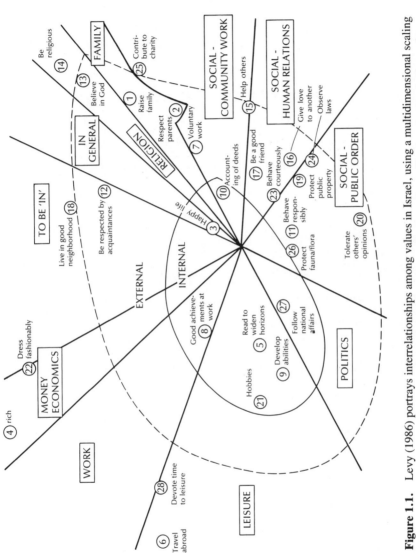

Figure 1.1. Levy (1986) portrays interrelationships among values in Israel, using a multidimensional scaling algorithm known as SSA-I. A two-dimensional cross section of a four-dimensional projection is shown here. "Be rich" is far distant from "Happy life" and very weakly correlated with other values. Similar results have been obtained for other countries.

Table 1.2
The Economics of the "Rat Race"

Billy, an $80,000-a-year executive, is in an income bracket inhabited by only a tiny fraction of Americans, yet feels pinched; he and his family have adopted such money-saving measures as adjusting the engine on their foreign car to run on regular gasoline, told the local druggist to cut by 20% the number of pills in all prescriptions filled for the family, buy underwear at a factory outlet with savings of 20-25%, stopped home milk deliveries, take the train instead of plane for short hops, use cold-water detergents to save hot water, and buy swimming pool purifying chemicals in bulk, to save $40 a year.

Here is the Family Budget

Food, Incidentals	$ 19,400
Car depreciation, upkeep	2,880
School tuition, transportation	10,944
Home mortgage, improvement loan	9,600
All insurance	3,576
Medical and dental bills	3,000
Social Security, pension contributions	3,000
Property taxes	2,880
Federal, state income taxes	24,720
	$ 80,000

Source: *Sylvia Porter's Money Book* (Avon: New York, 1975), pp. 150–51. The numbers have been adjusted for the inflation that occurred between 1974 and 1982.

Note: There is no special provision for the costs of vacation (the family has stopped taking them); "schools" is one of the family's budget expenses; and taxes amount to a fat 35 percent of the budget. Upper-income families are taking on more and more moonlighting jobs; men are urging their wives to go back to work; many are simply using for day-to-day living the capital they had accumulated toward college costs or retirement.

Mischel argues that people differ in all five dimensions. Two of the dimensions that seemingly overlap with expected-utility theory—expectancy and subjective value—in fact do not overlap at all; Mischel's model emphasizes that subjective probabilities may differ from the objective odds, and uses concepts of "value" that extend far beyond the economist's twice-differentiable utility functions with quantities consumed as their sole arguments.

Moreover, Mischel's model implies that individuals make decisions not only with respect to choice variables, but also, to some extent, with respect to their own tastes and some of the constraints upon their choice. In Mischel's words: ". . . people continuously select, change, and generate conditions just as much as they are affected by them" (1977, p. 350). A branch of microeconomics may be missing, one in which both the objective functions themselves and some of the constraints are in fact the decision variables, rather than the "givens."

Self-Regulatory Mechanisms

Why do people do things that ultimately cause them harm? The pervasiveness of such behavior—smoking, addiction, obesity, alcoholism, reckless driving—poses a major problem for choice theories that either preclude such behavior from the outset, on the grounds that it is irrational, or embrace it unabashedly because it is simply another instance of rational utility maximization (Stigler and Becker, 1977).

Dating from Freud, psychologists have been deeply interested in the acquisition of the ability to defer gratification; Freud saw what he called the transition from the pleasure principle (immediate gratification) to the reality principle (willingness to defer gratification) as an essential part of maturing.

According to this view, the primary function of the ego, or self, is to control impulsive behavior. There is intrapsychic tension between demands for immediate gratification and the need to postpone it:

The ego has the task of self-preservation . . . it performs that task by gaining control over the demands of the instincts, by deciding whether they are to be allowed satisfaction, by postponing that satisfaction to times and circumstances favourable in the external world or by suppressing their excitation entirely. (Freud, 1964, pp. 145–46.)

The tension between the desire for immediate gratification, and the knowledge that waiting for deferred, larger rewards is in some cases far more pleasurable, is a central theme of Freud's work. His famous 1911 essay, "On the Two Principles of Mental Functioning," talked about how we make the transition from the Pleasure Principle (immediate gratification) to the Reality Principle (deferred gratification). A generation later, Freud returned to this theme, in his "An Outline of Psycho-analysis" (1938). There, he noted that:

the immediate and unheeding satisfaction of the instincts . . . would often lead to perilous conflicts with the external world and to extinction. . . . it is an established fact that self-perceptions—coenaesthetic feelings and feelings of pleasure-unpleasure—govern the passage of events in the id with despotic force. The id obeys the inexorable pleasure principle. . . . the activity of other psychical agencies too is able only to modify the pleasure principle but not to nullify it; and it remains a question of the highest theoretical importance, and one that has not yet been answered, when and how it is ever possible for the pleasure principle to be overcome . . . . (p. 197.)

Psychodynamic theorists, from Freud, speak of "defense mechanisms"—ways by which the ego deals with "instinctual drives" for immediate gratification.

A practicing psychiatrist, George Ainslie, has in two brilliant articles (1982, 1984) interpreted and explained all of the Freudian defense mechanisms (repression, suppression, compulsiveness, denial, sublimation, projection) in terms of the eternal tension between impulse and control, or in Scitovsky's (1976) terms comfort and pleasure, and in particular in terms of the "matching principle." Ainslie calls his work "behavioral economics," as it explicates Freud's "economic" theory of behavior in which the key scarce resource is psychic energy. (In the next section, time preference is interpreted as a product of the attempt to conserve "cognitive attention," a kind of psychic-energy constraint.)

A major part of acquiring the ability to defer gratification is developing the skill of self-regulation. As Ainslie describes it:

A person's immense capacity for self-reward presents him with an equally immense problem of self-control. . . . A person is led by the basic shape of his reward delay function to exploit his sources of reward wastefully. If he does not bind his reward process to events outside his control . . . his every appetite is gratified, but so quickly that the anticipation which is necessary to harvest full satisfaction from a drive never develops, and so briefly that he must repeat the process indefinitely. A person cannot rid himself of the opportunity for this kind of regression; it must be, like the old idea of original sin, a constant factor in his motivation. He can only control it through the adoption of precommitting devices. . . . Thus can subtle appetites, e.g., for music, games and the varieties of human companionship, be understood not as the product of unnumerable separate drives but as disciplines we learn to adopt to protect ourselves from runaway self-reward. (p. 71.)

Ainslie (1982) argues that all precommitting devices fall into these categories, two of which are closely related:

1. Extrapsychic devices (which operate by physical or social means).
2. Attention-controlling devices, which keep the person from noticing the availability of occasions for speciously rewarded behavior. These are the intrapsychic equivalents of the wax in the crew's ear (Ulysses sailing past the Sirens).
3. Devices that change the future contingencies of reward by intrapsychic means. There seem to be two types of devices within this category:
   a) the control of affects which have intrinsic psychological momentum (. . . cultivation of affects incompatible with the impulse, and the inhibition of affects which facilitate it).
   b) private rules, often spoken of as will power, acting on principle, making promises to one's self, etc.

One of experimental psychology's more interesting and fruitful experimental paradigms has been the "now-vs-later" experiment, where pigeons, rats, monkeys, and of course human subjects are offered immediate rewards, often small, or much larger delayed rewards. The effectiveness of such rewards has been measured and compared, and a hyperbolic reaction established between reinforcement effectiveness and delay time (see Figure 1.2). The key finding is that the two hyperbolic curves intersect; that is, shorten the waiting period enough, and people (or animals) will shift from preferring the larger, delayed reward to the small, immediate one—a choice they may regret later.

Self-control is an attempt to recognize and forestall such future regret. In a famous experiment, Ainslie demonstrated the ability of self-control even in the pigeon (Ainslie 1984):

Pigeons were periodically offered a choice between a small immediate food reward and a larger one a few seconds later. All subjects chose the immediate

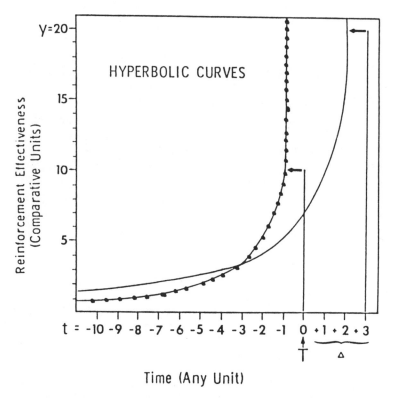

Figure 1.2. Reinforcement effectiveness of a small reward received at time *T*, compared with a larger reward received at time *T* + 3. The relative effectiveness of a small, early reward versus a reward twice as large available three units of time later, as predicted by Herrnstein's matching law. (Herrnstein, 1970, pp. 243–66; Formula 1). (Just before the rewards are due their curves become infinitely high; this portion is not depicted.)

reward on virtually all trials. If, however, several seconds before the choice was due to come up again they were allowed to make a response that rendered the smaller reward unavailable, some of the birds came regularly to choose this precommitment. These birds did not make this response in control conditions where it had no effects, where it was necessary to make the earlier reward available, or where it was made possible only a very short time before the choice was due to come up. This is evidence not only that preference for a larger reward can change to a preference for a smaller alternative just because the smaller alternative is drawing closer, but also that a device to forestall this change of preference can be learned in the absence of "higher" mental functions. Precommitting devices seem to be learned entirely on the basis of the differential effect of the larger reward before the smaller reward becomes dominant.

The Economics and Psychology of Constraints

The psychology of impatience has an important implication that it shares with *economy*. It has to do with how economics and psychology regard constraints. In economics, constraints are welfare-impairing. In the language of linear programming, if constraints are effective, the resource they represent is a nonslack variable and has a positive shadow price (value). If they are not effective, the resource they represent is worthless, having a zero shadow price.

In psychology, constraints are often welfare-improving. Psychologists of all denominations—Freudian, behaviorist, learning theory, experimentalists, and cognitive—are very concerned with impulsive behavior and self-control. Destructive impulsive behavior is often controlled by an interesting variety of self-imposed constraints. Often, the more numerous and innovative these constraints are, the better off we are. With respect to present-future choice, these constraints conserve a scarce resource—cognitive attention (see below)—and, like Ulysses bound to the mast as his ship passes the Sirens, help us pass the Straits of Temptation.

Consider the following types of behavior:

— My teenage son's bicycle, though perfectly usable, is to him unaesthetic, because the left pedal is different from the right one; our efforts to remove and replace the odd pedal have defied every tool, technique, and muscle. For the past three weeks, he has voluntarily denied himself the convenience and pleasure of using the bicycle, because ". . . if I use it, you and I will never feel the need to take the time to get it down to the bike shop."

— A large number of Americans have both substantial savings deposits, earning low interest, and large car loans, requiring payment of high interest; they are perfectly aware that this behavior reduces their income by hundreds of dollars a year . . . and are happy to continue the arrangement year after year.

—- As I write these words, a small mental transaction is in the works: If I spend three hours working on this article, I will reward myself with a half-hour jog. I consider the offer—and accept it. (But whether I actually spend the next three hours writing remains to be seen.) (See Bandura, 1982.)

Each of these small behaviors has a common element—in each case, individuals act to impose constraints upon themselves, where the objective of the constraints is to maximize their utility. Far from being a part of the welfare "problem," self-imposed constraints are, for a wide range of behaviors, in fact part of the solution.

This type of behavior is important, complex, and ubiquitous. Once self-imposed welfare-improving constraints are admitted, both the positive theory of microeconomic choice and the normative theory of welfare economics require major renovation.

It may be that the mathematical language of constrained maximization has caused—with important exceptions—the neglect of an important aspect of economic behavior: the conscious choice, creation, and strengthening of constraints, as part of the choice-set solution to welfare maximization rather than as part of the problem. In many cases, behavior is a result not of the choice of decision variables to maximize utility in the presence of binding constraints, but rather the choice of self-imposed constraints in order to maximize utility, where constraints are in fact the key decision variables themselves, and where our well-being often rests on how effective, ingenious, and binding our self-imposed constraints are.

PLEASURE VERSUS COMFORT

Assume that utility is a function of two attributes: Pleasure (P) and Comfort (C). For simplicity, let Comfort be represented by the initial level of consumption of good x, x_0. Let Pleasure be represented by the rate of growth of consumption, $x = \frac{dx}{dt} /x$. The rational consumer tries to maximize Utility $U(P,C)$, for a given lifetime wealth constraint, by choosing optimal values for x_0 and $\dot{x}$.

The wealth constraint is a convex transformation curve $F(x_0, \dot{x})$; it states that the integral of $x(t)$ [the amount of x consumed at time t] over time cannot exceed the terminal value of wealth. (For simplicity, a discount factor is not included, but can be added without altering the model's conclusions.) The transformation curve $F(x_0,\dot{x})$ will normally be concave, even though $P_{x'}$ and p_x decline as x' and x_0, respectively, increase; as x_0 increases, it can be shown that $p_{\dot{x}}$ declines more rapidly than p_x, hence $p_{x'}/P_{x'}$, the slope of $F(\dot{x}, x_0)$, will be an increasing function of x_0, for a given value of terminal wealth W_T.

In Figure 1.3, the optimal "mix" of Pleasure and Comfort is shown at point A. Myopic undervaluation of Pleasure can lead to suboptimal utility ($1b$) as wealth increases, where added wealth leaves utility unchanged; or, alternately, excessively high minimum demands for Comfort can also impair utility ($1c$).

The Quest for the Holy Gradient

The joyless economy may be a *dis*equilibrium state that will ultimately, perhaps soon, be remedied as soon as the search process in the untracked regions of

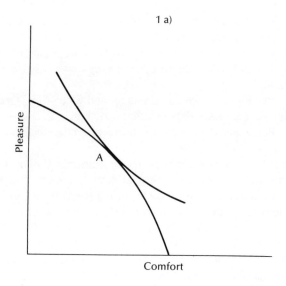

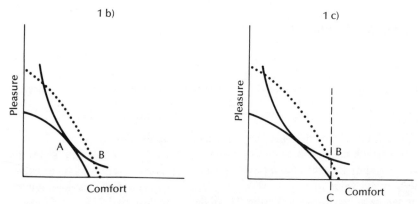

Figure 1.3. The microeconomics of pleasure-comfort choice. A fully rational, max-imizing individual would satisfy (3) by choosing point A. An outward shift of the pleasure-comfort curve, as wealth increases, may leave utility unchanged (point B, in 1b), either because the marginal utility of pleasure is undervalued (i.e., the de-nominator in the LHS of (3) is misperceived), or because the minimal comfort level C is constrained to be so high that it forestalls giving up x_0 in favor of $\dot{x}$. This, however, is superficial; the true message of *The Joyless Economy* is far deeper.

our preference maps comes to a successful end and a new equilibrium is attained. A theorem due to Irving Fisher can be used to explain this interpretation.

During doctoral studies at Yale, Irving Fisher studied vector mathematics with mathematician Willard Gibbs. He used it in his dissertation (1891) to prove a gradient theorem of consumer search: If an initial consumer equilibrium, in which all consumers face identical prices, is disturbed by an outward shift in the

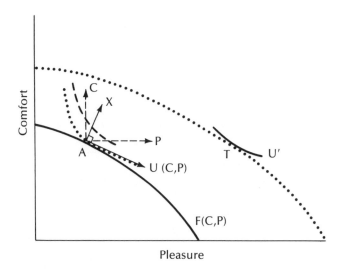

Pleasure

Figure 1.4. Vector *AX* is the resultant of "pleasure-force" *AP* and "comfort-force" *AC*. It is the gradient to *U(C,P)* at point *A*. If *A* is a utility-maximizing point, then slope *F(C,P)* at *A* equals the marginal utility of pleasure/marginal utility of comfort. The lower this ratio, the higher the slope of *AX*. Affluence shifts the transformation curve *F(C,P)* outward. Initial "search" emphasizes comfort, moving along the gradient *AX*. This search may lead to only small improvements in utility. Ultimately, as inert areas in our preference maps vanish, we shift direction, move toward the new optimum point *T*, and emphasize pleasure at the expense of comfort.

budget constraint, each consumer will increase his consumption of goods *X,Y* in exactly the same proportion, where *X/Y* equals the gradient (that is, the slope of perpendicular) of the isoutility curve at the initial equilibrium point.

As Figure 1.4 explains, an outward shift in the wealth constraint *F(C,P)* will induce a search process in which both comfort and pleasure are increased; initially, if the marginal utility of pleasure is perceived to be low, the additional wealth will be spent mainly on comfort, according to the gradient *AX*. Later, the direction will shift, as consumers adjust their spending, reduce comfort, and sharply increase pleasure, to move to the new equilibrium point *T*. Utility will rise quickly in the latter stages of the search process.

Some recent social trends are consistent with this interpretation (such as the new abstinence described above); but there is still little evidence that the comfort-addicted Western society is becoming any less so.

NOVELTY AS CUMULATIVE CONSUMPTION

Unlike the *New Yorker* cartoon (Figure 1.5), life is not a supermarket with clearly delineated "good for you," "bad for you" aisles. Most of what we

Figure 1.5. Drawing by Koren; © 1982 The New Yorker Magazine, Inc. Note that most consumption goods are sold both on aisle 1 and aisle 2.

consume is good for us in moderation and bad for us in excess. It is often unclear where the quantitative borders of "excess" lie. This suggests an alternate interpretation of Scitovsky's "novelty" argument in utility functions, measured by cumulative consumption. Nearing death, Keynes expressed only one regret—at not having drunk more champagne. We gain comfort from a glass of champagne, but lose novelty the more champagne we have consumed in our lifetimes. (Keynes' comfort-novelty trade-off apparently still favored comfort.) For some goods—cigarettes, drugs, alcohol, even food—the health-impairing effects are a function of the cumulative amount consumed. "Novelty," then, may be comprised of a psychological component—boredom—and a physiological one—health impairment. Boredom is underestimated because it may seem distant—today's glass of champagne will diminish the "newness" of tomorrow's—and health impairment is underestimated because it is both distant and perceptually uncertain. The obverse of habit is the reassurance and familiarity of habit.[3]

Increasing attention in the media to long-term health costs of excess caffeine, sugar, nicotine, alcohol, and drug consumption is having an effect on consumption patterns. In its typically understated style, *Fortune* magazine labels this trend "the new American abstinence" and suggests that we are consuming smaller amounts of things that are cumulatively bad for us. *Fortune* also notes that some corporations are cynically exploiting the shift in consumer tastes: Many products may be low in sugar content (duly noted in advertisements) but high in sodium (duly ignored). Declining consumption of sugar, caffeine, cigarettes, alcohol, and pork suggests that the underweighting of "novelty" (its health component) is somewhat in decline. Last year, the average American consumed 1,425 pounds of food, 3 percent less than the year before.

THE JOYS OF CREDIT

Lester Thurow once used 1961 census data to show that actual consumption over the life cycle is distributed much more closely to actual income than it is to "ideal" consumption—the latter measured as the annual income at which persons between the ages of 20 and 70 earn exactly what they spend. He concluded that improving imperfect capital markets to enable more intertemporal transfer of income, from later ages to earlier ones when families are growing and needs are high, would improve well-being. However, the past generation has seen such mechanisms become widespread; though I do not yet have the data to prove it, I suspect actual consumption over the life cycle is in 1985 much closer to "ideal" consumption than it was in 1961. This should be an unmitigated gain in well-being. Yet it has a cost. It has deprived an entire generation of much of the pleasure of working hard, saving and scrimping for material comforts, then seeing the fruits of their labors after, say, five or ten years. Debt availability offers immediate comfort, and annihilates delayed pleasure. On balance, removal of this constraint may have cost us more utility than it gained.

In *The Joyless Economy*, Scitovsky argues:

Is there not another reason for our increasing frustration with our freely chosen lives? Could it not be that we seek our satisfaction in the wrong things or in the wrong way and are then dissatisfied with the outcome? Economists today consider [what man chooses to get and what will best satisfy him] synonymous. . . . This approach overlooks the fact that tastes are highly variable, easily influenced by custom and suggestion, constantly changed by the accumulation of experience, and modified by changing prices and the availability of some satisfactions and the unavailability of others. (pp. 4–5.)

The widespread availability of credit has, despite deep-rooted instincts that decry its use, made possible immediate comfort and has lowered a key barrier that once helped us choose pleasure over comfort. The joyless economy is mired in debt.[4]

The welfare-improving attribute of credit constraints modeled using the Pleasure-Comfort trade-off was developed above. The argument is summarized in Table 1.3. In condensed form: Previous generations were constrained by un-availability of credit essentially to spend only up to their incomes, in each period. This constraint was utility-improving, since it forestalled the temptation to choose excessive comfort (x_0) over future pleasure ($\dot{x}$). Today, a wide range of credit is available, removing the income (t)-spending (t) constraint, and permitting us to embrace the Siren of comfort. Self-imposed constraints exist but may not be sufficiently developed, or they may have atrophied.

The American people—along with people in most European countries—are extremely conservative about debt-financed purchases. A large majority of Americans, when asked whether it is all right to make a major purchase on credit, say no. At the same time, consumer credit is growing by leaps and bounds and indeed is powering the current [1985] American economic recovery. In *Minds, Markets & Money* (1982), I reconciled these two facts by noting that sophisticated credit vendors have learned to lend people money without actually having them explicitly borrow. If your checking account has an automatic loan provision, you can overdraw your account up to your credit limit. That makes the zero point in the account of little consequence, whereas once it was of great consequence, representing the point where checks bounced. Borrowing money by automatic overdraft may not appear to be borrowing, if you simply do not know what your account balance is: The capacity for self-delusion is large, and defeats the self-control mechanism inherent in bounced checks.

Purchases on credit cards can also be rationalized as "I will pay the full amount at the end of the month, so it is not as if I were borrowing or going into debt." The end of the month comes, of course, and large bills often mean the minimum monthly payment is made. Plastic money, too, encourages buying on impulse, on credit, without the necessity of recognizing that we are doing so.

Performing an act we think is wrong—despite the camouflage of rationaliza-tion—should ultimately, after many repetitions, lead to a change in the attitude that the act is wrong. It is somewhat surprising that after three years of credit-financed borrowing, most Americans still believe going in debt to consume is wrong, and there is no evidence of erosion in that view; in fact, the percentage who believe buying on credit is "not O.K., or never O.K." increased somewhat from 1978 to 1980 (see Figure 1.6).

Table 1.3
Utility maximization under pleasure myopia and credit constraints

---

MODEL I.

$$\underset{x_0,\dot{x}}{\text{MAX}}\; U(x_0,\dot{x}) \quad \text{S.T.} \quad \int_0^T x_0 e^{\dot{x}t}dt \le W_T$$

$$x_t \le y_t$$

Description: Credit-market constraints prevent people from intertemporal transfers of income. This will impose "damage-control" on pleasure-myopia, and, when initial income is low and growing fairly quickly, impose a similar consumption path.

MODEL II.

$$\text{MAX}\; U(x_0, \dot{x}) \quad \text{S.T.} \quad \int_0^T x_0 e^{\dot{x}t}dt \le W_T$$

Description: Credit-market constraints are removed. It is now possible to spend future income today, by credit card purchases, bank loans, second mortgages, etc. Removal of this constraint for a fully rational individual cannot impair utility, but will likely increase it.

MODEL III.

While the true utility function is $U(x_0,\dot{x})$, the individual discounts pleasure ($\dot{x}$) and solves the maximization problem:

$$\text{MAX}\; U(x_0) \quad \text{S.T.} \quad \int_0^T x_0 e^{\dot{x}t}dt \le W_T$$

Description: Pleasure-myopia leads the individual to want high values of x_0 (which may be ex-post utility-impairing), and freely available credit aids and abets this error. Increases in wealth lead to immediate increases in x_0, perhaps up to the satiation point. Lifetime utility here may be less, for comparable wealth levels, than for Model I.

MODEL IV.

As in Model III, except: the credit constraint is restored:

$$\text{MAX}\; U(x_0) \quad \text{S.T.} \quad \int_0^T x_0 e^{\dot{x}t}dt \le W_T$$

$$x_t \le y_t$$

Description: The credit constraint can offset pleasure-myopia. While we may seek to overly emphasize comfort (x_0), lack of resources and the inability to transfer resources from the future to the present constrains us against doing so.

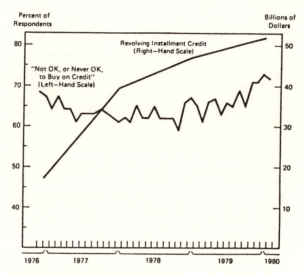

Figure 1.6. Attitudes Toward Credit, and Amount of Revolving Installment Credit in the United States, 1976–80.
Source: Attitude Toward Debt: Gallup Poll Survey, August 1979; Installment Credit, *Statistical Abstract of the United States,* U.S. Bureau of the Census.

The opulent economy creates the joyless one in part by accelerating the satisfaction of wants, and by making such instant satisfaction almost obligatory. It is difficult to buy summer clothing in early July, because department stores are launching their fall lines. Each year, fall clothing appears a little earlier in the summer. In this Prisoner's Dilemma race among stores to corner the consumer's fall clothing dollar, display-window clothing is not synchronized with the prevailing season, and all stores may lose, as does the consumer, who is asked to satisfy an *anticipated* want rather than an immediate one. The down parka I saw in a window on Beacon Street, on a sunny late June morning, is a forlorn symbol of the joyless economy.

Not only are we cajoled to satisfy future wants long before they materialize, but we are enjoined to satisfy *current* wants at all costs. In the throwaway society, where human relationships have become as discardable as milk containers, we are initially offered the *opportunity* for happiness and self-fulfillment inherent in wealth. Samuel Johnson said that a man searching for his dinner and trembling from his creditors is unlikely to develop great thoughts. Opulence offers the opportunity for great thoughts. But, by a remarkable transmutation, opportunity becomes obligation. We are impelled by social pressure to seek immediate happiness and fulfillment and urged to clear from our path any perceived obstacle, including long-standing bonds with other people. The chance for great thoughts is destroyed by the compulsion of mean ones. I wonder if this is not the single most important source of unhappiness in the comfort-obsessed society.

One of the assumptions of conventional economics is that of "institutional transparency"—for example, how we save and spend should not be influenced by the manner in which we are paid our salaries (pay envelope or bank deposit). The new theoretical institutional economics, inspired in part by organizational theory (Herbert Simon, James March, Oliver Williamson), denies this premise. Consider the high-saving Japanese. The Japanese worker is paid his or her monthly wages in cash, in a pay packet. That sum is brought home and doled out in small piles among various budget items. Automatic teller machines are ubiquitous—but spending is paid for by cash. Credit card use is minimal, and so are bank loans. The fabled end-of-year bonus, too, is paid in cash, and may amount to several months' salary. Unlike America, Christmas bonuses are spent only after they are earned. The constraint on monthly consumption to be less than or equal to monthly cash income must be a powerful restraint on impulse buying. Surely the high savings rate in Japan has something to do with this. Are the Japanese less happy because they must wait to make major purchases until they have saved up enough for them?

MODELING WELFARE-IMPROVING CONSTRAINTS

So far, it has been argued that *The Joyless Economy* storms the ramparts of constraints that should be strengthened rather than dismantled. How ought welfare-improving constraints to be modeled? The psychology literature previously cited suggests the existence of an "internal psychic marketplace," one in which the "planning" part of the individual offers rewards, punishments, and incentives, in return for various types of behavior on the part of the "doer." Impulsive "doers" may be successfully constrained by clever "planners." The way these transactions work could in fact be modeled as a kind of market, with supplier (doer) and demander (planner) operating under various assumptions about utility, information, and so forth. The behavior of an individual in conventional markets, under this model, would be seen as the net result of a prior set of transactions, internal to the individual, between the two "agencies." A burgeoning literature exists on "two-self" theory, aimed at explaining behavior which is self-destructive; see Thaler and Shefrin (1981); Winston (1983); Schelling (1984a, 1984b).

Cognitive Attention as a Scarce Resource

Not all psychologists, however, accept the two-self "planner" versus "doer" model of subjective time preference and impatience. Herrnstein (1981) suggests that the choice of small immediate rewards over large delayed ones may be simply the result of saving a scarce resource—cognitive attention.

Let the consumer choose between an immediately available good X, and a delayed, but superior good, Y: The price of the respective goods is p_x and p_y, and the individual has an amount of income I to allocate between the two goods. The standard textbook problem is therefore:

$$\text{MAX } U(X,Y) \qquad \text{S.T. } p_x X + p_y Y = I$$
$$XY$$

and, for a Cobb-Douglas utility function $U(X,Y) = XY$, the proportion:

$$\frac{X}{Y} = \frac{P_y}{P_x}$$

will be chosen.

Now, assume, with Herrnstein (1970, 1981), that the individual has another scarce resource, in addition to income, which we might call cognitive attention or processing capacity—a limited ability to do, in Hernnstein's phrase, "cognitive bookkeeping" (see also Navon and Gopher 1979). Then,

> Self control versus impulsiveness is sometimes cast in terms of rationality versus irrationality. At first look, it may seem irrational to choose a smaller reinforcer just because the larger one is later. The deeper insight of a hyperbolic theory uncovers a differing view, however. Being later, the larger one is probably less certain. It may not be delivered as promised, or we may not be there to collect. Moreover, being later, it requires cognitive bookkeeping to keep track of, or to discover at all, and cognitive capacities are finite. The advantage in reinforcement for the later alternative may be more than offset by the cost in psychological effort and preoccupation. (Herrnstein, 1981, p. 19.)

Now, let the delay time required before X is received be D_x, and let D_y be the delay time (in hours or days) for Y, with $D_x \leq D_y$. Suppose that our cognitive capacity, measured in units of time, is finite and equal to Z:

$$D_x X + D_y Y \leq Z$$

Adding this constraint on the income constraint makes the consumer-choice problem:

$$\text{MAX } U(X,Y) \qquad \text{S.T.} \qquad p_x X + p_y Y \leq I$$
$$X,Y \qquad\qquad\qquad\qquad D_x X + D_y Y \leq Z$$

The *effective* constraint on our consumption may not be income at all, but cognitive attention (see Figure 1.7). Thus, in the diagram, consumption is constrained by the discontinuous dotted line, and utility may be maximized at point A.

An increase in income may result in no increase in utility, unless there is an accompanying increase in resource Z.

A more likely course of events is this: Tangency between isoutility curves and the *I-Z* constraints occurs at the point of discontinuity. An increase in income (without change in Z) shifts that discontinuity downward and to the right, moving along the Z constraint line. This leads to an increase in the "immediate" good,

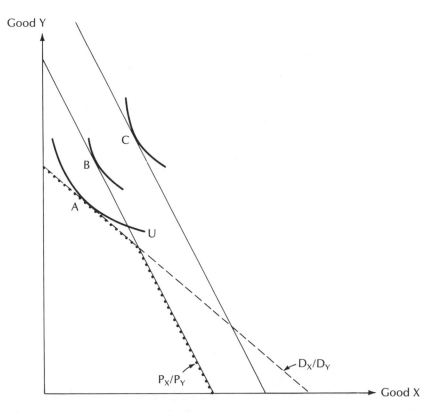

Figure 1.7. Utility Maximization under Income and Cognition Constraints. An individual maximizes $U(X,Y)$ subject to a conventional income constraint $p_xX + p_yY = I$ and a cognitive attention constraint $D_xX + D_yY = Z$, where D_x and D_y are the amounts of time one must wait to get one unit of X and Y, respectively, and Z is the total amount of cognition-attention resource (in hours) available. Increases in income may not increase utility unless there is a comparable increase in resource Z (ability to wait for deferred rewards).

X, and a decrease in the delayed good, Y. Utility may in fact rise, but by far less than the growth in income might be expected to generate in the absence of the Z constraint.

JOYLESS WORK

An individual's well-being depends only in part on spending and consumption. Another important determinant of our well-being is how we earn the income to support that spending. Work itself can be an important source of satisfaction, or a major cause of unhappiness. Some of the most interesting parts of *The Joyless Economy* discuss why the utility of work, as well as the utility of consumption, fades in the face of opulence. What follows is a theory of wealth-induced anomie (based on work by learning-theory psychologists) that Karl Marx should have thought of—and somewhere in *Capital*, probably did.

The Assistant Professor Syndrome

Consider a newly appointed assistant professor. With the ink still fresh on his (or her) diploma, he bashes into old ideas and sprints after new ones with vigor and zest, driven by curiosity, interest, and, naturally, ambition. The young assistant professor is at least in part motivated by intrinsic rewards (utility derived from the pursuit of ideas itself, rather than rewards that pursuit brings). If this were not true, less intellectual employment would pull him away from the campus. The utility function at this stage is a rocket powered by its own fuel. Soon, the assistant professor learns that external rewards—tenure, salary, grants, prestige, travel—accrue to success in the game of ideas. Moreover, one of those external rewards (tenure) is a necessary condition for the right to continued enjoyment of intrinsic ones. This should pose no problem: Extrinsic and intrinsic rewards are more powerful motivators than intrinsic ones alone. The difficulty is, there are "hidden costs" to rewards, as Lepper and Greene (1978) show. In the learning-theory version of Gresham's law, extrinsic motivation drives out intrinsic. When you pay someone to do a job he enjoys, in certain cases he comes to enjoy the job solely because of the pay, and ultimately, when the marginal utility of pay declines, finds he does not enjoy the job at all. The associate professor, successful, honored, tenured, and financially secure, comes to value intellectual pursuits for their external rewards. All too soon, those rewards pall, and so does the joy of writing and thinking. Society has created a joyless economist.

This phenomenon is common in education. It is often mistaken for "burn-out," fatigue from persistent unrewarded effort, but in fact it is the opposite— fatigue from persistent *rewarded* effort. The blame for posttenure blahs is often laid at the feet of the institution of tenure. This, too, I believe, is an error. Tenure is only one of a series of extrinsic rewards for academic performance, and perhaps not the most important one.

Can the assistant professor syndrome be generalized? In a market economy we are allegedly paid the value of our marginal product, in competitive labor markets. If the net after-tax wage exceeds the value of the leisure displaced by work, at the margin higher pay should induce greater quality and intensity of effort. As Leibenstein (1986) noted, time clocks measure labor hours but do not measure *effective* effort: Owing to X inefficiency, it is difficult to link pay and true effort empirically. There is, however, evidence that monetary incentives for greater effort often prove very weak. The backward-bending labor supply curve is an extreme example. Intrinsic-extrinsic reward trade-offs offer an alternate explanation to the standard income versus substitution effects. Suppose higher pay acts negatively on intrinsic reward and increases the disutility from a labor hour. A dialectic emerges where higher productivity generates higher pay, which displaces job satisfaction as the driving force behind effort. High pay soon becomes a good that disappoints, as we yearn for the time when we worked for work's own sake, and wealth displaces the irreplaceable contentment of doing things because we enjoy them. This is a closed-loop system (see Figure 1.8), and in

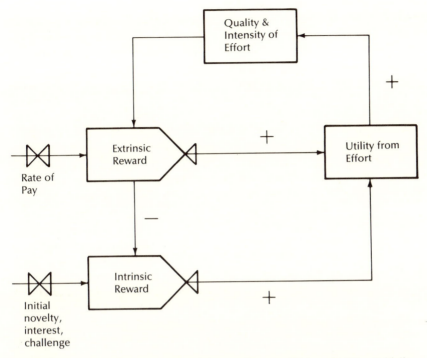

Figure 1.8. A closed-loop system relating work, pay, effort, and utility. Initially, we get utility from a task because it is new, interesting, and challenging, and do it even without pay; this is the "intrinsic reward" motive. Then, we are paid for doing the task (extrinsic reward). The higher the extrinsic reward, the lower the intrinsic reward becomes. As extrinsic rewards annihilate intrinsic ones, higher and higher rates of pay may become necessary to induce the same effort levels, and to maintain the level of utility. Higher income is thus associated with the same level of effort and the same amount of utility.

some cases, if the negative loop is powerful enough, may leave us at a utility level below that from which we began.

Lepper and Greene (1978) propose three main empirical reasons why extrinsic and intrinsic rewards may be enemies. First, being paid for doing a task focuses our attention on aspects of performance that elicit payment. This distracts our attention from other performance aspects that may be pleasurable but that are not rewarded. Make tenure contingent on achieving a certain *quantity* of publications (uniformly denied in theory and affirmed in practice) and the joy of polishing a paper's *quality* is impaired. Second, external rewards are a measure of a person's competence or success. When our own self-worth is dependent not on internal feelings under our control, but on external rewards that may be uncertain, we live with the fear that our self-worth and value to society may disappear with our wealth. I believe even exceedingly wealthy people are afflicted with this uncertainty. (The famous song in the musical *Hair*, that exults in having eyes, arms, nose, and hair, though no wealth, is in a sense a rebellion against linking self-worth with wealth.) Finally, intrinsic rewards are subject to our own direct volition. This provides us with freedom and independence that can have great value. External rewards are subject to the will of other people. They constrain our freedom, and hence impose costs.

The latter "hidden cost of reward" raises an interesting issue. In economics, income and wealth are invariably treated as constraints. Nonslack constraints always impair utility; constrained resources have positive shadow prices. In psychology, relaxing *economic* constraints may *impair* utility. More pay shifts the budget constraint outward—in economics, utility-improving—but by making us more dependent on the employer, *increases* the psychological constraint on our freedom of choice. The net effect may be a decline in utility. The theme that some economic constraints have a positive psychological benefit, and that relaxing them can harm our well-being, recurs again and again in this paper, as in fact it does in *The Joyless Economy*.

The Joyless Economy argues that, owing to the Puritan ethic, people invest too much time and effort in production and too little in consumption. But perhaps this problem is too *little* Puritan ethic rather than too much; too little work for work's sake, and too much work for pay's sake. Admittedly, McCullers (1978) notes, this is hard to test empirically. If you ask someone who works hard for low pay whether or not he enjoys his work, chances are he will say, "Yes," owing to cognitive dissonance—the need to justify ex post an action undertaken perhaps unwillingly ex ante.[5]

CONCLUSION

Goethe said that thinking is more interesting than knowing—but less interesting than looking. By looking intensively at our society and economy, Tibor Scitovsky has set us thinking; despite the enormous inertia inherent in a closed system of microeconomics that the vast majority of economists regard as almost without blemish, we may end up less confident in what we know about the link between wealth and utility, and more willing to rethink what we know.

Wordsworth noted that wisdom is often nearer when we stoop than when we soar. Scitovsky (1985) notes how far the Greeks got in using pure introspection. One day, mainstream economics will stoop to rediscover the power of direct observation, and the fascination of backward science—theorizing about interesting observations, rather than observing where theory has pointed. When they do, they will find trails broken by Tibor Scitovsky.

I am indebted to two anonymous referees for incisive criticism: to Paul Albanese for suggesting and soliciting this paper and then resolutely overcoming my indolence in revising it, and to Richard Herrnstein and Harvey Leibenstein for stimulating conversation on the topic. Colleen Mahan typed the final draft expertly. The Technion Vice President's Fund provided partial financial support. The paper was revised during a summer visit to the Management of Technology Program, Sloan School of Management, Massachusetts Institute of Technology.

NOTES

1. The late Harry Johnson once remarked that the next revolution in economic theory would come from someone steeped in the history of economic thought. At the time, I found that very strange, when most of the kudos were going to young mathematically brilliant economists whose knowledge went as far back as the Beach Boys. Reading Scitovsky's 1985 paper, I began to see how an intimate knowledge of the past is a precondition to changing theories of the present and foreseeing those of the future.

2. In his 1983 paper, Richard E. Creel heralds "Eudology: The Science of Happiness," and proposes a new science of happiness based on eudaemonism, the belief that happiness is the highest form of good. In a critique, Mihaly Csikszentmihalyi notes the "Columbus" effect, rediscovering America, and suggests that the study of the causes and nature of happiness has been underway for many years or even centuries. (Csikszentmihalyi, 1983.)

For a bibliography on happiness, see: E. Diener and S. Griffin, "Happiness and Life Satisfaction: A Bibliography," *Psychological Documents,* July 1984.

3. A 1934 Act of Congress required the Federal Reserve to collect and disseminate information on interest rates in several cities. As a test, the Fed asked banks, credit unions, finance companies, and thrifts to submit their interest rates on personal loans, auto loans, and first and second mortgages. The Fed then organized the rates in a chart, which it published in local newspapers. This was done in Akron, Ohio; Sacramento, California; and Rochester, New York. An economic analysis of the plan would be highly approving, increasing the efficiency of credit markets and their competitiveness. A psychological analysis, along the lines of this paper, would suggest that disseminating information about credit availability might have the effect of reducing barriers to using it, and hence remove a valuable constraint on impulse buying and on pleasure-myopia. (See *Wall Street Journal,* Friday, July 26, 1985.)

4. An example of the force of habit in consumption patterns is Legal Sea Foods, a chain of restaurants of which one is near the Massachusetts Institute of Technology. Friday lunch is always especially crowded. Though the fish-on-Friday rule was rescinded long ago by the Catholic Church, the habit seems to remain. The same restaurant also illustrates the capacity for change and novelty. Three centuries ago, many indentured servants had clauses in their contracts which limited the amount of salmon they could be fed to five times a week. The same dish today is, in Legal Sea Foods, a costly delicacy. (Of course, supply conditions help create a delicacy, as well as demand.) I am grateful for this point to Professor Dan Holland.

5. According to Professor John D. Owen, writing in *Monthly Labor Review,* working adults ". . . have had no net gain in their leisure time in 30 years." He notes that the long-term trend in hours worked fell from 58.4 hours a week to 42 hours in 1948, but since then there has been "little or no change." Owen believes that hours worked have not declined as pay rises for two reasons: child-rearing costs on families following the baby boom, and the rising costs of college that have "greatly increased the average cost of raising a child." (Cited in the *Wall Street Journal,* 7 Sept. 1976.)

REFERENCES

Ainslie, George. "A behavioral economic approach to the defense mechanism: Freud's energy theory revisited." *Social Science Information* 21 (1982):735–79.

Ainslie, George. "Behavioral economics II: Motivated, involuntary behavior." *Social Science Information* 23, No. 1 (April 1984):47–78.

Bandura, Albert. "Self-efficacy mechanism in human agency." *American Psychologist* (February 1982):122–47.

Creel, Richard E. "Eudology: The science of happiness." *New Ideas in Psychology* 1 (1983):303–12.

Csikszentmihalyi, Mihaly. "Response." *New Ideas in Psychology* 1 (1983):313–14.

Diener, Ed and Griffin, Sharon. "Happiness and life satisfaction: A bibliography." *Psychological Documents* 14, No. 1 (1984):81.

Fisher, Irving. "Mathematics in Economics." Ph.D. dissertation, Yale, 1891.

Freud, Sigmund. "Formulations on the two principles of mental functioning.: *The Standard Edition of the Complete Psychological Works of Sigmund Freud*, vol. 12, pp. 226–39. Translated under the general editorship of James Strachey in collaboration with Anna Freud et al. London: Hogarth Press, 1959.

Freud, Sigmund. "An Outline of psychoanalysis." In *The Standard Edition of the Complete Works of Sigmund Freud*, vol. 23, pp. 144–205. Translated under the general editorship of James Strachey in collaboration with Anna Freud et al. London: The Hogarth Press, 1964.

Galbraith, John K. *The Affluent Society.* Boston: Little, Brown, 1957.

Herrnstein, Richard. "On the law of effect." *Journal of the Experimental Analysis of Behavior* 13 (1970):243–66.

Herrnstein, Richard. "Self-control as response strength." *Quantifications of Steady-State Operant Behavior*, edited by C. M. Bradshaw and C. F. Lowe. Amsterdam: Elsevier, 1981.

Kahneman, D. and Tversky, A. "Prospect theory: An analysis of decision under risk." *Econometrica* 47 (1979):269–91.

Leibenstein, Harvey. "On relaxing the maximization postulate." *Behavioral Economics of the Firm: Journal of Behavioral Economics*, edited by Roger Frantz. Spring 1986.

Lepper, Mark R. and Greene, David. *The Hidden Costs of Reward: New Perspectives on the Psychology of Human Motivation.* Hillsdale, NJ: Erlbaum, 1978.

Levy, Shlomit. "Israel: Values 1984." Paper presented to the International Conference in Economics and Psychology: "Choice and Exchange," Kibbutz Shefayim. Israel, July 1986.

Linder, Stefan. *The Harried Leisure Class.* New York: Columbia University Press, 1970.

Maital, S. *Minds, Markets and Money: Psychological Foundations of Economic Behavior.* New York: Basic Books, 1982.

McCullers, John C. "Issues in learning and motivation," The Hidden Costs of Reward: New Perspectives on the Psychology of Human Motivation, edited by M. R. Lepper and D. Greene. Hillsdale, NJ: Erlbaum, 1978, 5–19.

Mischel, W. "The interaction of person and situation." In *Personality At the Crossroads: Current Issues in Interactional Psychology*, edited by D. Magnusson and N. Ednler, pp. 333–52. Hillsdale, NJ: Erlbaum, 1977.

Navon, D. and Gopher, D. "On the economy of human-processing system." *Psychological Review* 86 (1979):214–55.

Porter, Sylvia. *Sylvia Porter's Money Book.* New York: Avon, 1975.

Schelling, Thomas C. "Self-command in practice, in policy and in a theory of rational choice." *American Economic Review* (May 1984a):1–11.

Schelling, Thomas C. "The Intimate Contest for Self-Command." In *Choice and Conse-quences.* Cambridge, MA: Harvard University Press, 1984b.

Scitovsky, Tibor. *The Joyless Economy.* New York: Oxford University Press, 1976.

Scitovsky, Tibor. "Psychologizing by economists." Paper for presentation to the Eighth Annual Middlebury College Conference on Economic Issues, 1985.

Smith, Adam. *The Wealth of Nations.* New York: Random House, 1937 (orig. pub. 1776).

Stigler, G. and Becker, G. "De gustibus non est disputandum." *American Economic Review* 67 (1977):76–90.

Thaler, Richard H. and Shefrin, H. "An economic theory of self control." *Journal of Political Economy* (April 1981):392–406.

Tversky, A. and Kahneman, D. "Causal schema in judgements under uncertainty." In *Progress in Social Psychology,* edited by M. Fishbein. Hillsdale, NJ: Erlbaum, 1977.

Von Neumann, John and Oskar Morgenstern. *Theory of Games and Economic Behavior.* Princeton: Princeton University Press, 1944.

Winston, Richard H. "Using mental accounting in a theory of consumer behavior," Cornell University, May 1983.

APPENDIX: THE MICROECONOMICS OF THE PLEASURE-COMFORT TRADE-OFF

Terms:

$U(P,C)$ = life-cycle utility (measured over the life span) is a function of Pleasure (P) and Comfort (C)

x_0 = the initial level of consumption at time t_0

$\dot{x}$ = the (constant) rate at which consumption is growing (continuous)

T = length of life span

W_T = value of wealth at time T

An individual with given terminal wealth W_T must, at time t_0, choose control variables x_0 and $\dot{x}$ in order to maximize lifetime utility:

$$(1) \qquad \underset{\dot{x},\, x_0}{\text{Max }} U(P,C)$$

$$\text{S.T. (a)} \quad P = P(\dot{x})$$
$$\text{(b)} \quad C = C(x_0)$$

$$\text{(c)} \quad \int_0^T x_0 \exp(\dot{x}t)dt \leq W_T$$

The first two constraints are definitional, and simply say that pleasure depends on the *rate of change* of consumption, with $P_{\dot{x}} \geq 0$, and comfort depends on the initial (and subsequent, therefore) *levels* of consumption, with $C_{\dot{x}_0} \geq 0$. The third constraint states that you cannot during your lifetime spend more than your wealth, though (c) would not prevent you from going deeply into debt initially and later paying back that debt. Constraint (c) can be simplified to:

$$(2) \quad x_0(e^{\dot{x}T} - 1)/\dot{x} \le W_T$$

The first-order condition for maximum utility can be expressed as:

$$(3) \quad \frac{\partial U/\partial x_0}{\partial U/\partial \dot{x}} = \frac{\partial W/\partial x_0}{\partial W/\partial \dot{x}}$$

The LHS is the marginal rate of substitution of comfort for pleasure. The RHS is the relative price of comfort (x_0) with respect to pleasure $(\dot{x})$, measured as the incremental increase in x_0 (x).

The RHS of Eq. (3) is

$$(4) \quad \frac{P_{\dot{x}_0}}{P_{\dot{x}}} = \frac{(e^{\dot{x}T} - 1)(\dot{x})^2}{\dot{x}} \quad \frac{1}{(x_0)(e^{\dot{x}T} - 1)(\dot{x}T - 1)} = \frac{\dot{x}}{x_0} \frac{1}{(\dot{x}T - 1)}$$

where P_i is the "price" of an added unit of i.

Closed solutions for the pleasure-comfort choice, for three special cases, are:

A. Pleasure and Comfort are log-linear functions of x and x_p, respectively:

$$(5) \quad C = a \, \log x_0, \quad P = b \, \log \dot{x}$$
$$U(C,P) = a \, \log x_0 + b \, \log \dot{x}$$

In this case, there is nonsatiation in both comfort and pleasure, and utility is a separable function of each component. The optimal rate of growth in consumption spending is:

$$(6) \quad \dot{x}^* = \left(\frac{b}{a} + 1 \right) /T$$

Here, persons with shorter life spans will, as expected, consume at a faster rate of growth. The value of $\dot{x}^*$ is *independent* of terminal wealth; people with more wealth will choose a higher value of x_0 (assuming that their values of a and b are the same). The greater the value of a, the smaller the value of x.

Now, assume with Scitovsky that the utility of pleasure is undervalued, so that, in the extreme case, $b = 0$. Equation (6) becomes:

$$(7) \quad \dot{x}^* = 1/T$$

Suppose $T = 50$. Consumption, therefore, will be growing at a rate of $1/50 = 0.02$ percent a year.

Suppose the "true" (ex ante) value of b is such that $b = a$. The optimal path of $x(t)$ will then be twice as steep. For a given wealth constraint, initial x_0 will be lower, but consumption will be growing more rapidly, at 4 percent a year.

B. Pleasure and Comfort are simple linear functions of x and x_0:

(8) $\quad C = ax_0, \quad P = b\dot{x}$
$$U(C,P) = ax_0 + b\dot{x}$$

The optimal, utility-maximizing relation between $\dot{x}$ and x_0 is:

(9) $\quad \dot{x}^* = 1/(T - v), \quad v = b/ax_0$

Here again, when $b = 0$ (pleasure myopia), $\dot{x}^*$ collapses to $1/T$. It can be shown, using Eq. (9), that $\dot{x}^*$ varies inversely with x_0, as expected, and that the optimal ratio of $\dot{x}^*/x_0$ depends on the relative marginal utilities of Pleasure and Comfort, b and a, respectively.

C. Comfort is a quadratic function of x_0, with satiation at $x_0 = d/2a$, Pleasure is a log-linear function of $\dot{x}$:

(10) $\qquad P = b \log \dot{x}, \quad C = dx_0 - ax_0^2 + h$
$$U(C,P) = dx_0 - ax_0^2 + h + b \log \dot{x}$$

The optimal relation between x_0 and $\dot{x}$ is found from:

(11) $\quad (dx_0 - 2ax_0^2)(\dot{x}T - 1) = 1, \quad x_0 \leq d/2a$

2

HOW THE OPPONENT-PROCESS THEORY OF ACQUIRED MOTIVATION CAME INTO ECONOMICS

Richard L. Solomon

I don't know where to begin. First I must confess that I'm truly an imposter here. Many of us think that we are captains of our own fate. That definitely is not the case. Let me tell you how you can be a victim. When I first started publishing material on opponent processes and acquired motivation for psychologists, the articles were presented as an opponent-process theory of motivation, and the various experiments that were done in the animal laboratory were recorded. That went on for about ten years, and then after a dozen years I published a summary article in *The American Psychologist,* which is a publication for psychologists of all persuasions, and I sent in the article entitled "An Opponent-Process Theory of Acquired Motivation." The article was bounced back for revision. The editor was a very, very astute lady who at the time was terribly interested in the article. She said, "You've got to spice it up." She invented the title as follows: "An Opponent-Process Theory of Acquired Motivation: The Costs of Pleasure and the Benefits of Pain." Now the fact that the words "costs" and "benefits" were included in that title (and not included by me) resulted in a flood of correspondence from economists. And at first, since I had very little interest and formal training in economics—I didn't realize what was going on. Gradually, over a period of five years, it has dawned on me: The problems in motivation which I was viewing in the laboratory were related to major concepts in economics.

I sense that today we are dealing with tastes, preferences, and the commitment of resources for goods and services, and our attention has been drawn to matters such as compulsive and addictive behavior. Those behaviors are intriguing because they don't fit anyone's pattern of rationality. Let me give you some examples of how opponent-processes theory evolves. A person experimenting with drugs mainlines heroin and has an immediate delicious experience. If you have ever had opiates, you know what it's like. There's just nothing like it on this earth. But there are individual differences among the people who shoot these drugs. Generally, the experience is pleasurable, even though at first there might be some nausea and upset. But as the drug wears off, a relatively unpleasant state follows, even after the first shot.

However, if the drug is repeatedly administered with short interdose intervals, two major phenomena occur. One is that the capacity of the drug to make you euphoric decreases. That is called drug tolerance, or habituation—habituation to a stimulating event which initially produced intense euphoria but now, after several repetitions of dosing, gradually loses its capacity to produce an experience of the same intensity. While this is occurring, the unpleasant after-effects of the dose begin to intensify and expand in duration so that the so-called withdrawal syndrome or the abstinence unpleasantness becomes more intense with each successive dose and lasts longer. Now you have a very remarkable situation in which an individual continues to use a drug—no longer to make him or her feel very good but instead to terminate the bad experience. This is a dynamically changing relationship between a repeated stimulating event and mood change in the subject. When the withdrawal syndrome becomes intense, the particular individual learns that the quickest and easiest way to terminate that unpleasant event is to re-dose. This causes immediate termination of the bad experience— and the individual is hooked. He or she is on the addictive cycle, and both the tolerance and the withdrawal syndrome proceed and grow and become asymptotic. The individual now has a new problem, a new source of unpleasantness that never could have been introduced into his or her life if he or she hadn't experienced the pleasantness in the first place. That's a cost of pleasure.

Now you say, "Oh, well, that's a drug. That has nothing to do with everyday events to which we're exposed." Well, I could list over fifty-five types of experiences not involving drugs which also produce the same outcome. For example, falling in love: With repetition of the same stimuli over and over again, the ecstasy declines. That's a tolerance or habituation phenomenon. At the same time, the capacity to experience misery when the loved one is not there increases, and the duration of the misery also increases with repetition, till the individual who started out in a social attachment because of the marvelous pleasures involved ends up staying in the relationship because it's too unpleasant to terminate it. This shift is also seen in experimental laboratories which study social attachment. The duckling, when it's hatched, falls in love with the first moving object around it. Usually, that's the mother. This makes the duckling very happy. We know that the mother is a positive event because the duckling will learn to stamp on a treadle in order to make the mother appear, and it gives distress calls when the mother disappears. If you study this relationship quantitatively, you discover that the greater the frequency of exposure to the mother, and the shorter the intermother presentation time—that is, the times between which it sees the mother—the more intense is the withdrawal agony of the duckling, as measured by the intensity and duration of its distress calls. You can work out all your quantitative relationships there, and the growth of distress calling will be related to the duration of each exposure and the interexposure interval. This is exactly the same set of relationships that you can study experimentally in drug addiction in animals.

In general, drug addiction will proceed more rapidly if the drug is given in larger doses or at short interdose intervals. Indeed, for any given species, and any given drug, you can prevent the development of addiction or stimulate compulsive behavior, by adjusting the interdose interval properly. If you get a long-enough interdose interval, the individual will become a casual user of the substance. If you make the interexposure interval long enough, the duckling can take or leave its mother. It won't give any distress calls if the mother disappears, but it will look happy when the mother is there. Even though the duckling may press a pedal in order to see the mother (that is, develop an instrumental act in that setting), it may suffer absolutely no separation distress as measured by distress calls, if the exposures to the mother are far enough apart in time. That parameter of interstimulus exposure is controlled mostly by the innate organization or wiring of the species and by the quality and intensity of the stimulation and the number of times that the stimulus has been repeated.

Now, given the situation where the powerful emotion-arousing effect of a constantly repeated event, or stimulus, or object declines with repetition, or habituates when the subject becomes tolerant, and also given that the termination or withdrawal or separation syndrome becomes more and more intense and longer-lasting, it's clear that you have two correlated events. It's almost inconceivable that a person convulsing due to alcohol withdrawal does not already have a high tolerance for alcohol. These phenomena are correlated.

It is also inconceivable for you or for me to grieve at separation from a loved one if we have not become used to that person. This kind of correlation requires a theory, the simplest kind of which is an opponent-process theory, a simple control system whereby, whenever you arouse some type of big mood change, an opposing change comes in to reduce it. The opposing change is sluggish in its recruitment and its approach to its asymptote, and it is slow to decay. Under those circumstances, what will happen when stimuli are presented is that the opponent process will be exercised, and thus strengthened—like a muscle. And when the opponent process becomes strengthened, two things happen: Since it opposes the primary process, the total effect of the stimulus is decreased—that is, the drug or the presence of your loved one no longer makes you as ecstatic. But, since the opponent process is slow to decay, if you terminate the experience or remove the stimulating event, the opponent process reveals itself, although you can't tell in advance what the process will be. It's a completely empirical matter as to what will happen when you remove a substance that initially produced a big mood change.

It's not unusual that we need empirical information to determine the process. With the duckling, it's distress calling. In love, it's grief and loneliness. With drug addiction, it's abstinence agony. They bear *some* relationship to each other—they are all unpleasant—but their qualities are different. It shouldn't surprise you that this is an empirical matter. The concept of opponent process goes far back in the history of psychology. Its greatest success is in the area of color vision. If I shine a bright red light in your eye for a short time, the perceived redness decreases—that is, it looks less saturated. And then, if I suddenly terminate that red light, instead of seeing the color on the wall there, I see a green after-image which peaks and then declines and fades away. Or if I shine a blue light in your eye and do the same thing, the blueness decreases, and then when I terminate the light, you see a yellow after-image.

From those empirical events we deduce that green is the opponent of red and that yellow is the opponent of blue. It is not surprising, since the brain has this kind of wiring mechanism in it, that such relationships are found for emotions, for motivational states, and for moods. The process of addiction then can proceed whenever that mechanism is called into action. And if the process of addiction proceeds, the individual begins to act irrationally because he or she is being constantly exposed to an object or event which results only in unpleasantness—habituation to the stimulus removes the original pleasure and all that is left is the displeasure.

Those who talk about the integration of rewards and punishments in time should look closely at addictive behavior. By the laws of association, it would seem that any rational person ought to quit when a little bit of pleasantness is followed by great unpleasantness. Watch an alcoholic screaming in agony during a withdrawal convulsion. You say, "Why on earth would a person drink if it's going to produce this kind of an outcome?" And the answer is: We don't know exactly why, but obviously the laws of integration of rewards and punishments in time aren't working from the point of view of a rational system. There are overwhelming emotional events, which we call mood changes, that have their own laws; and you must take those laws into account when you begin talking about the development of tastes and preferences. Reasonableness is not going to be an element in this, I can assure you.

I think that is why I happen to be here. I think that rational models have lost their charm for economists interested in psychology. And anywhere in psychology you can find a Freudian or an opponent-process irrationality model, I think it's going to help economists in their thinking.

3

A MODEL OF CONSUMPTION AND DEMAND BASED ON PSYCHOLOGICAL OPPONENT PROCESSES

Lester D. Taylor

> If all wants were reducible to a single want, *utility,* we could not explain why in any American household water is consumed to the satiety of thirst—and therefore should have a zero "intensity" of utility at that point—while, since water is not used to satiety in sprinkling the lawn, it must have a positive "final degree of utility." Yet, no household would go thirsty—no matter how little—to water a flower pot. In other words, if a commodity satisfies several wants, it may very well happen that its "marginal utility" with respect to some wants may be zero (because these wants are completely satisfied) and yet the "utility" of the last unit not be null.
>
> —Nicholas Georgescu-Roegen

INTRODUCTION

Traditionally, economists have avoided questions concerning wants. Wants are taken as fixed, and their origins are left to psychology.[1] Moreover, since Pareto, it has not been considered necessary to distinguish between consumption and expenditure. By reducing all wants to a single want—utility—consumption and expenditure are merged, and the empirical implications of one cannot be distinguished from those of the other. The problem with reducing all wants to a single, all-encompassing want is that (cf. the quote from Georgescu-Roegen) the hierarchical nature of consumption is ignored.

While it may be proper in a narrow sense for economists to focus on expenditure—because the *economic* problem is how consumers allocate income among market goods and services—expenditure nonetheless originates from consumption, and a theory of expenditure must therefore be rooted in a theory of consumption. Focusing narrowly on expenditure entails unavoidable implicit assumptions about consumption, and there is great danger of these assumptions being psychological nonsense.

My purpose in this paper is to discuss a theory of consumption which has a credible basis in psychology. The vehicle for this will be the opponent-process model that has been developed in recent years by the psychologist Richard L. Solomon and his associates at the University of Pennsylvania.[2] The basic features of the opponent-process model are discussed in the next section. A consumption model is then developed, in which a consumer's choice set is assumed to consist of a collection of consumption activities, each of which is an opponent process. The bridge between consumption and expenditure (or demand as we conventionally think of it) is then established and, finally, the chapter concludes with some remarks related to consumption, time, and the quest for novelty.

THE PSYCHOLOGICAL OPPONENT-PROCESS MODEL

The point of departure for the opponent-process model is the observation that many feelings of pleasure or pain seem to be followed by a contrary aftereffect—pain by a pleasant feeling of relief, pleasure by a feeling of letdown or emptiness. Solomon and Corbit (1974) illustrate the phenomenon with the following example.[3]

A woman at work discovers a lump in her breast and is terrified. She sits still, intermittently weeping, or she paces the floor. After a few hours, she slowly regains her composure, stops crying, and begins to work. At this point, she is still tense and disturbed, but no longer terrified and distracted. She manifests the symptoms usually associated with intense anxiety. While in this state she calls her doctor for an appointment. A few hours later she is in his office, still tense, still frightened: She is obviously a very unhappy woman. The doctor makes his examination. He then informs her that there is no possibility of cancer, that there is nothing to worry about, and that her problem is just a clogged sebaceous gland requiring no medical attention.

A few minutes later, the woman leaves the doctor's office, smiling, greeting strangers, and walking with an unusually buoyant stride. Her euphoric mood permeates all her activities as she resumes her normal duties. She exudes joy, which is not in character for her. A few hours later, however, she is working in her normal, perfunctory way. Her emotional expression is back to normal. She once more has the personality immediately recognizable by all of her friends. Gone is the euphoria, and there is no hint of the earlier terrifying experience of that day. (Solomon and Corbit, 1974, p. 119.)

The dynamics in this example can be described as follows: Normal (or baseline) behavior is interrupted by the discovery of the lump, which triggers a state of intense fear and anxiety. This state is succeeded by a state of euphoria when the lump is disclosed to be harmless. However, the euphoria eventually dies and normal behavior resumes. More generally, the sequence can be characterized as: Baseline Behavior → State A → State B → Baseline Behavior, where State B is the hedonic opposite to State A. In the example, State A is painful, while State B is pleasurable, but there are numerous examples where the states are reversed. Birthday parties that end in tears and the hangover which follows a night on the town are two examples.

The salient characteristics of the opponent-process model are given in Figure 3.1. The model consists of three components: a primary process which is initiated by a stimulus, an opponent process which is aroused by the primary process, and a summator which sums the hedonic effects of the primary and opponent processes. Solomon refers to the primary process as an *a* process and the opponent process as a *b* process. State A referred to in the example is associated with the *a* process, while State B is associated with the *b* process. The magnitude of the *a* process is postulated to correlate closely with the intensity, quality, and duration of the stimulus. An *a* process is phasic and sensitive to small changes in the stimulus. The function of the *b* process is to oppose or suppress the state generated by the *a* process. The *b* process is postulated to be (i) of sluggish latency, (ii) inertial, or slow to build to its peak intensity, and (iii) slow to decay after the stimulus has terminated and the *a* process has stopped. Since it is an opponent process, the hedonic quality of the *b* process is opposite to that of the *a* process.

The hedonic state at any moment is postulated to be the difference, without regard to sign, between the magnitude of the *a* process and that of the *b* process. The sign of the *b* process is opposite to that of the *a* process. Let *a* denote the hedonic intensity of the *a* process and *b* the hedonic intensity of the *b* process. The *state rule* (per Solomon and Corbit), then, is simple: if $|a| > |b|$ the organism

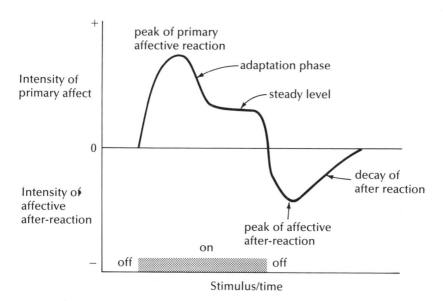

Figure 3.1. Opponent processes.

is in State A, while if $|b| > |a|$, the organism is in State B. Furthermore, if being in State A is positively reinforcing (pleasant, desirable), being in State B will be negatively reinforcing (aversive, undesirable), and vice versa.

There is a great deal of evidence from laboratory studies of opponent processes that when a stimulus of medium intensity is repeated many times within relatively short intervals the reaction to the stimulus tends to diminish.[4] This is a habituation, or ''getting used to'' process that can be seen as arising from a strengthening of the b process. This is illustrated in Figures 3.2 and 3.3. In the extreme, the tolerance to a stimulus may be so strong that there is no movement above the baseline. As will be discussed below, opponent processes with this pattern are strong candidates for addiction.

OPPONENT PROCESSES BASED ON CONSUMPTION BEHAVIOR

Let me now turn to a theory of consumption which is based on the model just described. My point of departure will be the assumption that at any point in time an individual's relationship to the world, both internal and external, can be described by a set of state variables. Included in the state variables will be stocks of durable goods, stocks of financial assets, and a (possibly long) list of psychological quantities. Consumers are assumed to select their consumption from among a set of consumption activities. A consumption activity is taken to be a

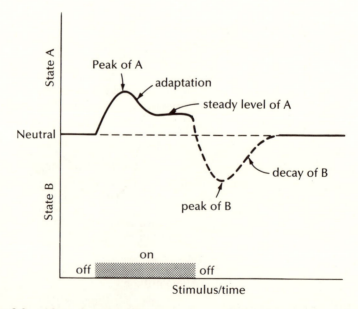

Figure 3.2. After a few stimulations.

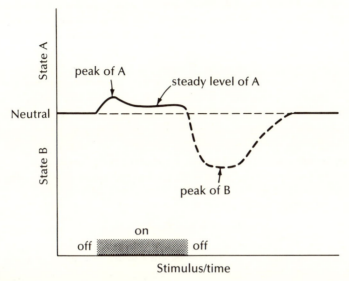

Figure 3.3.   After many stimulations.

well-defined production process which (per Lancaster and Becker) has market goods and time as inputs. An activity may be simple (such as eating an apple) or complex (such as giving a dinner party), and it may involve just a single good or a combination of goods.

The analysis allows for activities to occur simultaneously or, more accurately, within the same interval of time, such as drinking and eating while watching television. When two or more technically uncoupled activities take place in the same time interval, that with the longest time requirement will be taken as the "controlling" activity. Such activities can quite clearly be treated as complementary. In contrast, activities which compete for the same time slot will be substitutes. This form of substitution and complementarity, however, differs from the substitution and complementarity which arises from goods being inputs (along with time) into consumption activities.

We now assume that each consumption activity has associated with it a pair of opponent processes, an *a* process which is initiated by the stimulus which defines the activity and a *b* process which is triggered by the *a* process. For convenience, it will be assumed that the *a* process is hedonically positive and the *b* process negative. A consumption activity will be defined in terms of the goods which are inputs into it and the associated stimulus will be identified with the actual physical consumption of the goods. The consumer is assumed to influence the *a* process by controlling the timing, intensity, and duration of the stimulus. The *b* process, however, is governed by its own dynamics.

For many consumption activities, the scope and duration of the activity are more or less predetermined. Movies and football games are of a certain length, apples are of a certain size, and so on, and once begun, the activity is pursued to its natural conclusion. The apples may be small and one is not enough. What determines how many apples will be eaten? The conventional answer to this question is that apples will be eaten to the point where the marginal utility from another apple (another bite?) divided by the price of apples is equal to the marginal utility of income. But this is a poor description of behavior; most people, if given the opportunity, will eat until the taste for apples has been sated. This suggests a natural way of defining the duration of an activity: Consumption ends at the point where the marginal utility from continuing the activity falls to zero. Taking consumption activities as the objects of choice thus enables satiation to be brought into the analysis in a straightforward way.[5]

Following Solomon and Corbit, let us assume that the hedonic function at time t that is associated with a particular consumption activity is given by

$$(1) \quad \phi(t) = \phi_a(t) + \phi_b(t)$$

where ϕ_a and ϕ_b denote the hedonic values of the a process and b process, respectively. For convenience, we will take ϕ_a to be positive and ϕ_b negative. The functions, ϕ, ϕ_a, and ϕ_b can be interpreted as utility functions. For ϕ_a, it is assumed that

$$(2) \quad \phi_a(t) = \beta d(t)q(t)$$

where β is a parameter, $d(t)$ is a stimulus indicator variable, and $q(t)$ represents the intensity of the stimulus. For ϕ_b, it is assumed that

$$(3) \quad \phi_b(t) = -S(t)$$

where:

$$S(t) = e^{-\delta t}S_0$$

S_0 = initial strength of the a process

$e^{-\delta t}$ = rate of decay of the b process.

As noted, the consumer is assumed to control the intensity and duration of the a process. However, the duration of the b process is determined by its "depreciation" rate. The only way that a b process can be "controlled" is through "redosing," that is, by reapplying stimulus. When there is redosing in order to kill the effects of a painful b process, the consumer has reached a state of addiction. Redosing to escape the withdrawal pains from heroin and drinking to kill a hangover are obvious cases in point.

There are several different forms of addiction. As starters, there are addictions that have a physiological basis and those that are psychologically induced.

Breathing, sleeping, and eating exemplify the former, while smoking, alcoholism, and drug dependence are instances of the latter. We must also distinguish
between addictions for which physiological, biological, or time constraints are
critical and those for which income is the binding constraint. With smoking, time
is the constraint. One can smoke continually, but the tobacco consumed would
be far less than that which could be bought with available income. Even the
poorest of the poor seem somehow to be able to feed their tobacco habits. With
heroin addiction, in contrast, the physical and biological limits on dosage are
much higher, as is also the cost per dose. As a consequence, the heroin addict's
budget constraint is almost always seriously threatened, with obvious and well-
known social externalities.

Redosing occurs when the discomfort associated with the b process reaches a
point where it can no longer be tolerated. The timing of a redose will therefore be
determined by the shape and height of the b curve. Three such curves are given in
Figure 3.4. The curve in the first panel corresponds to an activity that is not

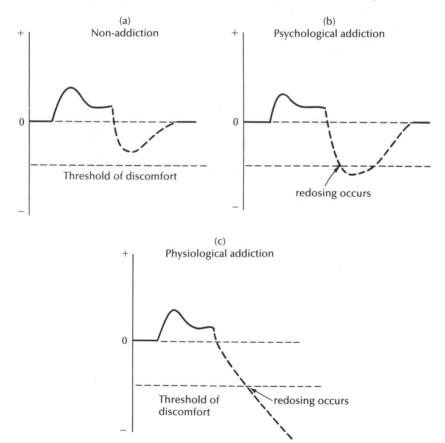

Figure 3.4. Apparent process theory of non-addiction, psychological addiction, and
physiological addiction.

addicting, as the curve does not reach the threshold level of discomfort. The second panel corresponds to an addicting activity such as tobacco consumption, for the curve drops below the threshold. Finally, the third panel corresponds to a physiologically addicting activity such as eating. The curve begins slowly, eventually passes the threshold, but then keeps on falling, reflecting the fact that endless fasting ultimately results in death.[6] The steepness of the discomfort curve in panels 2 and 3 explains the difference in time intervals between redosing for smoking and eating. The curve is much steeper for tobacco, which causes redosing to occur at much shorter intervals than for food. The extreme of course is chain-smoking, which corresponds to continual redosing.

It should be clear that, except for cases in which the *b* process decays instantaneously, each consumption activity involves a negative component. This is very much at odds with the conventional view, which holds that all consumption results in positive utility. Yet, that the conventional view is counter to common sense was recognized many years ago by R. G. Hawtrey when he distinguished between creative and defensive consumption:

The two classes of products, defensive and creative, are neither mutually exclusive nor exhaustive. The same product often fulfills purposes of both kinds. Food, for example, is needed to guard against hunger, weakness and ultimately death by starvation, but at the same time different kinds of food are designed to give the consumer positive satisfaction. This duality does not invalidate the distinction.

We may regard either class of product as meeting a *need*. In the case of the defensive product the need arises from the distress caused or threatened by some physical condition. No imaginative effort from within or prompting from without is required to awaken the need. In the case of the creative product on the other hand, the need can only arise from a knowledge of the possibility of the product. Obviously that knowledge cannot take the form of an original invention of something new, save in rare and exceptional cases. The ordinary man can only gain it from the experience of himself and his neighbors. [Hawtrey, 1925, pp. 189–90, italics in original.]

Hawtrey also notes:

An exhaustive classification of creative products is impossible, but it will be worthwhile to enumerate some of the principal types. To begin with, there are purely sensual pleasures, such as those of eating and drinking. We are stimulated to seek whatever is physiologically necessary for ourselves and our species by instinctive reactions to certain sensations. Some sensations, such as physical pain, cause us distress, and we are induced thereby to take whatever action we can to end them. Others cause us pleasure, and induce us so to act as to start them, or, if we already have them, to intensify and prolong them. Products of which the purpose is to promote physical pleasure are a part of those we have classed as creative. It is not easy to draw the line between products which prevent pain and those which promote physical pleasure, because it is characteristic of any physical need, which causes distress while it is still unsatisfied, to cause positive physical pleasure as soon as it is in course of being satisfied. We have all heard of the man who had a thirst he would not sell for ten dollars. The pleasure that arises *merely* from the removal of distress cannot be regarded as constituting the product that occasions it a creative product. But it is often possible by a suitable adaptation or elaboration of the product to procure much more pleasure than the satisfaction of the need alone would yield. Then the product will become creative. (Hawtrey, 1925, pp. 191–92, italics in original.)

In *The Joyless Economy*, Scitovsky, who clearly sympathizes with Hawtrey, distinguishes between comfort and pleasure. Scitovsky notes that a great deal of consumption activity, especially in the United States, is directed toward maintaining a desired level of comfort, and it is only after comforts are dealt with that there is consumption for pleasure. Comfort itself does not yield hedonic pleasure, but its absence clearly gives rise to displeasure. The rich man in his chauffeured Rolls Royce is not necessarily any happier than the middle-class merchant driving his Chevrolet, but put the rich man in the Chevrolet and he would almost certainly become unhappy. Consumption directed at maintaining comfort can accordingly be interpreted as defensive consumption, while pleasure-producing consumption represents creative consumption.

Comfort in Scitovsky's scheme refers not just to physical comfort but to comfort that arises through *acquired motivation*. People become habituated to certain norms of consumption activity, and when these norms are not maintained (or are even threatened), discomfort results. These norms clearly vary across individuals, and for the same individual they can vary over time, depending (among other things) on the level of income, the consumption history of the individual, and the social milieu. By conventional theory, the rich should be happier than the poor because they are able to consume more, but who really believes this to be the case? Indeed, the rich may in some cases even be less happy because their higher level of income offers a broader range of "comforts" to be maintained.

The only current empirically oriented demand model which seems to reflect the comfort/pleasure distinction is the Stone-Rowe linear expenditure system. As is well known, the Stone-Geary utility function, from which the linear expenditure system is derived, is a Cobb-Douglas (that is, double logarithmic) function with the origin translated to the point $\gamma = (\gamma_1, \ldots, \gamma_n)$. The γ_i's, which in most applications are assumed to be positive, are interpreted as "minimum required quantities." Utility is not even defined in this model until these minimum quantities, which are independent of prices and income (at least in the static case), have been consumed. In the present context, it is natural to interpret these quantities as expenditures to maintain comfort. The dynamization of the linear expenditure system of Phlips (1972) brings this system into even closer agreement with the comfort/pleasure dichotomy, for in the Phlips model the amount expended for "comfort" can vary with consumption experience and the level of income.

It was assumed earlier that at any point in time a consumer's relationship to the world is described by a set of state variables. These state variables, in conjunction with income and other external factors, affect the individual's consumption behavior. However, the state variables may themselves be affected by current consumption. Our assumption will be that a minimum of two state variables is associated with every consumption activity, one associated with the *a* process and the second with the *b* process. The *a*-process state variable can be viewed as a general stock of consumption capital for the activity, in the manner of Stigler and Becker (1977). Intangibles will always be contained in this stock, and in many cases physical capital as well. Included in the intangibles will be knowledge of the activity that has been acquired through research and previous experience, or what Scitovsky refers to as redundancy. Solomon and Corbit note the fear and trepidation (even panic) that can accompany an activity that has not been previously experienced. Skydiving provides a good example, for parachutists on their first jump are often terrified, but their responses are totally different after a few jumps. This demise of discomfort can be laid to the creation of a stock of consumption capital.

The stock of consumption capital will be assumed to be subject to depreciation. However, experience suggests that the "investment" process involved is in general not reversible, because once something is learned, relearning is usually much easier. Relearning the basic results of calculus is a case in point. Moreover, there are some things, such as riding a bicycle or driving a car, that never seem to be forgotten once they have been learned.

Let us now turn to the state variable for the *b* process. As we have seen, this is a slave process triggered by the *a* process, but which, once started, unfolds according to its own dynamics (unless interrupted by redosing). The *b* process tends to strengthen with repetition, and, except for physiological addictions such as eating and breathing, eventually wears off. The *b* process was represented earlier by

$$(5) \quad S(t) = e^{-\delta t} S_0, \; \delta > 0$$

where S_0 denotes the initial strength of the process. We shall now allow for a strengthening of the *b* process. To this end, let $B(t)$ denote the *b*-process state variable at time *t*, where *t* is assumed to be measured from the time of first exposure. We now assume that $B(t)$ is given by

$$(6) \quad B(t) = B_0 + \sum_{i=1}^{n^*} e^{-\eta i} q[i], \quad \eta > 0$$

where B_0 represents the strength of the process at the time of first exposure, $q(i)$ denotes the strength of the stimulus during the *i*th exposure, and n^* denotes the number of distinct exposures. The *b* process is thus assumed to increase with exposure, but at a decreasing rate.

The *b*-process utility for an activity at time (t, t') will accordingly be given by

$$(7) \quad -S(t,t') = -e^{-\delta(t' - t)} B(t)$$

where $B(t)$ is given by expression (6).

Note that two types of time are represented in this expression, historical (or chronological) time, which relates to consumption decision points, and process (or activity) time, which refers to the time interval over which a consumption activity occurs. The former is indexed by t and the latter by t'. It is assumed that $B(t)$ is independent of t', that is, that the state variable is affected only by the frequency and intensity of the stimulus which defines the activity.

Let the state variable for the a process be given by $A(t)$ and assume that A changes with t according to

$$(8) \quad \dot{A}(t) = q(t) - \eta A(t), \; \eta > 0$$

Note that the time argument in this expression is t rather than t'—that is, as with B, the level of A is affected only by the frequency and intensity of the stimulus, and not by the duration of an exposure.

The next task is to incorporate the A-state variable into the utility function. This is assumed to occur through the coefficient β in expression (2), so that the utility at time (t, t') for the a process will be given by

$$(9) \quad \phi_a(t, t') = \beta \, [A(t)]d(t' - t) \, q(t')$$

The utility for the consumption activity as a whole at time (t, t') will therefore be equal to

$$(10) \quad \phi(t, t') = \phi_a(t, t') + \phi_b(t, t')$$
$$= \beta[A(t)d(t' - t)q(t) - e^{-\delta(t'-t)}B(t)$$

where the "laws of motion" for A and B from expressions (6) and (8) are given by:

$$\dot{A}(t) = q(t) - \eta A(t)$$
$$\dot{B}(t) = e^{-\eta n^*}q[n^*]$$

Taking time t as the consumption decision point, we shall define the utility $\phi(t)$ for an activity as the utility of the a process minus the utility of the b process, viz:

$$(11) \quad \phi(t) = \int_t^{t+h} \emptyset_a(t, t')dt' - \int_t^{\infty} \emptyset_b(t, t')dt'$$

$$= \beta[A(t)]q(t) \int_t^{t+h} d(t, t')dt' - B(t) \int_t^{\infty} e^{-\delta(t'-t)}dt'$$

$$= \beta[A(t)]q(t)h - \frac{1}{\delta} B(t)$$

where h represents the length of time that the stimulus is on.[7]

The foregoing, which is applicable only to nonaddicting activities, assumes that the consumer is fully aware of the *b* process. This assumption may be questioned, for it might seem that consumers look only at the *a* process and ignore the negative utility of the *b* process. There are undoubtedly many instances where this is true, as exemplified in "Eat, drink, and be merry, for tomorrow we may die," but I do not believe that this is the case in general, else why does consumption not involve more regrets? The nonaddicted imbiber, for example, who occasionally "ties one on" is not surprised by the subsequent hangover. The person may lament this discomfort and swear never to do it again, yet there was an awareness of what was to come and the same decision would probably be made if it were all to be done again.[8]

EQUILIBRIUM OF THE CONSUMER

We come now to the tough part of the exercise, which is the specification of the rules by which a consumer selects a particular set of activities to consume and how this in turn is translated into the demand for goods and services. The assumption at this point is that an individual is really two people, a *consumer* concerned with obtaining as much satisfaction as possible given the time and income available and a *purchasing agent* who takes orders from the consumer as to the goods and services that are to be bought in the market. It is assumed that an individual's consumption behavior is affected by three types of constraints: income, time, and the state variables associated with the consumption activities. While the state variables are not constraints in quite the same way as income and time, it will be convenient to treat them as such since they evolve according to their own internal dynamics.

A consumer's choice of an equilibrium set of activities will be approached in two different frameworks. In the first, it will be assumed that the consumer selects activities in the order of their decreasing utility, while in the second it will be assumed that the consumer selects activities in accord with a preestablished hierarchical order of wants. For convenience, these two approaches will be referred to as utility-ordered and hierarchical-ordered, respectively.

Equilibrium with Utility Ordering

Earlier, the utility of an individual consumption activity was defined as the integral of the difference between the utility of the *a* process and that of the *b* process. Henceforth, when we speak of the utility of an activity, this will be the quantity in mind. Let I denote the set of consumption activities available to a consumer and let ϕ^i denote the utility for the *i*th activity in this set. Assume that I contains n activities and define the global (or total) utility function as

$$(12) \quad \phi = \sum_{i=1}^{n} \pi_i \phi^i$$

where

$$\pi_i = \begin{cases} 1 \text{ if activity } i \text{ is selected} \\ 0 \text{ otherwise.} \end{cases}$$

Next, let I^* denote an ordered index set such that, for all $i \in I^*$ and $j \notin I^*$, $\phi^i > \phi^j$.

The consumer's optimization problem can then be expressed as follows:

$$(13) \quad \sup_{i \in I^*} \{\phi = \sum_{i \in I^*} \pi_i \phi^i$$

subject to:

$$(14) \quad \sum_{i \in I^*} P_i \pi_i \leq x$$

$$(15) \quad \sum_{i \in I^*} t_i \pi_i \leq T$$

where:

p_i = price (that is, costs) of activity i

x = income

t_i = time required by activity i

T = total time available

The idea is simple: The consumer's task is to select a set of consumption activities that maximizes global (or total) utility subject to expenditure for the activities not being greater than the income which is available and subject to the time that is required by the activities not being greater than that which is available. Note that it is assumed that utilities are independent across activities, which means that the consumer can simply order activities by decreasing utility and then select sequentially until the income and time constraints are no longer satisfied. The solution is thus a straightforward programming problem.[9]

The price of goods enters the budget constraint indirectly through the cost of the individual activities. The price of an activity, p_i, represents the total cost of the activity, and will thus include the cost of the time required by the activity as well as the cost of the goods and services that are used as inputs. It is assumed that activities operate efficiently, that is, that "production" occurs on the efficiency frontier and that standard neoclassical least-cost conditions apply. Thus, it follows that a consumer's demands for goods and services are derived demands in exactly the same sense as a firm's demands for inputs.

Equilibrium with Hierarchical Ordering

As an alternative to the preceding equilibrium, it can be assumed that the consumer possesses a hierarchy of wants and that consumption activities are selected in accordance with this hierarchy.[10] To simplify the discussion, it will be assumed that activities and wants are isomorphic, so that each want is associated with a single activity and vice versa. With this assumption, it follows that a hierarchy on activities is induced by a hierarchy on wants. Further, it is assumed that at any point in time the hierarchy is a fixed feature of the consumer's preferences. This assumption does not rule out the possibility that the want hierarchy changes over time. Indeed, this is exactly what we should expect to occur through the dynamics of the underlying opponent processes. As the consumer is exposed to new activities, as will inevitably be the case in normal circumstances, new consumption capital (both positive and negative) will be created which will tend to reorder want priorities. Addicting activities are cases in point, with heroin an obvious extreme.[11]

Let A_i denote the ith activity. As before, it will be assumed that at any point in time the consumer has n activities available from which to select. Further, it is assumed that n is so large that the possibility never arises of all activities being consumed. Apart from the assumption that it is a fixed feature of the consumer's preferences, the only thing that will be assumed about the want hierarchy is that it is endless, that once a want has been satisfied there is always another to take its place. Global satiation is thus ruled out.[12] Let $A^* = (A^1, A^2, \ldots, A^n, \ldots)$ denote the ordering on activities that is induced by the consumer's hierarchy on wants. Finally, as before, let p_i denote the cost of the ith activity, t_i the time required by the activity, T the total time that is available, and x the amount of income that is available.

The consumer's optimization problem thus reduces to moving into A^* as far as possible without violating the constraints on income and time, or, more formally, to find the maximal advancing subset of A^*, $A^{**} = (A^1, A^2, \ldots, A^k)$, $k < n$, such that:

$$(16) \quad \sum_{i=1}^{k} p^i A^i \leq x$$

$$(17) \quad \sum_{i=1}^{k} t^i \leq T \quad \text{(See note 13.)}$$

Prices enter the budget constraint as before, although the notation is modified to account for the hierarchical ordering of activities. Also, as before, it is assumed that activities are operated efficiently and that whenever substitution possibilities exist, the least-cost combination of goods and services is available.

While the utility and hierarchical orderings involve different assumptions about the structure of a consumer's preferences, the mechanics of arriving at the

preferred set of consumption activities are virtually the same. The only difference is that in the first case the ordering is based on the net satisfaction that an
activity yields, while in the second case the ordering is determined by an a priori
hierarchy of wants. Once the ordering is determined, the consumer simply moves
along the ordering as far as the income and time constraints allow. We now take
a more detailed look at how this occurs.

As before, let A_i denote the ith consumption activity, except assume that the
activities have been ordered, so that A_i represents the activity in the ith place in
the order. Also, as before, let p_i and t_i denote the cost of A_i and the time required
by it as input. The total amount of time available will continue to be denoted by
T, but the budget constraint will be altered to allow for income to be endogenous.
In particular, the budget constraint will now be taken to be

$$(18) \quad \Sigma p_i \leq w(T - \Sigma t_i)$$

or

$$(19) \quad \Sigma(p_i + wt_i) \leq wT$$

where w is the consumer's market wage rate. Both of these expressions are
familiar. The term wT is referred to as full income in the labor-supply literature,[14] as it represents the potential income that the consumer has at his disposal
to purchase market goods and services and time as leisure and input into consumption activities. The term $w(T - \Sigma t_i)$ accordingly represents the amount of
money income available for the purchase of market goods.[15] The term $p_i + wt_i$ in
expression (16) represents the full cost of the ith activity, and consists of the cost
of market goods (p_i) and the opportunity cost of the time required as input
(wt_i).[16]

Let us now follow the consumer through the optimization process.[17] At his
first step, A_1 is selected, and the budget and time constraints are given by:

$$(20) \quad p_1 \leq w(T - t_1)$$

$$(21) \quad t_1 \leq T$$

At the second step, A_2 is selected, and the constraints are:

$$(22) \quad p_2 \leq w(T - t_1 - t_2) - p_1$$

$$(23) \quad t_2 \leq T - t_1$$

At the ith step, assuming that the constraints still contain some slack, A_i is
selected, and the constraints will be given by:

$$(24) \quad p_i \leq w\left(T - \sum_{j=1}^{i} t_j\right) - \sum_{j=1}^{i-1} p_j$$

$$(25) \quad t_i \leq T - \sum_{j-1}^{i-1} t_j$$

This will continue until one (or both) of the constraints is violated.

If we make the simplifying assumption that each activity uses only one good as an input, a simple graphical exposition becomes available. Accordingly, let us turn our attention to Figure 3.5. The good used as input to A_1 is measured on the vertical axis in panel a, while the time is measured on the horizontal axis. The time constraint is represented by the vertical line at T, while the budget constraint is represented by the straight line labeled x_1^* with slope equal to $-w/p_1$. The activity

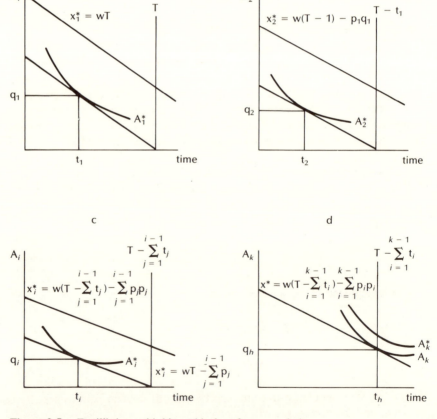

Figure 3.5. Equilibrium with hierarchical preference ordering.

A_1^* is represented by a family of convex curves with the curve labeled A_1 being the satiated level of the activity. Activities are represented as isoquants with conventional substitution technologies in order to underscore the point that activities represent production processes. Right-angled isoquants are not ruled out, as indeed would frequently be the case when there is only a single good and time as inputs. Equilibrium occurs in panel a at the point A_1^*, in which case q_1 units of the good are consumed and t_1 units of time.

Moving now to panel b, which represents the consumption of activity A_2, the time constraint is now the vertical line t_1 units to the left of T and the budget constraint, x_2^*, has a vertical intercept at $[w(t - t_1) - p_1 q_1]p_2$ and slope $-w/p_2$. Equilibrium occurs at the point a_2^*, with q_2 units of good 2 being consumed and t_2 units of time. Panel c depicts the consumption of activity A_i.

The time constraint is now moved $\sum_{j=1}^{i-1} t_i$ to the left of T, while the budget constraint has slope equal to $-w/p_i$ and its vertical intercept at $[w(T - \sum_{j=1}^{i-1} t_i) - \sum_{j=1}^{i-1} p_j q_j]/p_i$. Equilibrium occurs at A_i^*, at which point both costraints still contain slack. Finally, panel d depicts the terminal consumption activity, and illustrates a case, which in general will be atypical, where both constraints are just met.

FROM CONSUMPTION TO DEMAND

The demand for goods and services in this model is a derived demand. Goods and services, together with time, are inputs into consumption activities, whose initiation is controlled by the consumer. The consumer gives orders for the goods that are to be stocked, and they are then obtained by the purchasing agent at least cost. Functions relating quantities demanded to prices (including the price of time) and income thus exist in this model but, in general, they cannot be derived analytically from first-order conditions as with neoclassical demand theory.

In his doctoral dissertation at the University of Arizona, Donald Coursey examined the comparative statics of the demand functions and Engel curves for the case where preferences are hierarchical and goods and activities are isomorphic.[18] The principal results are as follows:

1. A price change for the ith good (that is, the good used by the ith activity) will not affect the demands for the first $i - 1$ goods, nor will it affect the demands for goods $i + 1$ through $k - 1$ (assuming that equilibrium occurs in the kth activity). This follows from the independence imposed by the technology of the problem and the fact that neither the budget nor time constraint is binding for these activities.

2. If the isoquant for A_i is smooth, a change in p_i will lead to a substitution of q_i for time

or vice versa. This means, in turn, that both the budget and time constraints for A_k will be affected and possibly the demand for q_k, depending upon whether the constraints were binding. At an extreme, a decrease in p_i may allow consumption to move to A_{k+1}, while an increase in p_i may cause terminal consumption to drop to A_{k-1}.

3. However, if the isoquant for A_i is right-angled, a change in p_i will not affect the demand for q_i. Its only effect will be on the budget constraint in A_k. The time constraint is nowhere affected; the only possible effect in this case is an income effect in the terminal activity.[19]

4. A change in the money wage rate will change the slope of the price line in every activity. Thus, demand will be affected (through a substitution effect) in every interior activity with a smooth isoquant. Demand will not be affected in those interior activities with right-angled isoquants. Demand in the terminal activity will be affected through changes in both the budget and time constraints.

5. Finally, a change in nonlabor income will affect demand in the terminal activity only through an income effect. There is no effect on the time constraint.

The foregoing conclusions hold strictly only in a very stylized world where activities have only one good input and each good is used in only one activity. When activities are allowed to have multiple goods as inputs and goods can be inputs into multiple activities, the analysis becomes much more relevant to the real world, but also much more complicated. Goods can now become substitutes and complements in production, and the change in the price of a good will affect directly the costs of all of the activities for which it is an output. Price elasticities will be highest for those goods having many substitution possibilities. Moreover, price elasticities will be insensitive to the good's position in the want hierarchy. But this will not be the case for income elasticities; income effects will be largest for goods used primarily in low-want activities.[20]

CONSUMPTION, TIME, AND THE QUEST FOR NOVELTY

Despite the seminal work by Becker and his followers and the equally important work of Linder (1970), time as an input and complement to consumption has not yet attained its rightful place in consumer theory. One of the goals of this paper has been to integrate time into the theory of consumption in a way that not only reflects its traditional economic aspects but also its psychological role. Economics has traditionally taken the view that consumption and happiness are synonymous. However, the view that is adopted in this paper is that a person's main preoccupation is how to spend time rather than income. Unlike income, for which most of us have to work, time appears each day as a gift. The amount is fixed and its receipt cannot be escaped.

The physiology and psychology of the human organism are such that unless a certain number of neurons are firing at any time, the individual is uncomfortable. As psychologists say, arousal is at too low a level. In general, stimulation in some form is required to maintain arousal, and much of this occurs through the consumption of market goods and services. Since goods and services are scarce, some of the individual's time must be spent in acquiring the income needed for their purchase. However, when not asleep or at work, the basic question facing the individual is how to maintain arousal at the desired level, which amounts to deciding how to allocate time among consumption activities.

Since the time that is available is fixed, people typically run out of it, so that time itself becomes scarce. When this happens, time must be used more efficiently. Generally, this involves trading off time for market goods in consumption activities. For most people, the primary force in increasing the scarcity of time is increased efficiency at work (that is, an increase in the real wage rate).[21] Thus, in an important sense, the constraint on consumption behavior is time, rather than income. The individual decides what activities to consume, and the goods required as input are assumed to be on hand in the amount necessary for the activity to reach satiation. Income becomes a constraint when the purchasing agent receives orders for the goods to be stocked.

It was noted that pleasantly stimulating activities blend novelty and redundancy. Too much redundancy leads to boredom because everything has an aura of deja vu or "familiarity breeds contempt", while too much novelty leads to confusion and immobility because one does not know what to expect. Some surprise is highly desirable, but too much causes discomfort because of limited capacity to process new information. Redundancy can be identified with the state variable (or variables) associated with the a process, and its kinship with the Stigler-Becker consumption capital has been noted. Redundancy is created through exposure, and arises through the internal dynamics of the consumption activity. The quest for novelty, in contrast, is inherent in the psyche of an individual. It functions independently of exposure,[22] and provides the motivation for seeking new activities. It is the raison d'etre for wants being endless, and incites the continual appearance of new goods. Many years ago Keynes saw "animal spirits" as the major force for investment; the quest for novelty is the counterpart for consumption.

CONCLUDING REMARKS

As stated in the introduction, my primary purpose in this paper has been to formulate a model of consumer behavior that has a credible basis in psychology. An individual's consumption decision is assumed to involve selecting from among a well-defined set of consumption activities which use goods and time as inputs. A consmption activity is assumed to embody two psychological opponent processes, an a process which is identified with the stimulus which defines the activity and a b process which is triggered by the a process. The a process is under the control of the individual, but the b process is slave to the a process and, once initiated, proceeds according to its own dynamics. State variables are associated with each of the processes. They evolve in response to exposure, and evolution that largely determines the dynamical behavior of consumption through time.

Satiation is present in that it is assumed that consumption in activity proceeds to the point where marginal utility becomes negative. It is assumed that, once physical survival has been dealt with, an individual spends his time so as to maintain arousal at an appropriate level. Economic behavior emerges because maintaining arousal at a satisfactory level usually requires the consumption of scarce goods and services, which in turn requires income. Since the desire to maintain arousal is never ending, the constraint on consumption behavior over very short intervals of time is time itself. Goods are assumed to be available in inventory, having been placed there by the ''purchasing agent'' upon orders from the ''consumer.'' Over longer intervals of time, income is also a constraint, and the individual must choose how to allocate time between consumption and work.

The tradition in economics has been to equate consumption with satisfaction. Those with more income are able to consume more and therefore achieve more satisfaction. Both logic and common sense question this assumption, and the opponent-process framework presented here explains why. Every consumption activity is seen as consisting of two processes which are hedonic opposites. If the *a* process yields pleasure, the *b* process yields discomfort, and vice versa. Thus, it is possible for a high level of consumption expenditure to yield very little satisfaction. Indeed, at an extreme, satisfaction may actually be negative, as all of the income is directed at killing the discomfort of addicting activities. At the other extreme will be the case where all of the consumption activities embody very weak *b* processes. This is a happy circumstance that is probably achieved by few, primarily through luck.

While the theory that has been presented here makes some important departures from conventional demand theory, the analysis has many predecessors. Much of the theory is classical, especially in the assumption of a hierarchy of wants. In this, it is squarely in the tradition of Banfield, Jevons, Menger, Böhm-Bawerk, and Marshall, and Georgescu-Roegen and Ironmonger in this century. Approaching consumption behavior in terms of activities follows Lancaster, Muth, Becker, Ironmonger, and others, and the emphasis on time as a constraint on consumption is in keeping with Becker and Linder. Finally, the whole effort was greatly motivated by Scitovsky's *The Joyless Economy*. If nothing else, the exercise offers yet another instance of the absence of free lunch: *There ain't no such thing as an endless chain of pleasures!*

I am indebted to Donald Coursey, Fernando Saldanha, and Peter Zweifel for comments and criticism and to Mary Flannery and Maureen DiTolla for secretarial assistance. An earlier version of this paper was given at the Madrid meetings of the Econometric Society in September 1984.

NOTES

1. See Friedman (1962, p. 13). I do not mean to disparage the interesting work on endogenous taste change of V. Weizsäcker (1971), Pollak (1978), Stigler and Becker (1977), and others or the work on preference formation of Kapteyn (1977). See also Manove (1973), Yaari (1977), Schelling (1978), Sen (1977), and Winston (1980).

2. This model was first brought to the attention of economists by Tibor Scitovsky in *The Joyless Economy*.

3. A shortened version of the Solomon-Corbit paper appears in the 1978 *AEA Handbook*.

4. This evidence is discussed in Solomon and Corbit (1974) and Solomon (1980).

5. Both Barbara Sands and Gordon Winston have suggested that it would be more meaningful to have an activity cease when the marginal utility of the activity dips below the marginal utility of some other activity. Certainly, there may be times when this is the case, but still it seems to me that much consumption activity is pursued to satiation. Anyway, this is the assumption that I wish to make here.

6. This is for normal eating patterns. Anorexia, which has recently received wide-spread attention, is an addiction similar in form to smoking and drug dependence.

7. As I have argued above, h can be viewed as being the value of t' at the point where $\partial\phi(t, t')/ \partial t' = 0$.

8. In this discussion paper, I am ignoring the possibility that individuals may be subject to two (or more) sets of preferences, which on occasion can be in conflict with one another. See Sen (1977), Schelling (1978), and Winston (1980).

9. The independence assumption which allows for this to be done seems reasonable since the reference is to activities as opposed to individual commodities. Activities which are dependent can be redefined as a single activity.

10. Hierarchical preferences have had a long but irregular existence in economics. A want hierarchy was an essential feature in much of classical theory, most notably in the writings of Jevons, Menger, and Böhm-Bawerk. It began to fall by the wayside with Marshall (although the notion is clearly still present in Book III), and disappeared entirely with Pareto. Hierarchical preferences have received little attention in the twentieth century, as they are absent altogether in neoclassical and revealed-preference theory, and have been kept alive largely through the efforts of Georgescu-Roegen (1954) and Iron-monger (1972). However, recent attempts to test the propositions of neoclassical theory by the methods of experimental economics have had to assume that wants are ordered.

11. One does not have to resort to extreme forms of "decadence" to make the point, for who among us has not seen consumption priorities change as a result of exposure to a new activity.

12. This is the standard assumption in hierarchical preferences, and is referred to by Georgescu-Roegen as the Principle of Subordination of Wants.

13. Because of the discreteness of consumption activities, it may be that the kth activity violates one or both of the constraints, but the $k + 1$st does not. In this case, the consumer might "jump over" a want in the hierarchy. This possibility also arises in the utility-ordered equilibrium.

14. See, among others, Becker (1965) and Burtless and Hausman (1978).

15. Nonlabor income is ignored.

16. See Becker (1965).

17. The presentation which follows was first developed by Donald Coursey in his Ph.D. dissertation at the University of Arizona. See Coursey (1982).

18. See Coursey (1982).

19. This result has some interesting implications for the way that consumers reacted to the large OPEC price increases in 1973 and 1979. For many consumers, the amount of energy consumed was not notably affected because energy-consuming activities were high in their hierarchy of wants. This slippage came in activities lower down in the hierarchy, many of which were unrelated to energy consumption, fewer "toys" bought, less eating out, and so on.

20. A want hierarchy provides a more natural framework for interpreting necessities and luxuries than is conventionally the case. Goods whose primary uses are far along in the hierarchy will clearly be much more sensitive to income than goods whose primary uses are early in the hierarchy. Defining necessities and luxuries in these terms seems much more satisfying than in terms of the value of income elasticities relative to one.

21. All of this is described in detail, with great insight and in a highly entertaining manner, by Staffan Linder in *The Harried Leisure Class*.

22. Although exposure to a new activity may remind an individual how pleasant novelty in fact is.

REFERENCES

Becker, G. S. "A Theory of the Allocation of Time." *Economic Journal* 75 (September 1965):493–517.

Burtless, G. and Hausman, J. A. "The Effect of Taxation on Labor Supply: Evaluating the Gary Negative Income Tax Experiment." *Journal of Political Economy* 86, no. 6 (December 1978):1103–40.

Coursey, D. L. "Hierarchical Preferences and Consumer Choice," unpublished Ph.D. dissertation, Department of Economics, University of Arizona, 1982.

Friedman, M. *Price Theory: A Provisional Text.* Hawthorne, NY: Aldine Publishing Co., 1962.

Georgescu-Roegen, N. "Choice, Expectations, and Measurement." *Quarterly Journal of Economics* 68, no. 3 (August 1954):503–34.

Hawtrey, R. G. *The Economic Problem.* New York: Longmans, Green and Co., 1925.

Ironmonger, D. S. *New Commodities and Consumer Behavior.* London: Cambridge University Press, 1972.

Kapteyn, A. *A Theory of Preference Formation.* Drukkeriz J. H. Pasmans, 'S-Gravenhage, The Netherlands, 1977.

Lancaster, K. *Consumer Demand: A New Approach.* New York: Columbia University Press, 1977.

Linder, S. *The Harried Leisure Class.* New York: Columbia University Press, 1970.

Manove, M. "Consumer Behavior and Preference Formation." CORE, Catholic University of Louvain, August 1973.

Phlips, L. "A Dynamic Version of the Linear Expenditure Model." *Review of Economics and Statistics,* 54, no. 4 (1972):445–58.

Pollak, R. A. "Endogenous Tastes in Demand and Welfare Analysis." *American Economic Review, Papers and Proceedings* 68, no. 2 (May 1978):374–79.

Schelling, T. C. "Economics, or the Art of Self-Management." *American Economic Review* 68, no. 2 (May 1978):290–94.

Scitovsky, T. *The Joyless Economy.* Oxford University Press, 1976.

Sen, A. K. "Rational Fools: A Critique of the Behavioral Foundations of Economic Theory." *Philosophy and Public Affairs* 6, no. 4 (Summer 1977): 317–45.

Solomon, R. L. "The Opponent-Process Theory of Acquired Motivation: The Costs of Pleasure and Benefits of Pain." *American Psychologist* 35, no. 8 (August 1980):691–712.

Solomon, R. L. and Corbit, J. D. "An Opponent Process Theory of Motivation: I. Temporal Dynamics Affect." *Psychological Review* 81, no. 2 (1974):119–35.

Stigler, G. J. and Becker, G. S. "De Gustibus Non Est Disputandum." *American Economic Review* 67, no. 2 (March 1977):76–90.

V. Weizsäcker, C. C. "Notes on Endogenous Change of Tastes." *Journal of Economic Theory,* 3 (December 1979).

Winston, G. C. "Addiction and Backsliding: A Theory of Compulsive Consumption." *Journal of Economic Behavior and Organization* 1 (1980):295–324.

Yaari, M. E. "Endogenous Changes in Tastes: A Philosophical Discussion." *Erkenntnis* 11 (1977):157–96.

4

THE INTIMATE RELATIONS OF THE CONSISTENT CONSUMER: PSYCHOANALYTIC OBJECT RELATIONS THEORY APPLIED TO ECONOMICS

Paul J. Albanese

THE TASTELESS CONSUMER: AN ELEVATION OF TASTE CONSIDERATIONS

An exploration of the psychological foundations of the economic behavior of the individual consumer provides a promising opportunity for broadening the behavioral basis of economic analysis. To accomplish this objective, two basic patterns of individual consumption behavior will be analyzed—a pattern of stable and consistent consumption behavior, and a pattern of alternating and contradictory consumption behavior. Stable and consistent consumption behavior is the pattern that economists are more accustomed to dealing with, since consistency is the basis of the rationality postulate in economic theory. A consistent consumer will make consistent choices and, therefore, will have a transitive preference ordering—the sine qua non of ordinal utility theory. Stable and consistent consumption behavior will simply be termed normal consumption behavior.

An alternating and contradictory pattern of consumption is described by the observation of the following behavior: Consumers behave as if they had two separate sets of contradictory preferences which are alternately expressed in their observable consumption behavior. It will be argued that this is the basis for compulsive consumption behavior and, in the extreme, addictive consumption behavior. In such cases the person is in conflict over his or her consumption behavior—at one point in time, he/she wants to consume the commodity, and at another point, not consume the very same commodity (Schelling 1980, 1984; Winston 1980). The person's consumption behavior oscillates between these two contradictory preference states, and this alternating and contradictory pattern of behavior results in an intransitive preference ordering. Ordinal utility theory should not be applied in this case, since inconsistent consumption behavior violates the behavioral postulate of rationality.

This is not as serious an indictment of the economic theory of the consumer as it may seem; it simply acknowledges that the theory is useful only when applied within appropriate limits of applicability. With this acknowledgment, however, comes the recognition that patterns of individual consumption behavior which do not fit the model of the rational consumer must be represented by different preference structures, and ultimately reflect very different ranges of individual behavior. The recognition of discrete ranges of behavior representing different patterns of individual consumption behavior carries with it the challenge of modeling each range of behavior in a fundamentally different mathematical optimization framework. An investigation of the psychological foundations of the normal, compulsive, and addictive ranges of consumption behavior broadens the behavioral basis of the economic analysis of the consumer.

This broadening, in turn, provides a promising opportunity for advances in expanding the limits of applicability of the economic theory of the consumer, since each preference structure must be modeled in a fundamentally different optimization framework. J. R. Hicks (1934) argued in "A Reconsideration of the Theory of Value," that the transformation from cardinal or ordinal utility theory, following Pareto's demonstration of the immeasurability of utility, "rested on the positive demonstration that the facts of observable conduct make a scale of preferences capable of theoretical construction" (Hicks, 1934, p. 52). Presumably a consumer's scale of preferences is known to us from the observation of actual market behavior; however, this approach has not been widely practiced by economists. With the outstanding exception of the growing movement of behavioral economics, the observation of behavior has been largely abandoned by economists.

While ordinal utility theory came to be based on the observable market behavior of the individual consumer, it also came to rest on a superficial conception of the consumer as simply a scale of preferences. Even knowing the individual consumer's scale of preferences from the observation of actual market behavior, however, still does "not enable us to proceed from the scale of preferences to a particular utility function" (Hicks, 1934, p. 52). This represents a substantive weakness of the foundation of ordinal utility theory. Nevertheless, as we shall see, it is a good theory of choice when applied within the appropriate limits of its applicability, and should not be abandoned, but instead expanded to accommodate the additional ranges of consumption behavior.

The failure to observe the actual market behavior of the consumer, however, has constricted the scope of the superficial conception of the consumer even further by the easy assumption that the consumer's scale of preferences is given. This is a scandalous assumption, and immediately calls into question the nature of the consumer's preferences that are being held constant by assumption. There is no harm in making this assumption provided that the nature of the consumer's preferences is known to be stable and consistent from the observation of actual market behavior. An application of ordinal utility theory would be appropriate, and the rational consumer will always maximize utility. However, if the consumer's preferences fit the alternating and contradictory pattern of consumption behavior—or any other observable pattern of consumption behavior which does not fit the economic conception of the rational consumer—conventional ordinal utility theory is not appropriate, and should not be applied.

Psychology is based on the broader conception of the personality as an abstraction to represent the individual. The incorporation of the systematic observation of individual behavior by psychologists into the formulation of theories of personality, especially the scrutiny of individual behavior in the clinical setting, provides economists with an enormous body of existing observations of behavior. By relating economics and psychology, we can borrow the theories of personality which are based on a body of actual observations of human behavior, and thereby broaden the behavioral foundations of the economic theory of the consumer.

As I see it, direct inferences can be drawn from the personality of the individual to his or her patterns of consumption behavior and, therefore, to the structure of his or her preferences. The personality is a central determinant of the preference structure, and, in general, the pattern of consumption behavior of the individual consumer. Further, differences in personality will determine differences in the pattern of consumption behavior and, therefore, differences in the structure of preferences. This is the essential explanation that is being offered for the interpretation of observable patterns of consumption behavior: The particular personality of the individual is reflected in a pattern of consumption behavior which results in a specific structure of preferences.

The personality of the individual is the central conception to be used in the explanation of patterns of consumption behavior; therefore, the methodological task of relating economics and psychology must begin with the establishment of a theoretical relationship between the consumer's scale of preferences and the personality of the individual. To accomplish this task, a common ground of analysis is required which can relate the consumer of economic theory to a conception of the personality of psychological theory, and upon this common ground of analysis an integrative framework must be established which brings the contributions of psychology into economics in a systematic way.

This is no small task given the superficial conception of the consumer we have to work with, which resolves into nothing more than a set of statements on whether the consumer prefers one commodity to another, or is indifferent. It is no wonder that preferences may appear to be ephemeral or capricious. Tastes can be considered more fundamental than preferences, while not as basic as the personality. An investigation of tastes is equivalent to searching for the individual's utility function and, ultimately, for a unique utility function. This is not a call for a return to cardinal utility theory, however, since ordinal utility theory is a good, albeit limited, theory of choice. The attempt to go beyond the consumer's scale preferences represents an elevation of taste considerations and the social factors entering into their formation.

The basis for my analysis of the psychological foundations of economic behavior is psychoanalytic theory and, specifically, the psychoanalytic or American object relations theory of Otto F. Kernberg. An object relation is a relationship with another person, or simply an interpersonal relationship, and this is the basis of personality development in this theoretical framework. Kernberg has argued that psychoanalytic object-relations theory represents a crossroad which bridges the gap between various theories of personality in psychology (Kernberg, 1972, pp. 243–44; 1976, p. 59). Elswhere object-relations theory is described as an integrative framework which relates his work to that of various other theorists (Kernberg, 1976, 58–59). According to Kernberg, "As I see it, object-relations theory, already implied in Freud's writings, transcends any particular psychoanalytic school or group and represents a general psychoanalytic development to which authors of very different orientations have contributed significantly" (Kernberg, 1976, p. 58).

By providing a general integrative analytic framework for psychology, psychoanalytic object-relations theory provides a variety of promising opportunities for establishing a theoretical relationship between preferences and the personality. The task is to systematically relate ordinal utility theory, based on the economic conception of the consumer as a scale of preferences, and psychoanalytic object-relations theory, based on the broader conception of a personality organization. The personality organization is a central conception of psychoanalytic object-relations theory, and it is comprised of the intrapsychic structure and the predominant defensive organization of the personality. The formation of the intrapsychic structure of the personality is the central focus of psychoanalytic object-relations theory. It represents the study of the systematic processes of the internalization of significant interpersonal relationships which characterize a person's life, beginning with the mother-and-infant relationship. The predominant defensive organization of the personality represents a set of techniques for dealing with difficulties in significant interpersonal relationships.

Kernberg has constructed a continuum of personality development using the level of structural formation and predominant defensive organization of the personality to array different personality organizations along the continuum. Each personality organization occupies a discrete position along the continuum, which is divided into different ranges based on similarities in the intrapsychic structure and defensive organization of the personality which characterize the level of personality development of the individual. Thus, specific inferences can be drawn from the particular personality organization of the individual, and general inferences can be drawn from the range of the personality continuum occupied by the personality organization.

The personality continuum represents an enormous source of theories and observations of human behavior which become available to economists by forging a theoretical relationship between economics and psychology. It will be argued that the psychoanalytic concept of an internalized object relation constitutes a common ground of analysis which brings psychology and economics together, and that the larger conception of the personality organization represents an integrative framework which brings the contributions of psychology into economics in a systematic way. The purpose of this paper is to provide an explanation for the observed patterns of normal, compulsive, and addictive consumption behavior. The explanation that will be provided for these patterns of consumption behavior is that they represent different ranges along the personality continuum, represent different personality organizations which occupy discrete positions on the continuum, and, in short, represent entirely different persons.

The remainder of the paper will be organized the following way: The following section will consider some limitations of the economic theory of the consumer, and begin the exploration of the uses of psychoanalytic theory in expanding these limits. The next section will concentrate on the formation of the intrapsychic structure of the personality as the common ground of analysis for relating economics and psychology. The following section broadens the behavioral analysis to a consideration of the entire personality continuum, using the concept of interpersonal intimacy to array different personality organizations in ranges along the continuum. The next section will focus on the intermediate range of the continuum of personality development, and probe into particular personality organizations as explanations of compulsive and addictive patterns of consumption behavior. The final section will offer some brief concluding remarks.

A CONSIDERATION OF SOME LIMITATIONS OF CONSUMER THEORY

The limitations imposed by the economic theory of the consumer stem from the behavioral postulate of rationality and the assumption of a consumer of given preferences. The postulate of rationality can be considered a positive limitation because the validity of its behavioral implications can be verified or refuted by the observation of market behavior. Our understanding of the nature of the consumer's preferences which are held constant by assumption is limited to the concept of rationality, which imposes the requirement of internal consistency on the consumer: If the consumer makes consistent choices he will be considered rational, and will maximize utility in this enchanted world of definitions (Sen, 1977, p. 323).

Consistency is a surprisingly powerful behavioral postulate, and the postulate of rationality does impose meaningful limitations on the shape of demand functions; more often than not, however, the lofty concept of rationality is simply a disguise for our lack of a deeper understanding of what it means. Psychoanalytic approaches to the personality do provide an understanding of the determinants of consistent behavior and, therefore, the limitations of the behavioral postulate of rationality can be circumscribed. It will be shown that consistent individual behavior reflects the achievement of a very definite level of personality development, and represents a distinct range along the personality continuum. This is designated as the normal range of the personality continuum, and the principal economic implication is that personality organizations which occupy a position in the normal range of the personality continuum are described by a pattern of stable and consistent individual behavior. It is in this sense that the postulate of rationality can be considered a positive limitation; it is a relevant limitation on the usefulness of the economic theory of the consumer as a description of observable patterns of consumer behavior. As we progress to the higher reaches of the normal range of the personality continuum, observable behavior becomes increasingly stable and consistent; therefore, the behavioral postulate of rationality is strongly supported by the normal range of the personality continuum.

This does not imply that the reality of the rationality postulate is that it represents an ideal level of personality development. The rational consumer is not a perfect person, although the theoretically perfect person would be a perfectly rational consumer. The implication that Economic Man does not represent the pinnacle of personality development should not be surprising; however, the implications of going beyond Economic Man will prove to be surprisingly illuminating.

The assumption of a consumer of given preferences should be considered a negative limitation and a substantive weakness in the foundation of economic theory. The limitation of this assumption made in the absence of actual observations of market behavior has already been discussed in the previous section. Another, and perhaps more constricting, limitation that stems from the assumption of a consumer of given preferences is the overwhelming individual orientation that it imposes on the theory. This limitation has been enshrined in the concept of consumer sovereignty and the individual pursuit of self-interest; the individual consumer is the ultimate authority on how to maximize his or her own utility. The theory cannot distinguish between various social groups such as the family, friends, peer groups, the local community, economic and social classes, society as a whole, or even the entire world; each group is treated as if it behaves like an individual. (For a similar statement see Sen, 1977, p. 318, and for a similar statement on the economic theory of the firm, see Coleman, 1984.)

It is precisely because of the individual orientation of economic theory that psychological theories, and, in particular, psychoanalytic theories, of the personality are so useful: There is a fundamental compatibility between the individual basis of observation in economic theories of the consumer and psychological theories of the personality. This is why borrowing the observations of behavior and theories of psychology can broaden the behavioral foundations of economic theory.

The crucial implication of this compatibility for economic theory is that psychological theories of the personality which have as their basis the significant interpersonal relationships which characterize a person's life automatically transcend the individual to the wider social system. Harry Stack Sullivan has provided a crisp, operational definition of personality from an interpersonal perspective: Personality is the relatively enduring pattern of recurrent interpersonal situations which characterize a human life (Sullivan, 1953, p. 111). Personality development is shaped by a series of significant interpersonal relationships which begin with the mother-infant relationship as the original interpersonal situation, and therefore, the first social relationship. Thus, we begin life as part of the mother and, therefore, as part of a social system, and this social system widens throughout our lives to include, to varying degrees, all of the social situations listed above.

Two additional negative limitations of the assumption of given preferences can be elaborated at this point—circularity and change. We cannot question the motivation for the choices made by the consumer, without the theory becoming circular: If market behavior is explained by preferences, which are in turn defined only by observations of market behavior, the result can be nothing more than a circular statement saying that we behave as we behave, or prefer what we prefer (Sweezy 1934, p. 181; Samuelson, 1947, p. 91). This is not a problem with the theory, but with the application of theory; as long as we do not question the motivation of the consumer, the theory is not circular. This is such an apparent limitation of the theory that it is often overlooked in the welter of assumptions and equations used to explain consumer behavior. If we may paraphrase Tennyson's admonition, "Ours is not to reason why."

What we have left to work with is the scale of preferences of the individual consumer. Therefore, one way out of this circularity is to investigate the formation of preferences; only then can we address the fundamental issue of motivation. The psychoanalytic theory of the formation of the intrapsychic structure of the personality is a superb theoretical framework to accomplish this fundamental objective (Albanese, 1982). The use of psychoanalytic theory here is quite clear—motivation is in the mind of the consumer.

A final limitation of the economic theory of the consumer concerns the concept of changes in preferences. Such changes are an undeniable fact of considerable importance, particularly in Western societies (Hirschman, 1982, p. 9). Given the superficial conception of the consumer as merely a scale of preferences, it is imperative to overcome this limitation; otherwise preferences may appear to be changing capriciously.

An understanding of the systematic way in which preferences change has proved to be an intractable area of economic theory. The reason for this strikes at the very foundations of the economic theory of the consumer. The theory had its origin in Jeremy Bentham's hedonic calculus, which was based on the belief that pleasure and pain could be quantified. When economists borrowed this theoretical framework only the pleasurable side of the equation was chosen, and the painful aspects of the theory were completely ignored. This omission has direct relevance for understanding the intractability of preference change: What possible motivation could a consumer have for changing consumption behavior if only pleasure is experienced from consumption? In the static analysis of ordinal utility theory, a consistent consumer will maximize utility, and thus there is no motivation for change.

Disappointment is the motivation for change; it is disappointment with one's choices that leads to changes in preferences. Yet this simple idea cannot be readily incorporated into consumer theory in a systematic way in its present form. This is why Hirschman's treatment of the subject is somewhat unsatisfying, and why the work of Richard L. Solomon on the opponent-process theory of motivation has gained increasing credibility as a way of reformulating economic theory (See Hirschman, 1982; Solomon, 1974, 1980; and Taylor in this volume).

Psychoanalytic theory can provide a way out of this limitation through the general organizational concept of interpersonal intimacy. Through this conception, psychoanalytic theory has transcended its origins in the problems of personality to provide a theoretical framework which can encompass normal personality development (Kernberg, 1976, p. 59). Intimacy in an interpersonal relationship is considered an achievement, and the degree of success or failure in achieving intimacy can be used as an overall organizational concept to compare variations in the level of personality development along the personality continuum (Kernberg, 1977, 1974a, 1974b).

An examination of the preconditions for the achievement of interpersonal intimacy provides a basis for the economic theory of the consumer which incorporates the good and bad aspects of a relationship with another person, and therefore can serve as the basis for investigating changes in preferences. The objective of broadening the behavioral foundations of economic theory is essentially an effort to make the consumer a whole person, and this is a profound way of doing just that as we shall see in the exploration of the intimate relations of the consistent consumer.

THE COMMON GROUND: INTERNAL OBJECT RELATIONS

Object relations theory had its origin in Freud's illuminating conception of the superego, which became the basis for personality development through the work of W. R. D. Fairbairn and British Object Relations Theory (Fairbairn, 1952, p. 82). In "The Dissection of the Psychical Personality," Freud used the metaphor of a crystal to enunciate the structural point of view: "If we throw a crystal to the floor, it breaks; but not into haphazard pieces. It comes apart along its lines of cleavage into fragments whose boundaries, though they were invisibile, were predetermined by the crystal's structure" (Freud, 1965, p. 59).

The substance of psychoanalytic object relations theory is the internalization of interpersonal relationships. An internalized object relation can be defined as an internalized organization of interpersonal experience. Internalization begins as a process based on the perception and memory of another person, and a persisting structure is formed which becomes part of the personality. This occurs in levels which are hierarchically organized and which change as the processes of perception and memory mature (Kernberg, 1976; Rapaport and Gill, 1959).

The basic methodological unit of an internalized object relation consists of three components: (1) an image or representation of the other person; (2) an image or representation of the self relating to that person; (3) the affective, or emotional experience of the relationship with the other person (Kernberg, 1976, p. 26). The changes in the levels of internalization and the structural formation of the personality can be apprehended through the changing relationship between the self, object, and affect components. Following Kernberg's use of terminology, the levels of internalization are designated as introjection, identification, and the formation of an ego identity (Kernberg, 1976).

Introjection is the earliest process of internalization, and the internalized object relations which result represent the basic level of the intrapsychic structure of the personality. The internalized object relation is characterized by a self-component that is undifferentiated from the object component, and the affective experience is intense and overwhelming (Kernberg, 1976, pp. 29, 35).

The behavioral manifestations of introjections are less apparent because the capacity of the early infant for emotional experience is limited to pleasurable and painful affective states only (Kernberg, 1976, p. 31). Whether we call the pleasurable experience positive, rewarding, or gratifying, or call the painful experience negative, aversive, or frustrating, the result is a basic quality of good and bad (Kernberg, 1980, p. 108). Whatever these opposite affective states are labeled, there are only two, and they represent biologically determined inborn affect dispositions (Kernberg, 1980, p. 108).

Michael Balint describes the pleasurable experience of the infant as a "tranquil quiet sense of well-being," which is observable only with difficulty; while the frustration of the infant's needs calls forth the most stormy reaction, and if these needs remain unsatisfied, gratification will be demanded very vehemently (Balint, 1952, p. 81). Balint's description of the behavioral manifestations of the early infant sheds light on the potency of Pareto's challenge to the cardinal utility theorists—"Show me a utility or satisfaction that is, say, three times as great as another." It would seem that utility, as pleasure or satisfaction, is not only immeasurable, but barely observable.

The affective experience of the early infant represents the major motivation for organizing the intrapsychic structure of the personality. This is stated by Kernberg in the following way: "Affect dispositions constitute the primary motivational systems which integrate the perception of (1) central (pleasurable or unpleasurable) states, (2) physiological discharge phenomena, (3) inborn perceptive and behavior patterns, and (4) environmental responses as they impinge on specialized extroceptive and introceptive perceptions" (Kernberg, 1976, p. 87).

For the new-born infant, the first interpersonal relationship is typically with the mother, and the two affect dispositions are the earliest motivation for internalizing the relationship with the mother as two separate, completely different mothers, one representing the all-good and the other the all-bad mother. They are not integrated because the infant simply does not have the physiological capacity to bring together the internalized good and bad mothers.

The first level of structural formation of the personality is made up of these two structures, and they are known as "part-object relationships," because each represents only a part of the whole relationship with the mother. The economic implications hark back to the discussion of the inadequacy of ordinal utility theory for explaining change, since the theory incorporates only the pleasurable aspects of consumption behavior. The foundation of the personality is the good and bad aspects of the relationship with the mother; thus, psychoanalytic theory provides a basis for understanding the process of preference change.

The next higher process of internalization is known as identification, and it begins when the physiological capabilities of the infant have matured to the point that the growing infant perceives that both the mother and the infant are separate persons. The internalized object relations that result represent a self-component which is increasingly differentiated from the object component, the internalization of the role aspects of the relationship between the object and self, and the affective experience becomes less intense, and more differentiated, demonstrating a wider range of more sophisticated emotions.

The physiological capacity to integrate the different selves and objects is still absent, and identifications still represent part-object relations; however, there are now multiple selves and objects, rather than just two. In late infancy, with the increasing differentiation of self and object, the mother is no longer "all-good" and "all-bad," but increasingly differentiated into various mothers reflecting the more elaborate emotional experience of the growing infant. The main implication for economic theory is that the analysis can no longer revolve solely around simple concepts of pleasure and pain. This was recognized by Vilfredo Pareto, and constitutes the fundamental observation behind the transformation from cardinal to ordinal utility theory, that is, a quantitative concept of utility is unnecessary, and was replaced by a scale of relative preferences.

The behavioral manifestations of identification become much more interesting from an economic point of view. The behavior is described as either wanting or not wanting to be like another person (Kernberg, 1976, pp. 78–79; Freud, 1965, p. 63; Jacobson, 1964, p. 66; Sullivan, 1953, p. 209). This must be considered a nascent expression of preference behavior; by behaving like another person, the child will express a set of preferences which represent the specific aspects of the role of that person in the interpersonal relationship.

An even more profound economic implication is the social basis of consumption behavior. It is through the process of identification that the growing child learns behavior that is socially acceptable and roles which are socially sanctioned, and the child comes to know the role in the social system into which he or she was born. Kernberg states the implications for personality development in the following passage: "As the self-concept develops, role integration and differentiation of the self occurs automatically with it; and as the child develops differentiated relationships with both parents and his siblings, these role differentiations acquire a highly sophisticated organization *embedding the developing personality in the social system within which it develops*" (Kernberg, 1972, p. 244).

Through the internalization of significant interpersonal relationships, the personality becomes embedded in the social system, which harks back to Sullivan's interpersonal definition of personality as the relatively enduring pattern of recurrent interpersonal situations which characterize a person's life (Sullivan, 1953, p. 11). This pattern of interpersonal relationships constitutes the social system of the person and, through the processes of internalization, the intrapsychic structure of the personality comes to reflect that social system. Thus, the consumption pattern of the individual is socially determined, and will reflect the social system in which the personality develops.

It is important to recognize that the social system in which the personality develops is a system of significant interpersonal relationships, and does not constitute society as a whole. Society is stratified into relative economic and social classes, or a hierarchy of status groups, and the social system of the individual will be contained within a specific stratum of society. Thus, through the internalization of significant interpersonal relationships, the consumption bundle of the individual will reflect his/her role in the social system and relative social status in society. This is stated incisively by Kernberg in the following passage: "In this way, the social system (represented by socially determined status-role bundles) becomes integrated into the personality from infancy on, and the mother-child interaction is considered, in effect, as a basic element of both the personality and the social system (Kernberg, 1972, p. 244).

I draw profound economic implications from this analysis: The socially determined status-role bundles represent the tastes of the individual consumer, which reflect his or her role in the social system and relative social status in society. It is through this process of embedding the personality in the social system that psychoanalytic object relations theory relates the fundamental concept of tastes to the expression of preferences in the market behavior of the consumer. A further critical implication is that relating preferences to the personality using object relations theory transcends the individual orientation of economic theory to provide a social foundation for the analysis of consumer behavior.

The highest level of internalization is the formation of an ego identity. Identity formation begins when the physiological integrative capacity of the child matures to the point that the child recognizes that all of the good mothers and all of the bad mothers are one person. This can be a startling discovery, and represents a stage of ambivalence for the child. This is a profound development of the personality, known as the integration of whole-object relations. The child must integrate contradictory images of the self and the object, thereby making them more realistic. If the child accepts the fact that there is but one mother, the integration of whole-object relations will be successfully achieved, and the internalization of an ego identity begins.

The integration of whole-object relationships is an achievement in personality development. It means that the mother becomes a whole, and therefore, more realistic person, who is both good and bad; however, this internal world of object representations never reproduces the actual world of real people with whom the individual has established relationships in the past and present (Kernberg, 1976, p. 33).

The fundamental achievement of the integration of whole-object relations begins the process of identity formation. Paraphrasing Kernberg, ego identity represents the highest level in the organization of internalization processes, and refers to the overall organization of identifications and introjections under the guiding principle of the synthetic function of the ego. According to Kernberg, this organization implies:

1. A consistent, overall conception of the "world of objects," and a sense of consistency in one's own interpersonal interactions; the behavioral aspects—that is, general consistency in the behavior patterns—being even more important aspects of ego identity than those of identifications.
2. A recognition of this consistency in interactions as characteristic of the individual by his interpersonal environment, and, in turn, the perception by the individual of this recognition by the environment (Kernberg, 1976, pp. 31–32).

The fundamental behavioral implication of the formation of an ego identity for economic theory is the *general consistency in the behavior patterns,* and the recognition of this consistency of behavior in the interpersonal relations of the individual. Consistent consumption behavior is the sine qua non of ordinal utility theory, and psychoanalytic object relations theory provides an analysis of the determinants of consistent behavior. This is a critical contribution to an exploration of the psychological foundations of economic behavior. The manifestation of a pattern of consistent behavior has been explained by a specific development in the personality, the significant interpersonal relationships which contribute to this development, and the formation of intrapsychic structure in the personality derived from the interpersonal relations.

This overly simplified overview of the structural formation of the personality is meant to serve as a bridge to a broader consideration of human behavior. The level of the structural formation of the personality can be used to array personalities along the continuum of personality development. A personality organization is constituted by the level of structural formation and by the predominant defensive organization of the personality. This can be elaborated at this point with the ultimate objective of contrasting consistent behavior with compulsive and addictive patterns of behavior.

The achievement of the integration of whole-object relations contributes to a consistent pattern of behavior. As an achievement in personality development it represents the maturation of a person's capacity to experience concern for another person, and the capacity to experience guilt for violating parental prohibitions and demands. Concern is an ego consideration and guilt is a superego consideration. The internalization of more realistic parental prohibitions and prescriptions constitutes a superego development, and represents the formation of the prohibitive superego (Kernberg, 1976). This corresponds to the superego Freud described as conscience: "There is scarcely anything else in us that we so regularly separate from our ego and so easily set over against it as precisely our conscience. I feel an inclination to do something that I think will give me pleasure, but I abandon it on the ground that my conscience does not allow it. Or I have let myself be persuaded by too great an expectation of pleasure into doing something to which the voice of conscience has objected and after the deed my conscience punishes me with distressing reproaches and causes me to feel remorse for the deed'' (Freud, 1965, pp. 59–60).

This function of the superego is quite properly a metapreference consideration, that is, preferences about one's own preferences (Sen, 1977, p. 337; Hirschman, 1982, p. 71). This structural formation in the personality also contributes to the increasing self-control over individual behavior (Kernberg, 1976, p. 32; Schelling, 1980). In general, at this level of development of the superego, the internalized parental prohibitions and demands constitute a moral system, which tells us what is good and bad, and helps us distinguish between right and wrong. The superego reinforces our self-control and enforces behavior which is consistent with our moral system through the experience of guilt.

A principal objective of this investigation is to demonstrate uses of psychoanalytic theory that strengthen the behavioral foundations of the economic theory of the consumer. What has been demonstrated is that there are personality organizations which support the postulate of rationality, and that these personality organizations can be arrayed along one range of the personality continuum. There are other ranges along the personality continuum which do not support this postulate. To broaden the behavioral considerations of the analysis, the next section will turn to an elaboration of the various ranges along the personality continuum. A subsequent section will explore the intermediate range of the personality continuum, and look at the borderline and narcissistic personality organizations.

THE PERSONALITY CONTINUUM—CLASSIFICATION OF PERSONALITY ORGANIZATIONS AND THE RANGES OF THE CONTINUUM

Personality organizations can be arrayed along the personality continuum by the level of personality development. This can be done in a number of ways. A personality organization can be classified by the level of structural formation and the defensive organization of the personality. Much has been said on the formation of the intrapsychic structure of the personality, and a consideration of the predominant defensive organization of the personality will be postponed until the intermediate range of the continuum is discussed.

The degree of success or failure in achieving intimacy in an interpersonal relationship can also be used to classify personality organizations according to the level of personality development. This brings the analysis around to the fundamental basis of personality development—the significant interpersonal relations which characterize a person's life—and moves the analysis into the realm of observable patterns of interpersonal behavior. It also represents a way in which psychoanalytic theory has transcended its origins in the problems of personality to offer a theory of normal personality development over the course of a person's entire life.

Kernberg has condensed the preconditions for the achievement of intimacy in an interpersonal relationship into two stages of development. The first precondition for intimacy is the integration of whole-object relations; another significant person must be perceived as both good and bad, that is, as a whole person. In the beginning the infant does not have the physiological capacity to integrate the good and bad aspects of the relationship with the mother; good and bad aspects of the relationship are internalized separately. With the maturation of perception and memory, the infant comes to recognize that the good and bad mothers are one person, that is, a whole person who is both good and bad.

This achievement in personality development is the basis for the capacity for concern for the well-being of another person, and, in terms of intimacy, it represents the capacity for falling in love. Kernberg describes the first precondition in the following way: The first stage develops gradually and subtly throughout the first five years of life. It is the normal integration of internalized object relations, which leads to an integrated self-concept and to an integrated conceptualization of others, and also leads to the concomitant capacity for relations in depth with significant others (Kernberg, 1974a, p. 486).

The second precondition for intimacy involves the role of genital sexuality in an interpersonal relationship. According to Kernberg, "The second stage of development corresponds to the successful overcoming of oedipal conflicts and the related unconscious prohibitions against a full sexual relation" (Kernberg, 1974a, p. 486). In short, satisfying sexual relations must be successfully integrated into an interpersonal relationship. This represents the capacity to remain in love.

The advantage of condensing the determinants of intimacy into two preconditions is that different personality organizations can be arrayed along the personality continuum based on external, and therefore, observable patterns of interpersonal behavior. The degree of achievement of interpersonal intimacy represents the level of personality development, which can then be related to the level of intrapsychic structural formation and the predominant defensive organization of the personality. The personality organization becomes the general integrative framework which can be used to explain variations in patterns of consumption behavior. Thus, psychoanalytic object relations theory provides an integrative framework and a common ground of analysis for expanding the behavioral foundations of economic analysis.

The personality continuum can be divided into four general ranges of personality development which will be designated in the following way: (1) normal range, (2) neurotic range, (3) intermediate range, (4) psychotic range. Each range will be dealt with in turn, and in the following section, emphasis will be placed on the contrast of the normal and intermediate ranges.

The Normal Range of the Personality Continuum

We have already dealt extensively with the critical concept of the integration of whole-object relations. This achievement contributes to the increasing consistency of behavior, represents the first precondition for intimacy in an interpersonal relationship, provides the basis for the capacity to experience concern and guilt, and, in general, supports the postulate of rationality. We can now build on this analysis by looking at the second precondition for intimacy, the integration of genital sexual relations into an interpersonal relationship, which marks the beginning of the normal range of the personality continuum. Satisfying this precondition means that parental prohibitions against genital sexual relations which have been internalized in the prohibitive superego have been overcome in an interpersonal relationship. The person has the capacity to fall and remain in love and, therefore, to form a stable, intimate relationship.

This defines the normal range of the personality continuum in terms of intimacy in an interpersonal relationship. Within the normal range of personality development there are differences in the degree of achievement of intimacy, and we are in a position to investigate the economic implications of some of these differences by investigating the highest position in the normal range of the continuum of personality development. Much of Kernberg's work is based on the relationship of the married couple, and this perspective will also be taken here to elaborate the consequences of satisfying both preconditions for intimacy. Sexual relations culminating in orgasm in an intimate relationship result in the subjective experience of transcendence. Transcendence involves abandoning the boundaries of the self during orgasm, and this is required for its full experience (Kernberg, 1977, p. 97). This creates a sense of oneness with the loved person, and represents an idealization, not of the body or even the person, but the values for which this person stands (Kernberg, 1977, p. 99; 1974a, pp. 507–508).

The shared value system forms a new common social boundary around the couple which protects them from the parental prohibitions and demands of the prohibitive superego. This results in the formation of an intrapsychic structure which is called the protective superego, and represents the internalization of a value system. A person with this personality organization has achieved the highest level of personality development, and would occupy the highest position on the personality continuum.

This represents the pinnacle of personality development, and provides many useful insights into the behavioral foundations of economic theory. The maturation of the protective superego, as the internalization of a value system, is the basis of the capacity for commitment, which is a critical metapreference consideration raised by Sen (1977). Commitment is a dynamic concept: We make a commitment for the future; therefore, we can make more accurate predictions of a person's future behavior (Kernberg, 1977, pp. 98–99). The protective superego is the intrapsychic structure which provides a person with a future orientation, and with this comes the foresight to plan for the future. This has direct relevance for the determination of the individual's rate of time preference, and the relative valuation of the present and future. It is also a firm foundation for altruism, and the concept of commitment gives substance to Becker's dynamic use of altruism to explain intergenerational wealth transfers (Becker, 1981).

It should be clear that the abstraction of Economic Man does not represent the highest level of personality development. The postulate of rationality requires only that behavior be consistent, which begins with the integration of whole-object relations, and becomes increasingly consistent as we move up the personality continuum. The achievement of intimacy in an interpersonal relationship represents the normal range of the continuum, and behavior becomes stable and consistent, and this goes beyond the description of consistent behavior; however, it does not go all the way to the highest position of the personality continuum.

The Neurotic Range of the Personality Continuum

Moving down the personality continuum, the next range below the normal range is the neurotic range. From the perspective of interpersonal intimacy, neurotic personality organizations represent sexual inhibition, and the failure to integrate satisfying sexual relations in an interpersonal relationship. A neurotic person has achieved the integration of whole-object relations, and has the capacity to fall in love, but not to remain in love. Thus, the neurotic person has the capacity for experiencing concern for another person and guilt for violating an internalized moral system.

There are two behavioral implications for economics. While the determinant for consistent behavior—the integration of whole-object relations—has been achieved, we should expect the degree of consistent behavior to vary, depending on the position occupied by the particular personality organization in the neurotic range of the personality continuum. A second behavioral implication is the ambivalence of neurotic personality organizations. The implications of ambivalence for ordinal utility theory is that an equally strong preference for two different commodities makes choice difficult, and, in fact, neurotic personalities are notoriously indecisive.

The multitude of personality organizations that occupy the neurotic range of the personality continuum are potentially the most useful source of insights for the investigation of variations in patterns of consumption behavior. In an effort to return to the contrast of the normal and intermediate range of the personality continuum, only a preliminary description of the neurotic range has been provided here.

The Intermediate Range of the Personality Continuum

Personality organizations in the intermediate range of the personality continuum represent the failure to integrate whole-object relations and, therefore, have neither the capacity to fall or remain in love. There are two predominant defensive organizations of the personality: repression and splitting. Behavior which is prohibited is repressed, and repression is the dominant defensive organization of a person who has had the good fortune to have achieved the integration of whole-object relations. The failure to achieve the integration of whole-object relations means that the child has not been able to accept that the mother is only one person who is both good and bad, and a more primitive defensive organization known as splitting must be used. Splitting is an active defense against anxiety which involves separating contradictory images of the self and object, as a way of denying that the mother is not all good, and therefore, protecting the fantasy of the ideal, all-good mother (Kernberg, 1976, pp. 40; 68).

The active use of splitting as the predominant defensive organization prevents the integration of whole-object relations. This places personality organizations characterized by the failure to achieve whole-object relations on a lower range of the continuum of personality development, designated as the intermediate range. This will be the focus of the last section.

The Psychotic Range of the Personality Continuum

The psychotic range of the personality continuum is perhaps less interesting to economists, and this fact in itself is important. There is a fundamental problem with the perception of reality of the psychotic personality organizations. There is a tendency for the intrapsychic structure of the personality to collapse and, therefore, is less reliably modeled. The lack of economic uses of the psychotic range indicates the misuse of the designation of behavior as "irrational" by economists. This emphasizes the crucial importance of investigating the numerous ranges of behavior along the personality continuum between the extremes of perfectly rational and completely irrational behavior from a psychological point of view. The implication is that there is a vast area between the extremes of the perfectly rational and the truly irrational person: This is a critical contribution that psychology can make to economics—the recognition that there are *ranges of behavior* that exist between the extremes of rationality and irrationality. These ranges represent behavior which does not conform to the conventional theory of the consumer but, nonetheless, represent patterned and persisting behavior which can be modeled in an optimization framework.

A RECONSIDERATION OF THE INTERMEDIATE RANGE OF THE PERSONALITY CONTINUUM—THE ORIGINS OF COMPULSIVE AND ADDICTIVE BEHAVIOR

In the normal range of the personality continuum, behavior can be described as stable and consistent, and this range provides strong support for the postulate of rationality and the economic theory of consumer behavior. Psychoanalytic object relations theory has provided a common ground of analysis and an integrative framework which permits us to investigate virtually every aspect of human behavior in the normal range of the personality continuum. The intermediate range offers a striking contrast to the normal range of the personality continuum. Personality organizations in the intermediate range of the continuum are characterized by patterns of compulsive, and, in the extreme, addictive behavior, rather than stable and consistent behavior.

In the previous section I provided an analysis of the basic intrapsychic structure of the personality organizations in the intermediate range. Personality organizations in the intermediate range are characterized by the active use of splitting as a defense against overwhelming anxiety in interpersonal relationships. This represents a failure to integrate whole-object relations, the determinant of consistent behavior; thus, personality organizations in the intermediate range violate the economic postulate of rationality, but hardly represent irrational behavior from a psychological point of view. In this section I will concentrate on a broader description of the observable patterns of behavior of two personality organizations in the intermediate range—the borderline and narcissistic personality organizations. The objective is to show that these personality organizations can be used to explain commonly observed patterns of compulsive and addictive behavior; the ultimate objective is to make each of these personality organizations a recognizable person.

Personality organizations in the intermediate range display an apparent lack of impulse control, which Kernberg attributes to the weakness of the ego resulting from the active use of the powerful defense of splitting. Kernberg describes the behavioral manifestations of splitting in the following way: "It was as if there were two selves, equally strong, completely separated from each other in their emotions although not in the person's memory and alternating in his conscious experience" (Kernberg, 1976, p. 23).

The consumer behaves as if he or she had two separate sets of contradictory preferences which are alternately expressed in his or her observable consumption behavior. According to Kernberg, "The mechanism of splitting is reflected in what appears on the surface as a simple lack of impulse control, rather than in alternating expressions of complementary sides of a conflict. Such 'lack of impulse control' is often of a highly selective, specific kind and represents the emerging into consciousness of a split identification system" (Kernberg, 1976, p. 47).

This pattern of alternating and contradictory behavior violates the rationality postulate of the economic theory of the consumer. However, the behavior is highly patterned and, in fact, the pattern of behavior is described as rigid (Kernberg, 1976, p. 20). The rigidity of the alternating and contradictory pattern of behavior stems from the intrapsychic structure of the personality; this is the basis for the central argument that the intrapsychic structure of the personality is reflected in the structure of the consumer's preferences. This also reinforces the fundamental argument that the intrapsychic of the personality, and the concept of the internal object relation, provides a common ground of analysis.

The primary implication for the economic theory of the consumer is that behavior which is patterned can be modeled, but must be modeled differently from stable and consistent consumption behavior. This has, in fact, been accomplished in an optimization framework by Winston (1980). The further implication for expanding the limits of applicability of economic theory is that every range along the personality continuum can be modeled in an optimization framework.

Descriptions of the borderline and narcissistic personality organizations will be drawn on to illustrate the origins of compulsive and addictive behavior, respectively. In Kernberg's view, the effects of drugs or alcohol vary according to the intrapsychic structure of the personality: "In general terms, the implication is that the psychological functions of alcohol or drugs are strongly influenced by the predominant nature of intrapsychic structuralized object relations" (Kernberg, 1975, p. 222).

For the borderline personality organization, "Drug intake activates a sense of well-being and goodness that activates the split-off 'all good' self and object images and permits the denial of 'all bad' internalized object relations, thus permitting an escape from intolerable guilt [anxiety?] or sense of internal persecution" (Kernberg, 1975, p. 22). In other words, the use of splitting as a defense against anxiety results in an alternating and contradictory pattern of behavior which is reflected in a lack of impulse control; the reason for the habitual use of drugs or alcohol by a person with a borderline personality organization is to bring the all-good self and object images into consciousness, and to deny the all-bad self and objects, thereby creating a sense of well-being.

In the case of narcissistic personality organizations, according to Kernberg, addictive potential is at a maximum (Kernberg, 1975, p. 222). A person with a narcissistic personality has an almost complete lack of capacity for intimacy in an interpersonal relationship, and is completely unable to really depend on anybody because of a deep distrust and depreciation of others (Kernberg, 1975, p. 17). Thus, the narcissistic personality becomes dependent on some chemical substance, because he or she cannot depend on another human being.

Narcissistic personalities do not have the capacity to feel concern for another person nor to experience guilt, and therefore they can be utterly ruthless in their behavior toward others, especially those closest to them. According to Kernberg, "It is as if they feel they have the right to control and possess others and to exploit them without guilt feelings—and behind a surface which very often is charming and engaging, one senses coldness and ruthlessness" (Kernberg, 1975, p. 17).

A fundamental economic implication is that a narcissistic person will pursue self-interest in a selfish way, without concern for the well-being of anyone else. This must be put in perspective by comparison with the normal range of the personality continuum, since the individual pursuit of self-interest is the main behavioral foundation upon which all economic analysis is based. The narcissistic personality organization occupies a position in the intermediate range of the personality continuum, and represents a rather low level of personality development. As we move up the personality continuum, the integration of whole-object relations marks the beginning of the neurotic range; with this achievement comes the capacity to experience concern and guilt, to fall in love, and to behave more consistently. As we continue to move up the personality continuum, the normal range of personality development begins with the integration of satisfying sexual relations into an interpersonal relationship; this represents the capacity to remain in love, and to form a stable, intimate relationship. In the normal range of the personality continuum, a person's behavior would be stable and consistent, and individual self-interest would be pursued with concern for the well-being of others; it is this range of the personality continuum which supports the economic theory of the consumer.

CONCLUSION

Psychoanalytic object relations theory has yielded many useful insights into the behavioral foundations of economic theory. It has provided a common ground of analysis and an integrative framework which broadens the behavioral foundations of consumer theory, and provides a promising opportunity for expanding the limits of applicability of economic theory.

The central argument is that the personality organization of the individual is reflected in his or her pattern of consumption behavior, and therefore, determines the structure of preferences. The conception of the personality organization provides a useful approach for comparing differences in personality, which can be arrayed along a continuum of personality development. This personality continuum represents an invaluable source of existing observations of behavior and theories from psychology, and every range along the personality continuum can be modeled in a mathematical optimization framework.

Relating the fields of psychology and economics has broadened the conception of individual behavior, and transcended the individual orientation of economic analysis to the social foundations of behavior. The next task is to array every person into a range along the personality continuum, and eventually to classify every person as a particular personality organization. The refinement of techniques for the classification of a population by personality organization would provide an enormous amount of information about individual economic behavior for economists.

REFERENCES

Albanese, Paul J. "Toward a Methodology for Investigating the Formation of Preferences." Unpublished Ph.D. Dissertation, Harvard University, 1982.

Albanese, Paul J. "The Nature of Preferences: An Exploration of the Relationship Between Economics and Psychology." *Journal of Economic Psychology,* 8, no. 1 (March 1987): 3–18.

Balint, Michael. *Primary Love and Psychoanalytic Technique.* London: Hogarth Press, 1952.

Becker, Gary S. *A Treatise on the Family.* Cambridge, MA: Harvard University Press, 1981.

Coleman, James S. "Introducing Social Structure into Economic Analysis." *American Economic Review* 74, no. 2 (May 1984): 84–88.

Fairbairn, W. R. D. *Psychoanalytic Studies of the Personality.* London: Rutledge & Kegan Paul, 1952.

Freud, Sigmund. "The Dissection of the Psychical Personality." In *New Introductory Lectures on Psychoanalysis,* edited by James Strachey, pp. 57–80. New York: W. W. Norton, 1965.

Hicks, John R. "A Reconsideration of the Theory of Value." *Economica* 1, no. 1 (February 1934): 52–76.

Hirschman, Albert O. *Shifting Involvements: Private Interests and Public Action.* Princeton: Princeton University Press, 1982.

Jacobson, Edith. *The Self and the Object World.* New York: International Universities Press, 1964.

Kernberg, Otto F. "Early Ego Integration and Object Relations." *Annals of the New York Academy of Sciences* 193 (1972): 233–47.

Kernberg, Otto F. "Barriers to Falling and Remaining in Love." *Journal of the American Psychoanalytic Association* 22 (1974a): 486–514.

Kernberg, Otto F. "Mature Love: Prerequisites and Characteristics." *Journal of the American Psychoanalytic Association* 22 (1974b): 743–68.

Kernberg, Otto F. *Borderline Conditions and Pathological Narcissism.* New York: Jason Aronson, Inc., 1975.

Kernberg, Otto F. *Object Relations Theory and Clinical Psychoanalysis.* New York: Jason Aronson, Inc., 1976.

Kernberg, Otto K. "Boundaries and Structure in Love Relations." *Journal of the American Psychoanalytic Association* 25 (1977): 81–114.

Kernberg, Otto F. *Internal World and External Reality: Object Relations Theory Applied.* New York: Jason Aronson, Inc., 1980.

Rapaport, D. and Gill, M. "The Points of View and Assumptions of Metapsychology." *International Journal of Psycho-Analysis* 40 (1959): 153–62.

Samuelson, Paul A. *Foundations of Economic Analysis.* Cambridge, MA: Harvard University Press, 1947.

Schelling, Thomas C. "The Intimate Contest for Self-Command." *The Public Interest* 60 (1980): 94–118.

Schelling, Thomas C. "Self-Command in Practice, in Policy, and in a Theory of Rational Choice." *American Economic Review* 74 (1984): 1–11.

Schumpeter, Joseph A. *History of Economic Analysis.* New York: Oxford University Press, 1954.

Sen, Amartya. "Rational Fools: A Critique of the Behavioral Foundations of Economic Theory." *Philosophy and Public Affairs* 6 (1977): 317–44.

Solomon, Richard L. and Corbit, John D. "An Opponent-Process Theory of Motivation: Temporal Dynamics of Affect." *Psychological Review* 81, no. 2 (1974): 119–45.

Solomon, Richard L. "The Opponent-Process Theory of Acquired Motivation: The Costs of Pleasure and the Benefits of Pain." *American Psychologist* 35, no. 8 (August 1980): 691–712.

Sullivan, Harry Stack. *The Interpersonal Theory of Psychiatry.* New York: W. W. Norton, 1953.

Sweezy, Alan R. "The Interpretation of Subjective Value Theory in the Writings of the Austrian Economists." *Review of Economic Studies* 1, no. 3 (1934): 176–85.

Winston, Gordon W. "Addiction and Backsliding: A Theory of Compulsive Consumption." *Journal of Economic Behavior and Organization* 1 (1980): 295–324.

5

PERSONALITY, CULTURE, AND ORGANIZATION

Manfred F. R. Kets de Vries and
Danny Miller

THEME AND SCOPE

All of us in dealing with the vicissitudes of life have specific styles, "ways of thinking and perceiving, ways of experiencing emotion, modes of subjective experience in general, and modes of activity that are associated with various pathologies" (Shapiro, 1965, p. 1). We all possess certain patterns of dealing with the environment which are deeply embedded, pervasive, and likely to continue over long periods of time. Human functioning is generally characterized by a mixture of these often neurotic styles. The same person may possess elements of many different styles, each of which is triggered in different circumstances. Among many individuals, however, one specific neurotic style dominates and comes consistentjy to characterize many aspects of behavior. Extreme manifestations of any one style can signal significant psychopathology that seriously impairs functioning. Our experience with top executives and organizations revealed that *parallels could be drawn between individual pathology*—the excessive use of one neurotic style—*and organizational pathology,* the latter resulting in problems and poor performance. This is the speculative theme of this paper.

We shall be concentrating on relatively dysfunctional top executives—that is, those who have significant neurotic tendencies that influence their managerial behavior. Thus, our framework will be useful mainly to help us understand dysfunctional rather than healthy organizations. These are, of course, very numerous. Our model will be especially applicable to firms in which decision-making power is centralized in the hands of a top executive or a small, homogeneous dominant coalition. Where power is broadly distributed throughout a firm, its culture and strategies will be determined by many managers, and the relationship between neurotic style and organizational pathology becomes more tenuous. Contextual influences then become the more dominant ones. Finally, we shall be concerned with the highest level of management, and with top "corporate"-level rather than "business"-level strategies (Schendel and Hofer, 1979, pp. 12–13). Top managers normally have the most impact on their organizations, so it is wise, at least as a first step, to focus our attention on them. Their concern is usually with corporate-level issues and strategies, but where their neurotic tendencies prevent such a focus, and redirect it toward business-level policies, our attention will shift accordingly. We believe that neurotic styles can have an impact at all levels of organization but we wish here to limit our scope to top management. At this stage it is not at all clear how the neurotic styles of different organizational members interact to influence overall strategy and structure.

NEUROTIC STYLES AND ORGANIZATIONS

Strategy and even structure can be strongly influenced by the personality of the top manager (Miller, Kets de Vries and Toulouse, 1982). So can organizational culture (Kernberg, 1979; Jaques, 1951, 1970; Maccoby, 1976; Payne and Pugh, 1976; Zaleznik and Kets de Vries, 1975; Kets de Vries, 1980, 1984). The literature is filled with evidence to support this contention. Much of the research, however, has examined simple aspects of personality and related it to one or two organizational variables (Vroom, 1960; Tosi, 1970). Such studies have led to oversimplification of often very complex phenomena.

In our attempt to broaden the treatment of personality in management we have drawn on the psychoanalytic and psychiatric literature (especially as represented by the works of Fenichel (1945), Laplanche and Pontalis (1973), Shapiro (1965), Freedman, Kaplan, and Sadock (1975) and Nicholi (1978)). These studies provide a more complete and far more integrated view of intrapsychic functioning and behavior than is found in the traditional psychological literature. Our focus will be on clusters of behavior patterns, personality styles which remain relatively stable over the years, as opposed to simple dimensions of behavior. These patterns may better enable us to make a link between what happens in the inner world of the executive and his actual behavior in organizations.

Our central thesis in this paper is that the rather stable and global psychological orientations (Klein, 1948; Sandler and Rosenblatt, 1962; Laplanche and Pontalis, 1973; Mahler, Pine, and Bergman, 1975) of key organization members are major determinants of "neurotic styles" of their organizations and have many consequences. Top executives may create shared fantasies that permeate all levels of functioning, influence organizational culture, and make for a dominant organizational adaptive style (Kernberg, 1976). This style, we believe, will greatly influence decisions about strategy and structure.

The original idea behind our framework was that parallels could be drawn between common neurotic styles of behavior and common modes of organizational failure, particularly those delineated by the empirical taxonomy of Miller and Friesen (1978, 1980a, 1984). The pathological organizational types seemed in many ways to mirror the types of dysfunctions common to the most widely discussed neurotic styles among individuals (Shapiro, 1965; APA, 1980). For example, Miller and Friesen's (1978, 1984) stagnant bureaucracies were without clear goals, lacked initiative, reacted very sluggishly to any external changes, and were pervaded by managerial apathy, frustration, and inaction. The depressive personality style exhibits very similar features. The anecdotal literature as well as our experiences with organizations led us to the conclusion that depressive chief executive officers (CEOs) ran firms that fit Miller and Friesen's (1984) stagnant bureaucracy types.

One more example will further illustrate this theme. Miller and Friesen's (1978, 1984) impulsive firms are characterized by centralized power, bold and risk-embracing decisions, and a tremendous urge for growth and expansion, often by acquiring other firms. The dramatic personality reflects many of these traits—the need to dominate others, to display prowess through major projects, and to impress with dramatic action. Again there seemed to be a link between a common mode of organizational failure and a very prevalent neurotic style.

We shall refer to these and other of Miller and Friesen's (1984) types in greater detail later in the text since they have served as the basis for the strategic and structural descriptions of many of the situations we describe. In general, what unites our approach with Miller and Friesen's (1984) is its "holistic" orientation. We too are seeking representative common configurations that characterize many organizations and appear to be internally consistent, unified, and thematic. We have added personality and cultural dimensions in an attempt to explain some of the sources of this unity.

It is important to note that we do not believe that Miller and Friesen's (1984) pathological types necessarily *require* that the CEO involved exhibit the neurotic styles that we discuss. Clearly, some organizations might employ such strategies for other reasons. For example, a depressive firm might be found in a declining industry that has dwindling markets or too much foreign competition, or in a firm that has been acquired and dominated by a conglomerate or that has too few resources to be able to initiate a significant turnaround.

We have identified a number of very common fantasies and neurotic styles, well established in the psychoanalytic and psychiatric literature (Shapiro, 1965; Fenichel, 1945; Nicholi, 1978; Millon, 1981), and in the listing of personality disorders found in the latest *Diagnostic and Statistical Manual of Mental Disorders* (DSM III) published by the American Psychiatric Association (1980). We have also employed the common pathological organizational strategies and structures isolated by the empirical work of Miller and Friesen (1984). We will develop conjectures on the relationship between each style, its predominant motivating fantasy, the emerging organizational culture, and the strategy and

Table 5.1
Summary of the Five Constellations

Fantasy	Neurotic Style	Culture	Organization
persecution	vigilant	paranoid	paranoid
helplessness	depressive (avoidant/dependant)	avoidant	depressive
grandiosity	dramatic (histrionic/narcissistic)	charismatic	dramatic
control	compulsive	bureaucratic	compulsive
detachment	detached (schizoid/avoidant)	politicized	schizoid

Table 5.2
General Hypotheses

1. The more centralized the organization and the more powerful the CEO, the greater the impact of his personality (that is, fantasy and neurotic style) on culture, strategy, and structure.
2. The more similar the personalities of the top executives, the purer the cultural and organizational types—that is, the more closely they will adhere to the five types we have discussed.
3. The purer and more pronounced the personality type of the CEO (as measured by the DSM III (APA, 1980) or the Millon (1981) Inventory) the more it will be reflected in the culture, structure, and strategy of his firm. This will be especially true in smaller centralized organizations.
4. Healthy firms will have a mixture of personality types which will not be as dysfunctional. Our hypotheses will not be borne out in such samples.

structure of the overall organization (see Table 5.1). The discussion is speculative, as its major grounding stems from Miller and Friesen's (1984) empirical analysis and from experience with many sick organizations and their top executives. Our account should be treated as a series of complex *hypotheses,* not as any final word or rigid framework (see Table 5.2). Also, it is worthwhile to remember that we are discussing common gestalts found in many failing firms. These are by no means the only dysfunctional types, and mixed types are quite common.

THE PERSECUTORY PREOCCUPATION

The predominant concern associated with this vigilant style is the fantasy that nobody can really be trusted; that somewhere a menacing, superior force exists which is "out to get" one. Thus a major preoccupation is to be on guard, to be ready for any attack—real or imagined. This vigilant style is characterized by suspiciousness, mistrust of others, hypersensitivity, and hyperalertness. Guardedness and secretiveness are pervasive (Nicholi, 1978). Vigilant-style executives are constantly prepared to counter perceived threats. They may take offence easily and respond in anger. Envy and hostility are ever-present. These executives are overly preoccupied with hidden motives and special meanings. The actions of others are easily misread and distorted. Minor slights become magnified; mountains are made out of molehills. Vigilant-style executives expect to find trickery and deception everywhere, seeking out facts that confirm their worst expectations. They possess an intense, narrowly focused attention span and may come across as cold, rational, and unemotional (APA, 1980). Our experience indicates that top executives with this style often give rise to the following dysfunctional organizational setting.

Paranoid Cultures—Paranoid Firms

In the paranoid organization the interpersonal relationships between the leader and his subordinates are often characterized by a persecutory theme. The boss may feel hostile to those who report to him—he may want to harm or attack others as a defensive reaction to his own feelings of persecution and mistrust. Clearly, this is one of the most destructive attitudes of a leadership situation. The leader sees his/her subordinates as malingerers and incompetents, or as people who are deliberately out to raise his/her ire. As a consequence, he/she is likely to gravitate toward two extremes. He/she might try to exert a tremendous amount of control through intensive personal supervision, formal controls and rules, and harsh punishments. This will take away all initiative from managers, lower their self-esteem, and perhaps cause them to engage in a contest of wills with the boss. The absence of opportunity for growth or development may induce the most promising managers to leave.

The second, less common reaction of the hostile leader toward his/her subordinates may be one of overt aggression. He/she may be reluctant to provide emotional or material rewards, striving always to come out on the winning side of any "trades." Morale can suffer a good deal under these conditions, as subordinates hold back their contributions and concentrate mostly on protecting themselves from exploitation.

Vigilant-style top executives generate group cultures, that is, cultures which are pervaded by distrust, suspicion, and the identification of enemies. Bion (1959) has called these fight/flight cultures. In these cultures the members come to fear the same things as the top executive. An atmosphere of fear of attack exists and there is an identification of an enemy on whom one blames everything. The world and the people inhabiting it are split into good and bad parts: those who act in accordance with the group members' needs or against them. Group members deny responsibility for their own actions. They lack insight into their weaknesses. Again, fear and suspicion are the predominant emotions.

It is important to note that Bion (1959) believed that all groups have these fight/flight and various other phases as part of their normal evolution. But paranoid cultures become arrested at this level, so that the fight/flight fantasy endures and comes to dominate perceptions.

The paranoid culture tends to be uniform. The leader is careful to hire, reward, and promote only those who share his/her views. People who differ or dissent from his/her opinions are mistrusted. They are ignored or denied promotions. Thus the dominant coalition will generally see things the same way—sharing the same fears and common enemies.

In fact, the search for the enemy results in a great mobilization of energy and a strong sense of conviction among the organizational members about the correctness of their actions. Unfortunately, too much stereotyping can lead to rigidity in decision making. "Enemies" are vigorously analyzed and explicitly countered with a competitive strategy. Employees suspected of disloyalty are fired. Power is centralized in the hands of the leader since "no one can be trusted."

The suspicious atmosphere in these organizations will often carry over to interpersonal, and even interdepartmental, functioning. A premium is placed on information as a power resource and so departmental personnel may be reluctant to discuss common problems. An adversary relationship can develop that makes coordination difficult as secrets abound and a "protect yourself" ethic prevails.

In this type of company, which is derived from Miller and Friesen's (1984) "under fire" firms, managerial suspicions translate into a primary emphasis on organizational intelligence and controls. Managers develop sophisticated information systems to identify threats by the government, competitors, and customers, and they develop budgets, cost centers, profit centers, cost accounting procedures, and similar methods to control internal activities. The elaborate information-processing apparatus reflects their desire for perpetual vigilance and preparedness for emergencies.

This paranoia also influences decision making. Frequently, key executives decide that it may be safer to direct their distrust externally rather than withold information from one another. They share information and make concerted efforts to discover organizational problems and to select alternative solutions for dealing with them. Unfortunately, this type of decision making can become overly cautious, with different people being asked for similar information. Such "institutionalization of suspicion" sometimes ensures that accurate information gets to the top of the firm, but it may also lower morale and trust as well as waste valuable time and energy.

Paranoid firms tend to react rather than anticipate. If competitors lower prices, the firm may study the challenge and, eventually, react to it. If other firms introduce a product successfully, the paranoid firm will probably imitate them. But strategic paranoia carries with it a sizable element of conservatism. Fear often entails being afraid to innovate, overextend resources, or take risks. This reactive orientation impedes the development of a concerted and consistent strategy. The paranoid firm's direction has too much to do with external forces and not enough with consistent goals, plans, or unifying themes and traditions.

Paranoid firms frequently try product diversification, to reduce the risk of reliance on any one product, but because diversification requires more elaborate control and information-processing mechanisms, it actually reinforces the firm's paranoia.

Corporate paranoia often stems from a period of traumatic challenge. A strong market dries up, a powerful new competitor enters the market, or damaging legislation is passed. The harm done by these forces may cause managers to become very distrustful and fearful, to lose their nerve, to recognize the need for better intelligence.[1] These hypotheses are summarized in Table 5.3.

Table 5.3
Hypotheses for the Paranoid Constellation

1. The persecutory fantasy and the paranoid style will go together.

2. The more pronounced these are in the CEO and his top managers the more the organizational culture will be plagued by suspiciousness and mistrust, the search for and identification of enemies in the environment, poor morale, fight/flight attitudes, uniform but distorted perceptions, and the use of information as a power resource.

3. The more pronounced these personality and cultural factors, the more the structure of the organization will use sophisticated control and information systems, centralize power for decision making, and evolve a sophisticated scanning apparatus to study the environment.

4. The more pronounced these personality and cultural factors, the more wariness enters into decision making, the more reactive and fragmented the strategy, and the greater the proclivity to diversify.

HELPLESSNESS AND HOPELESSNESS

The fantasy that the course of events in life cannot be changed and that one is just not good enough dominates this depressive neurotic style. Depressive-style managers lack self-confidence and initiative. Using the DSM III as a guide, depressive-style managers are often dependent-avoidant mixed personalities. Psychiatrists claim that these dependent and sometimes avoidant personalities have a strong need for affection and nurturance, and possess very little self-esteem (Jacobson, 1971; Nicholi, 1978).

In this depressive style, feelings of guilt, worthlessness, and inadequacy are pervasive. Individuals tend to downgrade themselves; they are self-deprecating and feel inferior to others, claiming a lack of ability and talent. They abdicate responsibility. A sense of helplessness and hopelessness prevails. External sources for sustenance are needed to combat insecurity. Depressives submerge their individuality and look for protectors. They try to be ingratiating, adapting their behavior to please those upon whom they depend and allowing others to assume responsibility for major areas of life.

Depressive-style leaders are subject to feelings of persecution. They sometimes believe, often as a result of unpleasant past relationships, that people are out to get them, and this can lead to political infighting. Usually, however, there is no sound basis for these suspicions and depressive CEOs begin to feel guilty—to blame themselves. They turn their hostility inward in a phenomenon known as *moral masochism*. They seek psychic pain as a redemptive act, as a means of assuaging their guilt over unacceptable wishes. Defeat is seen as a just reward (Jacobson, 1971).

At the same time, such leaders seem to be looking for a messiah, someone to protect them from the dangers around them (Bion, 1959). They experience a need to idealize others, be it consultants, members of their constituency such as bankers or directors, or other figures with whom they are in regular contact.

Those in charge thus display incompetence and fail to show any imagination. They wait for others to take the initiative, often fearing success because they think it will make people envious and hostile. This sometimes prompts them to "snatch mediocrity from the jaws of victory." Executives adopt a passive orientation, shying away from action and becoming reclusive (Kernberg, 1979).

Avoidance Cultures—Depressive Organizations

The culture of the firm can be characterized as "avoidant." The executives look at the organization as a machine which simply has to be fed with routine input. There is a pervasive sense of futility, as executives try to reduce their contributions to the minimum required of them. The CEO sets a climate of negativity and lethargy and the second-tier executives take their cues from this. In some cases the boss's personality alone causes the depressive atmosphere. In others, an external force, such as the loss of the founder or a takeover by a conglomerate, causes healthy executives to lose their sense of control, their authority, their self-esteem, and, consequently, their initiative. In either event, an avoidant culture is permeated by unmotivated, absentee executives, buck-passing, delays, and an absence of meaningful interaction and communication among managers. There exists a "decidophobia." Things just continue along the same path as always, even when the firm begins to run into trouble.

Depressive firms are characterized by inactivity, lack of confidence, extreme conservatism, and insularity. There is an atmosphere of passivity and purposelessness. What gets done is what has been programmed and routinized and requires no special initiative. Miller and Friesen's (1984) stagnant bureaucracies exhibit the typical strategies and structures of depressive firms.

Most depressive firms are well established and serve a mature market, one that has had the same technology and competitive patterns for many years. Trade agreements, restrictive trade practices, and substantial tariffs are the rule. The primary steel industry and agricultural or industrial chemical businesses are the kinds of markets in which depressive firms are most commonly found. The low level of change, the absence of serious competition, and the homogeneity of the customers make the administrative task fairly simple.

Although formal authority is centralized and based on position rather than expertise, the issue of power is not very important. Control is really exercised by formalized programs and policies rather than by managerial initiatives. Suggestions for change are resisted and action is inhibited. It is almost as if the top executives share a sense of impotence and incapacity. They just don't feel they can control events or that they have what it takes to revitalize the firm.

Content with the status quo, these organizations do little to discover the key

Table 5.4
Hypotheses for the Depressive Constellation

---

1. The fantasy of helplessness and the depressive (avoidant/dependent) style will be found in the same CEOs.

2. The more pronounced these are in the CEO and his managers, the more the organizational culture will be characterized by a lack of initiative, unmotivated absentee executives, buck-passing, delays, "decidophobia," passivity, and a sense of futility.

3. The more prominent these personality and cultural factors, the more the structure of the firm will be bureaucratic, rigid, impersonal, and based on formal position—in short, mechanistic. There will be very little scanning of the environment or communication among managers.

4. The more prominent these factors, the more moribund the strategy, which will be less likely to have changed materially in a long time, and which will be anachronistic even in the mature industries in which these firms are usually found. Extreme conservatism, a very vague set of goals and strategies, and an absence of plans will also be more common.

---

threats and weaknesses in markets. It is difficult to say whether stagnation causes inattention to information gathering or vice versa. In either event, the two aspects go hand in hand in the depressive firm.

The sense of aimlessness and apathy among top managers precludes any attempt to give the firm clear direction or goals. Strategy is never explicitly considered, so no meaningful change occurs. Yesterday's products and markets become today's, not because of any policy of conservatism, but because of lethargy. Managers spend most of their time working out routine details while procrastinating on major decisions. These hypotheses are summarized in Table 5.4.

THE NEED FOR GRANDIOSITY

Central in this dramatic style is the need to draw attention to oneself and a fantasy that revolves around grandiosity. This style seems to mix characteristics of two personality types: the histrionic and the narcissistic. Although the genesis of these two personality types is quite different, there are many behavioral similarities which make it difficult to differentiate between the two types in action. Consequently, for expediency we have lumped them together. Dramatic individuals experience a great need to get attention from and impress others. They often exaggerate their achievements and talents and display excessive emotion. Their behavior has an exhibitionistic quality (Kets de Vries, 1981). Dramatic people seem to be driven by a need for excitement and stimulation that is often without substance. They lack self-discipline.

There is an incapacity for concentration and a tendency to overreact to minor events. Many of these individuals possess a sense of entitlement. They may be superficially warm and charming, but in fact often lack sincerity and are inconsiderate of others. Exploitation is not uncommon and empathy is usually lacking (Kernberg, 1979). Often unwittingly, these CEOs take others for granted. Relationships thus tend to be unstable. In many instances they alternate between extremes of overidealization and devaluation. When fantasies of unlimited power, success, and brilliance are cut short, dramatic CEOs may experience marked feelings of rage and anger and act vindictively.

The dramatic style may give rise to a specific role constellation in the firm. Dramatic leaders often attract subordinates with a dependent personality structure. Their action-orientated, grandiose style suits the dependency needs of insecure subordinates, allowing the latter to take responsibility for major areas of functioning and subordinating their own needs to those of the dramatic leader. The results are frequently as follows.

Charismatic Cultures—Dramatic Firms

Subordinates tend to *idealize* the charismatic leader, to ignore his faults and accentuate his strengths (idealization is often motivated by feelings of insecurity and unworthiness in the absence of a figure who can be admired). They become highly dependent on the idealized person, feeling a need to appeal to, support, and ingratiate themselves with him. They are prone to be very flattered by a few words of praise, and are devastated by the mildest of reprimands. They thus become extremely dependent on the leader and very easy to control and manipulate. This is generally the exact situation that the dramatic leader wants to encourage. He wishes others to ''nourish'' him with their confirming and admiring (''*mirroring*'') responses. Mirroring superiors in fact seek out idealizing subordinates—they demand not only conformity but praise and adulation (Kohut, 1971).

In the charismatic culture, everything seems to revolve around the leader. The hopes and ambitions of the other executives and managers all center around this idealized person. Charismatic leaders are persons of action who strive aggressively and single-mindedly to implement a central goal that becomes a focal concern for the followers. A tremendous uniformity exists that derives from the leader's ''charisma''—there is only one leader and many followers. There is thus an unquestioning, trustful climate of subordinacy among group members. Zealous followers help create an atmosphere in which the leader is seen as infallible. There is too little reflection or analysis as managers rely on the inspired judgment of the boss. The leader's power—both formal and informal—is so great that he has a great deal of latitude to make very bold and unilateral decisions. Typically, the leader does not permit any resistance or dissent from subordinates. Independent-minded managers cannot last very long in this culture.

Dramatic firms are hyperactive, impulsive, dramatically venturesome, and dangerously uninhibited. Their strategies, structures, and decision-making approaches are those of impulsive firms. Impulsive decision makers live in a world of hunches and impressions rather than facts as they haphazardly address an array of disparate markets. Their dramatic flair encourages the top people to centralize power, reserving their prerogative to initiate bold ventures.

Audacity, risk taking, and diversification are the corporate themes. Instead of reacting to the business environment, the top decision maker attempts to create his/her own environment. He/she enters some markets and leaves others; he/she constantly switches to new products while abandoning older ones, placing a sizable proportion of the firm's capital at risk. Unbridled growth is the goal, reflecting the top manager's considerable narcissistic needs and his/her desire for attention and visibility. He/she wants to be at center stage, showing how great an executive he/she really is.

The structure of the dramatic organization is usually far too primitive for its broad markets. First, too much power is concentrated in the chief executive, who meddles even in routine operating matters because he/she wants to put his/her personal stamp on (and take credit for) everything. A second problem follows from this overcentralization—namely, the absence of an effective information system. The top executive does little scanning of the business environment because he/she has too little time and prefers to act on intuition rather than facts.

Finally, the leader's dominance obstructs effective internal communication, which is mostly from the top down. These hypotheses are summarized in Table 5.5.

Table 5.5
Hypotheses for the Dramatic Constellation

1. The fantasy of grandiosity and the dramatic (histrionic/narcissistic) style will be found in the same personality.

2. The more pronounced these are in the CEO and his managers, the more the organization culture will be characterized by dependent subordinates who idealize the leader, hold him infallible, and never question him. There will be an enthusiastic adherence to the beliefs and goals of the CEO, and few independent-minded executives. In short, a charismatic culture will prevail.

3. The more prominent these personality and cultural factors, the more the structure of the organization will be extremely centralized, too informal for its administrative task, too primitive in its scanning and information-processing apparatus, and too constrained in bottom-up communications.

4. The more prominent these factors, the more intuitive, impulsive, and risky the decision making, and the more procreative, expansionist, and acquisitions-oriented the strategy.

THE NEED FOR CONTROL

Compulsive-style executives feel a need to counteract their fear of being at the mercy of events. Mastering and controlling whatever may affect their lives becomes an overwhelming preoccupation. These people see relationships in terms of dominance and submission; they insist that others submit to their ways of doing things. They can be deferential and ingratiating to superiors, while at the same time behaving in a markedly autocratic way toward subordinates. There is a sense of perfectionism that interferes with their ability to see the big picture. Compulsives are preoccupied with trivial details, rules, and regulations. They are attracted by routines and find it difficult to deviate from planned activity. The unfamiliar is upsetting and form takes precedence over substance. Meticulousness, dogmatism, and obstinacy are common traits. Compulsives demonstrate an excessive concern about order, organization, and efficiency. They lack spontaneity and are unable to relax. Although they may come across as industrious, their behavior is rigid, making for a lack of imagination and much repetition. Compulsives are excessively devoted to work, to the exclusion of pleasure and meaningful relationships. Indecisiveness and procrastination for fear of making mistakes are other elements of their style (Fenichel, 1945; Shapiro, 1965). But what sorts of organizations do these managers create?

Bureaucratic Cultures—Compulsive Organizations

In the compulsive firm, there is a degree of mistrust between the leader and his subordinates. To effect coordination, he/she would rather rely on formal controls and direct supervision than the goodwill, shared objectives, or talent of his management team. As a result, there are overtones of suspicion and manipulation. There is a constant preoccupation about losing control. Controls, however, can rob subordinates of their sense of discretion, involvement, and personal responsibility. The prescription of work and the atmosphere of suspicion saps executives' enthusiasm and robs them of initiative.

The bureaucratic group culture is above all depersonalized and rigidified. It is permeated by top management's preoccupation with control over people, operations, and the external environment. The rules may be legacies of the past, codifying the original founder(s) notions about how to run the company to be successful. Formal policies, standard operating procedures, and detailed specifications for the accomplishment of tasks and the management of personnel prevail. These are all vehicles that the top managers use to control the firm. They manage by rules rather than through personal guidance or directives. They wish to avoid surprises and to determine what is to happen throughout the firm. The only managers who can survive happily in this setting are "bureaucrats" who love to follow rules and fear taking the initiative. Independent managers will find that they do not have enough latitude to act on their own, and leave. The controlling top executive is not willing to relinquish sufficient control over operations to allow for a deliberative, participative mode of decision making. Instead, policies are the manifestation of compulsive features rather than objective adaptive requirements. They are, as such, not subject to discussion. We hasten to add that we are not using the term bureaucracy in the strictly Weberian way. Our notions do not so much conform to a sociological construct describing an ideal form of formal organization, as to a mode of operation that is highly ritualistic and inwardly focused.

The compulsive firm is wed to ritual. Every detail of operation is planned carefully in advance and carried out in routinized fashion. Thoroughness, completeness, and conformity to established procedures are emphasized (see Mintzberg's, 1979, machine bureaucracies).

Like the paranoid firm, the compulsive firm emphasizes formal controls and information systems. But there is a crucial difference. In compulsive organizations, controls are really designed to monitor internal operations, production efficiency, costs, and the scheduling and performance of projects, while the paranoid firm is interested chiefly in external conditions.

Operations are standardized as much as possible, and an elaborate set of formal policies and procedures evolves. These include not only production and marketing procedures but dress codes, frequent sales meetings, and even suggested employee attitudes.

The compulsive organization is exceedingly hierarchical, a reflection of the leader's strong concern with control. The compulsive person is always worried about the next move and how he/she is going to make it. Such preoccupation has often been reinforced by periods when the firm was at the mercy of other organizations or circumstances. To prevent this from happening again, compulsive-style executives try to reduce uncertainty and to attain a clearly specified objective in a carefully planned manner. Surprises must be avoided at all costs.

Compulsive firms show the same preoccupation with detail and established procedures in all their business strategies. They generally create a large number of action plans, budgets, and capital expenditure plans. Each project is designed with many checkpoints, exhaustive performance evaluations, and detailed schedules.

The compulsive firm has a particular orientation and distinctive competence, and its plans reflect them. This orientation, rather than what is going on in the world, serves as the major guide for the firm's strategy. For example, some organizations take pride in being the leading innovator in the marketplace; they try to be the first out with new products, whether or not they are called for by customers. Innovation may be inappropriate in the light of new market conditions, but the firm's strong inward focus prevents any realization of this fact. Change is difficult. These hypotheses are summarized in Table 5.6.

Table 5.6
Hypotheses for the Compulsive Constellation

---

1. The fantasy of control will conjoin with the compulsive style.

2. The more pronounced these are in the CEO and his managers, the more the organization culture will be centered around issues of control, with efficiency or the slavish adherence to some other archaic set of standards, and the prevalence of risk-averse, bureaucracy-loving managers. Ritual will come to rule.

3. The more prominent these personality and cultural factors, the more the structure of the organization will be bureaucratic, hierarchical, rigid, rule-oriented, inwardly focused, formalized, and centralized. Programmed, routinized, and standardized practices will dominate. Cost controls will monitor efficiency but there will be very little analysis of the environment.

4. The more prominent these factors, the more decision making will be focused on details and established procedures. A fixed strategy will most likely prevail, which is never questioned but is merely "implemented" through action plans, capital budgets, and so on.

THE NEED FOR DETACHMENT

Some individuals are guided by a detached style and fantasize that the outside world does not offer them any satisfaction. They sense that all interactions with others will eventually fail and cause harm; that it is safer to remain distant. Psychiatrists have identified avoidant and schizoid personalities who are often beset by such preoccupations. Both personality types center around a pattern of social detachment. Avoidant personalities have had experiences of interpersonal rejection and deprecation that have led them to be mistrustful of others and to avoid close relationships; however, they long for closer attachments and greater social acceptance. In contrast, schizoid personalities often have cognitive and emotional deficits that render them unconcerned about social isolation (Kernberg, 1975; Kets de Vries, 1980). Given the similarity in the behavioral manifestations of the two types, however, it is difficult to differentiate between them since both tend to be socially hesitant and unresponsive (APA, 1980).

What characterizes this detached style is the degree of noninvolvement and withdrawal. Detached individuals are most unwilling to enter into emotional relationships. They prefer to be by themselves and to feel no need to communicate. They distance themselves from close personal attachments and pursue noninvolvement. Although on the surface there may be great indifference to praise, criticism, or the feelings of others, this behavior is often a defensive maneuver against being hurt. Whatever the underlying reasons, these individuals appear to be cold and aloof. They display emotional blandness and an inability to express enthusiasm or pleasure. Detached managers are unable to engage in the give-and-take of reciprocal relationships; they appear to possess minimal human interest. To protect themselves, they refuse to enter into relationships and minimize involvements for fear of social derogation. The following type of organization may result.

Politicized Cultures—Schizoid Organizations

Miller and Friesen's (1984) headless firms suggest the strategies, structures, and decision-making approaches of these organizations. The politicized corporate culture is a product of a withdrawing executive who abdicates his responsibilities as a leader. His detached style causes him to avoid contact with others and so the management of the firm is left up to second-tier managers, none of whom is very clear about his/her responsibilities. The members of the second tier are "gamesmen" (Maccoby, 1976; Lasch, 1978) who spend their time jockeying for position and power against their "rivals" in other departments. They fill the leadership vacuum by politicking for their parochial interests with the detached leader. In this, they see opportunities for enhancing their spheres and resource bases. Needless to say, problems of coordination, cooperation, interdepartmental rivalry, and vacillating strategy are quite common here.

Strategy making resides in a shifting coalition of careerist second-tier managers who try to influence the indecisive leader and simultaneously advance their pet projects and minor empires. The firm muddles through and drifts, making incremental changes in one area and then reversing them whenever a new group of managers wins favor. The initiatives of one group of managers are often neutralized or severely blunted by those of an opposing group.

The divided nature of the organization thwarts effective coordination and communication. Information is used more as a power resource than as a vehicle for effective adaptation; in fact, managers erect barriers to prevent the free flow of information. But this is not the only shortcoming of the information system. Another is the absence of information on the outside business environment. The company's focus is internal—on personal ambitions and catering to the top manager's desires. Second-tier managers find it more useful to ignore real-world events that might reflect poorly on their own behavior or conflict with the wishes of the detached leader. These hypotheses are summarized in Table 5.7.

Table 5.7
Hypotheses for the Schizoid Constellation

---

1. The fantasy of detachment will coincide with the detached (schizoid/avoidant) style.

2. The more pronounced these are in the CEO, the more the culture of the organization will be characterized by a leadership vacuum, and dominance by a second tier of politicized "gamesmen" who jockey for power and position. Coordination and cooperation will be neglected.

3. The more prominent these personality and cultural factors, the more the structure of the organization will be fragmented into uncooperative "fiefdoms." Political battles will cause information systems to be used as power resources and effective communication and collaborations will be thwarted. Power will be spread among an altering coalition of second-tier managers.

4. The more prominent these factors, the more fragmented, vacillating, and inconsistent the strategies. The absence of consensus will make concerted and adaptive change less possible. Politics will be a far more important influence on decisions than rationality, and a muddling-through orientation will be much more common.

CONCLUSION

In describing the five dysfunctional types we have, for simplification, focused on the characteristics of "pure" constellations. In reality, however, the clinical picture is usually much more complicated. Combinations or mixtures among types often occur. The pages of *Fortune, Forbes, Business Week,* or the *Wall Street Journal* constantly portray hybrids such as the paranoid-compulsive type, the depressive-compulsive type, or the schizoid-depressive type. To make matters even more complex, we also find movement across organizational types, depending on who is in power, and the stage of the organization's life cycle. In addition, the style of the leader or of the dominant coalition may change through interactions with the evolving organization.

We must stress that, although the personality of the top manager can vitally influence his organization, a reverse relationship will also exist. A failing organization that is rife with disappointment can cause a leader to become depressed. A series of vicious threats from the competition can awaken dormant paranoia.

Clearly, then, the influence between organizational orientations and managerial disposition is reciprocal. Mutual causation is the rule.

It may be useful to highlight several advantages or strengths of our typology. First, it is holistic. It avoids the complexity of the "one variable at a time" approach by searching for common types and for the psychological and cultural factors that underlie these types. Second, it meets personality in a rather global way, looking for major adaptive styles that motivate and characterize much of behavior and eschewing narrow dimensions of affect or cognition. Third, we feel the framework gets at the roots of some strategic, structural, and cultural problems in organizations. Fourth, the assignment to a particular type proves useful by alerting the organizational analyst to a range of unobserved but frequently related manifestations, thus helping in the selection of the appropriate intervention strategy. Instead of dwelling on specific symptoms regarding the distribution of authority or the design of information systems, we are trying to search for the underlying cause of the conjunction of various symptoms. In doing so, we will become more effective as organizational diagnosticians, or at least more attuned to the limits of change.

One of the more pessimistic aspects of this research is that it seems to point to great areas of resistance to change. Neurotic styles of behavior are deeply rooted; CEOs are very hard to change, especially when they hold all of the power. In many cases, we would expect meaningful organizational turnaround to occur only after dramatic failure erodes the power base of the CEO, or after a new CEO takes over. This is consistent with the findings of Miller and Friesen (1980a, 1980b), who found that major organizational reorientations were motivated by extremely poor performance, changes in top management, or both. Therefore, much of the normative literature on policy, structure, and culture might do well to recognize that many managerial prescriptions will run counter to the personalities of the CEO and thus be resisted, or, where implemented, would not fit into the overall organizational configuration and thus be lacking in appropriateness and impact.

We close by using some directions for further operationalization and testing of the framework. It is possible to measure most of the CEO personality orientations using the instruments of Millon (1981) and the concepts developed in the DSM III (APA, 1980). Strategy-making, structural, and cultural variables can be measured using the instruments of Van de Ven and Ferry (1980), Miller and Friesen (1984), and others. Many strategy variables are suggested by Hofer and Schendel (1978). As we expect the associations between CEO personality and organizational variables to be statistically significant, correlation methods could be used to establish relationships. Alternatively, CEOs could be classified into various personality types. Analyses of variance could then be conducted on the organizational variables to see if the strategic, cultural, and structural orientations vary systematically among categories of CEOs. It may even be possible to use methods of taxonomy such as cluster analysis or Q-factor analysis to derive naturally occurring common types. We hope that our framework is sufficiently interesting to induce such further testing.

NOTE

1. More detailed descriptions of the structural correlates of this and the other four types can be found in Kets de Vries and Miller (1984a; 1984b).

REFERENCES

American Psychiatric Association. *Diagnostic and Statistical Manual of Mental Disorders,* 3d ed. Washington, DC, 1980.

Bion, Wilfred R. *Experiences in Groups.* London: Tavistock, 1959.

Fenichel, Otto. *The Psychoanalytic Theory of Neurosis.* New York: W. W. Norton and Co, 1945.

Freedman, Alfred M.; Kaplan, Harold J.; and Sadock, Benjamin J. (eds). *Comprehensive Textbook of Psychiatry,* Vols I, II. Baltimore: The Williams and Wilkins Co., 1975.

Hofer, Charles and Schendel, Dan. *Strategy Formulation: Analytical Concepts.* St. Paul, Minn: West Publishing, 1978.

Jacobson, Edith. *Depression.* New York: International Universities Press, 1971.

Jaques, Elliot. *The Changing Culture of a Factory.* London: Tavistock, 1951.

Jaques, Elliot. *Work, Creativity and Social Justice.* New York: International Universities Press, 1970.

Kernberg, Otto. *Borderline Conditions and Pathological Narcissism.* New York: Jason Aronson Inc., 1975.

Kernberg, Otto. *Object Relations Theory and Clinical Psychoanalysis.* New York: Jason Aronson Inc., 1976.

Kernberg, Otto. "Regression in Organizational Leadership." *Psychiatry* 42 (1979): 29–39.

Kets de Vries, Manfred F. R. *Organizational Paradoxes: Clinical Approaches to Management.* London: Tavistock, 1980.

Kets de Vries, Manfred F. R. "Leiderschap in een narcistisch tijdperk." *Management Totaal* 5 (1981): 20–25.

Kets de Vries, Manfred F. R. *The Irrational Executive: Psychoanalytic Explorations in Management.* New York: International Universities Press, 1984.

Kets de Vries, Manfred F. R. and Miller, Danny. "Neurotic Styles and Organizational Pathology." *Strategic Management Journal* 5 (1984a): 35–55.

Kets de Vries, Manfred and Miller, Danny. *The Neurotic Organization: Diagnosing and Changing Counterproductive Styles of Management.* San Francisco: Jossey Bass, 1984b.

Kets de Vries, Manfred and Miller, Danny. "Group Fantasies and Organizational Functioning." *Human Relations* 37 (1984c): 111–34.

Klein, Melanie. *Contributions to Psychoanalysis.* London: The Hogarth Press, 1948.

Kohut, Heinz. *The Analysis of the Self.* New York: International Universities Press, 1971.

Laplanche, J. and Pontalis, J. B. *The Language of Psychoanalysis.* London: The Hogarth Press, 1973.

Lasch, Christopher. *The Culture of Narcissism.* New York: W. W. Norton and Co., 1978.

Maccoby, Michael. *The Gamesman.* New York: Simon and Schuster, 1976.

Mahler, Margaret S., Pine, Fred, and Bergman, Anni. *The Psychological Birth of the Human Infant.* New York: Basic Books, 1975.

Miller, Danny and Friesen, Peter H. "Archetypes of Strategy Formulation." *Management Science* 24 (1978): 921–33.

Miller, Danny and Friesen, Peter H. "Archetypes of Organizational Transition." *Administrative Science Quarterly,* 25 (1980a): 268–99.

Miller, Danny and Friesen, Peter H. "Momentum and Revolution in Organizational Adaptation." *Academy of Management Journal* 24 (1980b): 591–614.

Miller, Danny and Friesen, Peter H. *Organizations: A Quantum View.* Englewood Cliffs, NJ: Prentice Hall, 1984.

Miller, Danny; Kets de Vries Manfred F. R.; and Toulouse, Jean-Marie. "Top Executives Locus of Control and Its Relationship to Strategy-Making, Structure and Environment." *Academy of Management Journal* 25 (1982): 237–53.

Millon, Theodore. *Disorders of Personality: DSM III, Axis II.* New York: Wiley-Interscience Books, 1981.

Mintzberg, Henry. *The Structuring of Organizations.* Englewood Cliffs, NJ: Prentice-Hall, 1979.

Nicholi, Armand M. (ed). *The Harvard Guide to Modern Psychiatry.* Cambridge: The Belknap Press, 1978.

Payne, Roy and Pugh, Derek S. "Organization Structure and Climate." In *Handbook of Industrial and Organizational Psychology,* edited by M. D. Dunnette. Chicago: Rand McNally, 1976.

Sandler, Joseph and Rosenblatt, Bernard. "The Concept of the Representational World." *Psychoanalytic Study of the Child* 17 (1962): 128–45.

Schendel, Dan and Hofer, Charles. *Strategic Management.* Boston: Little, Brown, 1979.

Shapiro, David. *Neurotic Styles.* New York: Basic Books, 1965.

Tosi, Henry. "A Reexamination of Personality as a Determinant of the Effects of Participation." *Personnel Psychology* 23 (1970): 91–99.

Van de Ven, Andrew H. and Ferry, Diane L. *Measuring and Assessing Organizations.* New York: Wiley-Interscience Books, 1980.

Vroom, Victor H. *Some Personality Determinants of the Effects of Participation.* Englewood Cliffs, NJ: Prentice-Hall, 1960.

Zaleznik, Abraham and Kets de Vries, Manfred F. R. *Power and the Corporate Mind.* Boston: Houghton Mifflin, 1975.

6

DECISIONS, COALITIONS, AND THE ECONOMY OF THE SELF

Abraham Zaleznik

Della and Jim Young, a couple deeply in love, each bought a Christmas gift for the other without communicating their intentions. Della sold her long, beautiful hair for twenty dollars and bought Jim a platinum fob chain for his splendid watch. Jim sold his watch for the money he needed to buy Della a set of tortoise shell combs for her hair. In ending his short story of gift giving and exchange, O. Henry writes:

The magi, as you know, were wise men—wonderfully wise men—who brought gifts to the Babe in the manger. They invented the art of giving Christmas presents. Being wise, their gifts were no doubt wise ones, possibly bearing the privilege of exchange in case of duplication. And here I have lamely related to you the uneventful chronicle of two foolish children in a flat who most unwisely sacrificed for each other the greatest treasures of their house. But in the last word to the wise of these days let it be said that of all who give gifts these two were the wisest. Of all who give and receive gifts, such as they are the wisest. Everywhere they are wisest. They are the magi.[1]

The gift the Youngs had given each other was trust, an open-ended, mutual commitment to act with the best interests of the other in mind, no matter the personal sacrifice. There can be no finer gift than trust—imagine the consequences if both the United States and the USSR, unilaterally and without prior consultation or bargaining, each destroyed its stockpile of missiles and nuclear warheads!

Being singularly rational men, with keen regard for the hazards of open-ended trust (the problem being that the goal is desirable, but how to achieve this goal is unknown and complex), strategic planners, aided by game theory, concentrate on rational procedures for making decisions involving conflict and commonality of interest simultaneously among two or more parties. Let us convert the

Youngs' dilemma into the logic of game theory using the famous "Battle of the Sexes."[2]

A man and his wife have the choice of either going to the ballet or to a prize fight on Friday evening. Being a traditionally minded couple, the man would rather go to the fight and his wife would prefer to go to the ballet. But both would rather be together than spend the evening apart, even if they do not attend their preferred entertainment. Each must buy his or her own ticket separately. What should they do?

Before rationally analyzing this problem, we should examine the variety of perspectives one can take with respect to the class of problems represented in rational action and decision making. These perspectives, from mathematics, psychology, sociology, and political science, have preceded psychoanalysis in considering decision problems and the formation of coalitions. Psychoanalysis, as the science of the unconscious, has not been applied to how men make decisions or, for that matter, to most areas of everyday life.[3] When Freud wrote about everyday life, his intent was to show the ubiquitousness of the unconscious.[4] Its appearance, however, was in the familiar structure of the formation of neurotic symptoms. A slip of the tongue, or a moment of forgetting, involves the familiar model of neurotic conflict: the opposition of a wish and some force within the psyche that prohibits direct action to gratify the wish. The parapraxis represents simultaneously, as do all symptoms according to this model, the partial gratification of the wish, the defense against anxiety connected with the wish, and the payment of the price inherent in all forms of psychological symptoms.

The basic distinction between primary-process and secondary-process thinking runs precisely along the lines of a mind in control and able to calculate, reason, and decide, as compared with a mind dominated by visual and disconnected images, propelled by impulses, and under the sway of the pleasure principle. Descriptions of ego function, according to secondary-process thinking, follow closely other descriptions of rational problem solving[5] and utility theory.[6] An optimal decision, according to utility theory, is one that maximizes satisfaction subject to a budget constraint. The formal logic of such a decision is expressed in economics in terms of the principle of marginal utility: An individual will (should) behave in such a way that the last dollar spent on each commodity yields the same additional utility. Such a principle is not distant from the notion expressed by Waelder in his discussion of multiple function of the ego.[7] From the standpoint of the economy of ego function, the course of action considered most desirable is that which achieves many ends simultaneously, with the least expenditure of energy. What prepares the ego for the calculations involved is the binding of discharge, and the use of thought as an experimental prelude to action.

These principles of secondary-process thinking, or norms of the mature ego function, when applied to the description and explanation of action in the clinical sense carry investigation hardly any distance. The more interesting problem is how the ego achieves this type of maturation. Once posed, this problem leads us back to the surer ground of psychoanalytic inquiry, toward the neuroses and other psychopathologies. Human action in decision-making structures seems like infertile ground either for the application of psychoanalytic theory or for providing new material for the development of psychoanalysis as a science or as a general psychology. The burden of this paper is to show just the opposite.

MODELS OF DECISION MAKING

From the standpoint of psychology in general, the terms of economic theory, particularly utility theory and the principle of marginal utility, are closely allied to the assumptions and propositions of behaviorism and learning theory. According to these propositions, an individual continues to emit certain behaviors until the cost and reward connected with a unit of action are equal. The terms of the equation are affected by principles such as satiation (the more one gets of a particular reward, the less desirable it becomes) and repetition (the more one repeats a behavior, the more bored one becomes and, consequently, the more costly the action).

Rational models of decision making, including the principle of multiple function of the ego, involve complex calculation. In the case of the more traditional models of decision making, one assumes that the calculation is conscious, although how the calculation occurs and how the ego arrives at the point of decision and choice are not understood. There is no such assumption in the case of the principle of multiple function. Complex calculations, especially those governed by conscious thought processes, demand elaborate search procedures to isolate the factors involved, to determine preferences and utilities, and to assign probabilities to the various outcomes. This form of search and reason is itself a costly human activity and establishes limits on how far thought will precede decision and action. The practical limitations of solving problems lead to a revision in defining the goals of action, from optimizing (the outcome in marginal utility analysis) to satisficing (reaching a point where the subjective response of a payout for action results in closure).[8]

One of the main characteristics of economic theory as applied to decision making is the assumption of a market. Here, one is bidding against impersonal forces and undertaking risks where the objects whose interests interact with ours are unknown. The wheat farmer sells in an impersonal market; he does not size up a particular individual whose interest is directly opposed to his (the buyer wants the lowest price possible, and the seller wants the highest). The market sets the price under circumstances, usually, where all the participants have equal access to the information that ultimately determines the price. That this assumption of equality of information does not hold is exemplified in the case of the Russian wheat deal of 1972 when the brokers knew how deeply the Russians wanted to get into the U.S. market while the farmers did not. By buying contracts in advance, before the information could affect the price, the brokers were able to increase their profits, much to the anger of the farmers.

Positions in the market can be translated to mean differences in power among participants in decision events. The purpose in back of the revision of classical economic theory and the development of the theory of monopolistic and imperfect competition was to take account of the fact that, as a result of market structure, certain participants could dominate bargaining through superior control of resources.[9] The effect of oligopoly, a market structure with few participants, is to eliminate the total anonymity of the marketplace. Thus, the Ford Motor Company must take into account how General Motors ''thinks'' before deciding on the design of a new line of automobiles. Ford actually lost millions in the presentation of the Edsel model because it not only misjudged what the consumer wanted, but also because its competitor influenced consumer preferences by the types of cars offered and the supporting advertising and sales promotion.

The ability to project oneself into the mind of an opponent in a decision event opens the way for new modes of calculating and weighing various utilities and probabilities and, ultimately, in reaching decisions. Game theory is designed to evaluate formally and assess the probabilities and effects of alternative outcomes when decisions involve comparing one's own preferences with those of another player.

The foundations of game theory were laid in 1944 by John Von Neumann and Oskar Morgenstern with the publication of their book, *The Theory of Games and Economic Behavior*. As the title implies, the concepts were originally developed to provide a new approach to economic problems. The authors set out to show that ''the typical problems of economic behavior become strictly identical with the mathematical notions of suitable games of strategy.''[10] In its short history, however, game theory has sparked interest and enthusiasm in diverse fields, and its effects have been felt not only in economics but in such areas as pure mathematics, psychology, sociology, business (particularly marketing and finance), and warfare.

Game theory may be described as a theory of rational decision making in situations of interest conflict. These situations involve the following:

— Two or more decision makers or players, whose interests partly or wholly conflict (a ''player'' need not be a single person but may be a group of individuals such as a team or a corporation).
— A well-defined set of possible strategies for each player.
— A well-defined outcome for every combination of strategies chosen by the players.

It is assumed that in every game there is a known, causal relationship between specific actions and their outcomes, and that all possible outcomes are known and specified. Further, each player is assumed to have well-defined preferences over these outcomes; each is assumed to be fully aware of the rules of the game. Finally, each player is assumed to be ''rational'' in a specific sense: that is, each always seeks to gain his most desirable outcome, and each assumes that the other players are rational in the same sense. Rationality requires that a player estimate the consequences of his own actions, taking into account not only his own preferences but the fact that the outcome also depends on the preferences of others over whom he has little or no control; thus, in deciding on a strategy, he must also estimate the most likely strategy that every other player will choose. Rationality also includes imputing the same type of rationality to other players because errors are impossible to predict and because it is unrealistic to assume that one's opponent will make the mistakes one would like him to make.

Given a situation that meets the preceding criteria, the basic questions of game theory are: How should each player behave to derive the greatest benefit from his partial control over the outcome, and, assuming this behavior takes place, what then should be the final outcome of the game? The answers to these two questions, when they exist, constitute the "solution" to a game.

The simplest competitive situation is the two-person, zero-sum (or constant-sum) game, so-called because the players compete for a constant amount of resources: One man's gain is another man's loss. Game theory has been most successful in its treatment of these situations, and in fact Von Neumann formulated a solution for all zero-sum games. Two examples follow:[11]

1. The Democratic and Republican candidates for a state governorship are drawing up their platforms. Each believes that his position regarding a controversial proposal for legislation will be the most important factor in determining the number of votes he will receive. Each must therefore decide whether to favor the plan, oppose it, or hedge; they will announce their positions simultaneously.

The wrong behavior of the electorate can be predicted from past experience and recent polls: Party regulars will vote for their candidate regardless of his position, others will vote for the candidate supporting their views and, if both take the same position, a certain number will probably abstain. On the basis of this information, each candidate calculates what will happen in every circumstance and comes up with the matrix below. Entries (payoffs) represent the number of votes the row player, in this case the Republican candidate, will receive if he and his opponent take the positions shown.

		Democrat		
		Favor	*Oppose*	*Hedge*
	Favor (f)	45%	50%	40%
Republican	*Oppose* (o)	60%	55%	45%
	Hedge (h)	45%	55%	40%

Note that the Republican will win the most votes if he opposes the bill, regardless of his opponent's position. Strategy (o) is his dominant strategy, and he should always choose it. From the Democrat's point of view, strategies (f) and

(o) are dominated by (h). Thus, if each player chooses his dominant strategy, the final outcome is predictable: The Republican will lose the election, gaining 45 percent of the votes to the Democrat's 55 percent.

Two strategies, such as (o) and (h), are said to be in equilibrium when neither player gains from changing his strategy unilaterally; their outcome, in this case the 45 to 55 percent payoff, is called the game's equilibrium point.

2. A real-life example of a zero-sum game occurred during World War II. In February 1943, General Kenney, Commander of the Allied Air Forces in the Southwest Pacific, was faced with a critical decision. He knew that the Japanese were planning to reinforce their army in New Guinea, and that they would choose between two alternative routes. They could sail either north of New Britain, where the weather was rainy, or via the south were the weather was generally fair. In either case the journey would take three days. General Kenney had to decide where to concentrate his reconnaissance aircraft. The Japanese wanted their ships to have the least possible exposure to Allied bombers, while Kenney, of course, wanted the reverse. The matrix below shows the problem, with payoffs expressed in the expected number of days of bombing exposure.

		Japanese	
		North	*South*
Allies	*North*	2 days	2 days
	South	1 day	3 days

Looking at this game from Kenney's position, at first glance the Allies do not appear to have a dominant strategy, but the answer becomes clear in the next step of the analysis. By looking at the matrix from the Japanese point of view, it is evident that their dominant strategy is to take the northern route, since no matter what Kenney does their losses will be less than if they go via the south. Kenney's answer was clear: He should take the northern route. (He did in fact do so, as did the Japanese.) As in the preceding example, two rational players should *always* choose this pair of strategies (north, north), whether the game is played once or a hundred times.

If one thinks about the characteristics of zero-sum games in the context of a specifically human situation, an image of total isolation comes to mind: Pure conflict as defined in the preceding two examples removes any possibility of a relationship between the two players. The absence of a relationship is reinforced by the uselessness of communication given the constraints of the situation. One should not, however, mistake the conditions of the zero-sum game to be an artifact that totally misrepresents life. Many of the attempts to solve human conflict lead to the imposition of constraints which limit relationships and minimize communication.

Modern scientific management developed by Frederick Winslow Taylor provides a system which, theoretically, holds no room for conflict, nor does it require communication between management and labor, so long as both parties are willing to abide by the rules of the scientific management system.[12] The fact that they are unwilling to do so arises from the introduction of power as a motive in human relationships. We shall say more about power later in this paper. The point to be stressed here is that decisions involving an equilibrium point among alternatives derive from the logic of the analysis and not the interaction of the players.

The case is different in the problem introduced earlier: the "Battle of the Sexes." The formal structure of this problem appears in the following matrix:

		Woman	
		B_1	B_2
Man	a_1	2, 1	$-1, -1$
	a_2	$-1, -1$	1, 2

The best outcome for the man is shown in cell a_1, B_1 where he enjoys both the fight and his wife's company. The opposite decision suits the wife best and is shown in cell a_2, B_2. The remaining two possibilities mean that the husband and wife spend the evening apart, which is the least desirable outcome for both. There is no equilibrium point where both parties maximize by adopting one and only one strategy. The solution to the problem involves communication of some sort. Suppose, for example, that the man is intent on having his way, the solution in cell a_1, B_1. He must preempt his wife's decision making by power play. He can do this by "stonewalling": I am going to the fight. *You* make up your mind and do what you want." If he has a reputation for stubbornness, his wife will believe him and to avoid a negative payout shown in cell a_1, B_2 she will comply and go to the fight. If the husband's preemptive position is not believable, he can demonstrate intent by showing his wife the ticket to the fight that he has already purchased. This move leaves her no room to maneuver. As Luce and Raiffa suggest, the communication of moves now changes the limits of the game and consequently the preferences. "But, to some spirited females, such an offhand dictatorial procedure is resented with sufficient ferocity to alter drastically the utilities involved in the payoff matrix. Preplay communication is considered outside the game structure of the payoff matrices, yet in some cases it may result in a radical change of one player's preference pattern and therefore of the payoff matrix."[13] For the game theorist, the problem can then shift to devising new payout matrices that include the woman's desire to get even with her husband for his peremptory behavior. The game theorist enlarges the utilities under consideration and constructs new matrices to determine the nature of the moves and the possible emergence of dominant strategies. In other words, game theory is normative and relatively uninterested in what goes on in the minds of actors beyond getting them to state preferences and subjective probabilities.

From a social scientist's point of view, the most interesting games, as well as those most frequently encountered in real life, are non-zero-sum, where there are elements of both conflict and cooperation. A major difference between these and zero-sum games is the potential value of preplay communication and agreements, hence the possibility of an alliance, however uneasy, between players.

There is no mathematical "solution," no prescribed method of finding an optimal strategy for these games. It is at this point that game theory begins to overlap into such areas as psychology and sociology, for analysis of these situations requires consideration of such factors as communication, the order of play, the nature of the information available to the players, threats, binding agreements, double crosses, and, inevitably, the personalities of the players.

Furthermore, while it was possible to define "rationality" (albeit somewhat arbitrarily) and then to determine what constitutes "rational" play in zero-sum games, in many non-zero-sum situations this is no longer possible: The structure of the games themselves prevents one from saying whether a given move is "rational" or not. Since there is no optimal strategy, and since our definition of rationality includes the desire *only* to maximize one's own payoffs, rational moves are difficult to isolate.

The most famous class of non-zero-sum situations is known as the Prisoner's Dilemma. These are situations in which the best outcome for all concerned results when each competitor *refrains from* trying to maximize his payoff.

The basic situation concerns two prisoners, Sam and Harry, who have been taken into custody and separated so that there is no communication possible between them. The sheriff is certain they are guilty of a particular crime (as indeed they are), but he lacks enough evidence to convict them. He makes them a devious proposition: Each prisoner has two alternatives, to confess to the crime or not to confess. If neither confesses, the sheriff will book them on a minor trumped-up charge and they will both receive lenient (½ year) sentences. If they both confess, he will recommend leniency and each will receive a moderate sentence of eight years. But if only one confesses, he will be released in exchange for turning state's evidence and the one who remains silent will receive the maximum sentence of ten years. The matrix below represents their respective payoffs in terms of years in prison (note that they want to *minimize* these payoffs).

		Harry	
		Don't Confess H_1	*Confess* H_2
Sam	*Don't Confess* S_1	½, ½	10, 0
	Confess S_2	0, 10	8, 8

Looking at the problem from Sam's viewpoint, if he could be sure Harry would not confess, perhaps it might be best for him not to confess either; but since he is a rational player who wants to maximize his own payoff, if Harry does not confess, why shouldn't Sam confess and thus avoid a term in prison? In fact, no matter *what* Harry does, Sam is better off if he confesses: Sam's Confess strategy dominates his Don't Confess strategy. The dilemma arises from the fact that, if Harry reasons the same, rational way, he too will choose his dominant, Confess strategy, with the result that both prisoners will spend eight years in prison. Yet this is not the optimal outcome, for both prisoners would be better off if neither confessed.

If they were allowed to communicate, they would probably decide to play the (S_1, H_1) pair of strategies, since neither prefers (S_2, H_2). But the situation is extremely unstable; such an agreement would provide a strong incentive to defect, for each can do better by unilaterally double-crossing the other. But, of course, if they both think this way, they will end up once again at (S_2, H_2) and eight years of prison. It is to their joint advantage if no one reneges, but to each individual's advantage to renege unilaterally. Thus even prechoice communication cannot help to resolve the dilemma unless there is some legal or moral force to bind the prisoners to their agreement.

Luce and Raiffa comment:

> The hopelessness that one feels in such a game as this cannot be overcome by a play on the words "rational" and "irrational"; it is inherent in the situation. "There should be a law against such games!" Indeed, some hold the view that one essential role of government is to declare that the rules of certain social "games" must be changed whenever it is inherent in the game situation that the players, in pursuing their own ends, will be forced into a socially undesirable position.[14]

It is striking to find that the solution proposed to such dilemmas of life, where individuals acting in self-interest end up with a worse solution than if they had in mind the interests of the other, calls forth the desire for some external control: "There ought to be a law against such games." The law has no great confidence in human nature and instead works on the principle of "Hope for the best, but expect the worst."

In any case, the problems of decision call for communication and throw the issue into the realm of psychology. The psychological bases of decision theory become even more apparent when the frame of analysis shifts from two-person to "*n*-person" situations involving the formation of coalitions.

COALITIONS

Georg Simmel wrote: "The essential point is that within a dyad, there can be no majority which could outvote the individual. This, however, is made possible by the mere addition of a third member."[15] This gives rise to the possibility of coalitions. The problem is that game theory never explicitly provides for the effects of communication and collusion, which are even more important in *n*-person games than in two-person, non-zero-sum games. There are also inherent practical problems arising from the fact that the number of possible coalitions increases rapidly as players are added. Nevertheless, a game-theoretic approach to *n*-person games yields some interesting insights.

One of the distinctions between two-person and *n*-person games is that in the latter the power of an individual—his ability to influence the final outcome—is much less predictable, and the value to him of cooperation with other players increases proportionately. In two-person, zero-sum games, as has been seen, the players essentially act alone, and the power of a player is limited to what he is sure of getting on the basis of his own resources alone. In two-person, non-zero-sum situations, the focus shifts somewhat as the players' dependence on each other increases. Now what a player can expect from a game consists of a guaranteed minimum payoff plus the *potential* power that resides in his ability to punish and/or reward his opponent; but his potential is hard to quantify because what he does with it depends to a large extent on his own personality, and its effects depend on the personality of his opponent.

In *n*-person games, the concept of power becomes even more elusive. A player's initial strength consists of the resources he has at his command, such as a number of votes or an amount of money; this is usually the minimum payoff he can expect. In addition, as in some two-person, non-zero-sum situations, he has the possibility of increasing his payoff by cooperating with other players, that is, by entering into a coalition; but unlike these situations, he now has no recourse if the others choose not to cooperate with him. He may acquire a degree of power over other players in the form of threats to defect from a given coalition and/or promises to share the winnings in a certain way, but these require that he be in demand as a partner by at least one other player.

Furthermore, the demand for a player—and hence his potential payoff—is not necessarily related to the resources he commands at the outset. In a three-person voting game, for instance, in which the winning coalition need only command a simple majority of the players' resources, two players may control forty-nine votes apiece while the third controls only two; yet the third, "weaker" player is logically just as desirable as a coalition partner as the two others. Hence the notion of "strength in weakness." Nor does a player's potential payoff rest solely with his ability to enter into a winning coalition: Still to be determined is the proportion of the gross winnings that will accrue to him.

Thus, in the *n*-person games there is both a parallelism of interests that gives rise to the formation of coalitions and the subsequent coordination of strategies, and a conflict of interests that arises between rival players or groups of players, and between coalition members when the winnings are distributed. The behavior of players can similarly be characterized as both cooperative and competitive. During coalition formation there is concern for the commonweal, whereas when the winnings are distributed individual interests predominate. These two orientations frequently coexist, of course, and a player's success in such games often depends on his bargaining ability.

Generally speaking, a coalition is a group of two or more players who combine their resources and coordinate their strategies in order to maximize their combined payoff. A distinction is drawn between a coalition and the cooperative relationship that sometimes occurs in two-person, non-zero-sum situations. According to Von Neumann and Morgenstern:

> In a 2-person game there are not enough players to go around: a coalition absorbs at least 2 players, and then nobody is left to oppose.[16]

Elsewhere, however, they show how players in a triad may form a "grand coalition" of all three members. The critical distinction, then, is not the presence of an opposing player or group of players, but the *possibility* that such an opposing force may exist. This reflects the fact that it is interesting to see not only who joins a coalition but who is left out.

This distinction also underlines the voluntary nature of a coalition and the possibility of choice that is open to its members. In a three-person game a player can at best choose between two possible coalitions.

> If, however, a player has only one possibility of forming a coalition . . . then it is not quite clear in what sense there is a coalition at all: moves forced upon a player in a unique way by the necessities of the rules of the game are more in the nature of a (one-sided) strategy than of a (cooperative) coalition.[17]

The expedient nature of a coalition, hence its intrinsic instability, its tendency to disintegrate once the "game" is over, should also be emphasized to distinguish it from relationships such as "friendship." A working definition might be that rewards are extrinsic to the relationship ("real income"), whereas the rewards of friendship are intrinsic to it ("psychic income"). This leads us to notions of "rationality" once again. Certain *n*-person games are classified as inessential, meaning that there is no rational reason to form any coalition, and Von Neumann and Morgenstern state that "a coalition need never be considered if it does not promise to every participant (individually) definitely more than he can get for himself."[18] These criteria may be applied to cases in which individuals persistently combine forces over a series of different games, in order to determine whether their alliance is a "rational" coalition or an "irrational" relationship of some other kind. They also suggest that some political blocs do not qualify as coalitions: If two people persistently join forces because they share the same ideologies or beliefs, much of the element of choice is removed from their behavior, and their cooperation may not be rational or essential as defined above.

Given the complexities of *n*-person games, and the impossibility of incorporating such critical factors as a player's bargaining ability in a formal mathematical theory, game theorists have given up hope of predicting *which* coalitions will form except in the simplest, most obvious cases where only certain coalitions can muster the strength to win. Instead, the emphasis has been on predicting the payoffs to individual members *assuming* a given coalition structure.

Von Neumann and Morgenstern assumed that the final set of payoffs—the manner in which winnings were distributed among members of a winning coalition—would be such that no other would permit all the players to do better simultaneously, and that it would be "individually rational" in the sense that each member would obtain at least as much as he could get by acting alone. In addition, they assumed it would be stable in that no other set of payoffs would be attractive enough to induce a majority of the coalition members to change it (only a majority has the power to bring about such a change). This generalized solution to the payouts within coalitions follows principles of rationality, and obviously excludes from consideration problems of bargaining, negotiation, and persuasion characteristic of all *n*-person coalition structures.

One of the most significant contributions to decision theory comes from Schelling in his book, *The Strategy of Conflict*. The significance of this study is that it provides an approach to the social sciences by emphasizing the limitations of mathematics in solving problems of behavior in mixed-motive situations. Most "games" of life resemble the "Battle of the Sexes" in which there is no optimal strategy to be derived from a payout matrix. The games of life also often resemble the Prisoner's Dilemma in which individuals acting in narrow self-interest will emerge with a payout inferior to one that will come about through cooperation. In Schelling's words, "This is not to say just that it is an empirical question how people do actually perform in mixed-motive games, especially games too complicated for intellectual mastery. It is a stronger statement: that the principles relevant to *successful* play, the *strategic* principles, the propositions of a *normative* theory, cannot be derived by purely analytical means from a priori considerations."[19] [Author's italics.] The dynamics of decision making become central to the problem because the moves that occur to a player stem from the effects on his thinking, both conscious and unconscious, of the unfolding of the game. In the "Battle of the Sexes," actors' intentions dominate the play and, ultimately, the outcome. If both actors want to accommodate themselves to the other and enhance their collective rewards, their problem becomes one of two parts: first, to communicate their intentions in such a way that the other cannot mistake the meaning of the action and, second, to coordinate their moves to reach the desired end. This coordination calls for signals that can be interpreted by the other and selections of meanings that can be tested. If, for example, both the husband and wife buy tickets for the activity favored by the other, they will each spend an evening apart. It becomes crucial to understand the meaning for them of this behavior. Did each assume the other was selfish and therefore elect to give way rather than spend an evening apart? Or, were they attempting to signal that they valued each other more than the particular favored activity? The problem involves now the selection of actions to make their intentions known. Subsequent trials make available the opportunity to arrive at an understanding and, presumably, coordination, by alternately going to the fight and the ballet. Again, Schelling's delineation of the general problem is to the point:

In a zero-sum game the analyst is really dealing with only a single center of con-sciousness, a single source of decisions. True, there are two players, each with his own consciousness; but minimax strategy converts the situation into one involving two essen-tially unilateral decisions. No spark of recognition needs to jump between the two players;

no meeting of minds is required; no hints have to be conveyed; no impressions, images, or understanding have to be compared. No social perception is involved. But in the mixed-motive game, two or more centers of consciousness are dependent on each other in an essential way. Something has to be communicated; at least some spark of recognition must pass between the players. There is generally a necessity for some social activity, however rudimentary or tacit it may be; and both players are dependent to some degree on the success of their social perception and interaction. Even two completely isolated individuals, who play with each other in absolute silence and without even knowing each other's identity, must tacitly reach some meeting of the minds.[20]

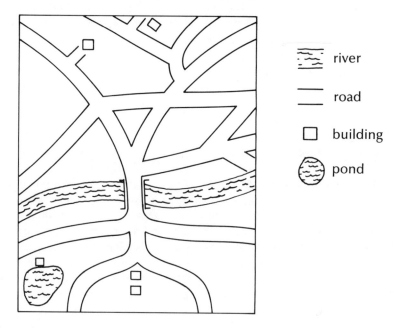

river

road

building

pond

Figure 6.1.   The Common Meeting Place?

Abandoning mathematics for the social sciences does not imply abandoning the assumptions of rationality and the optimization of returns. It does mean that attention shifts to areas of perception, communication, and the derivation of meaning from the actions of others. Here, certain cultural factors become important in arriving at some understanding of the "convergence of expectations" that enable people to arrive at mutually satisfactory solutions to problems.[21] In fact, mathematical formulations may become instrumental in helping people arrive at convergences, and therefore become one class of phenomena used as social information. As we shall discuss shortly, the convergence of expectation depends upon some shared cultural understanding but also on empathetic capacity, to know what the other expects by knowing what one would expect in turn if one were in the position of the other. Schelling offers the following example.

Two people parachute into the area shown on the map in Figure 6.1. Each has this map and knows the other has it. Where do they go to meet? Most people would go to the bridge without prior commitment to do so, simply out of a common expectation that the other would seek out a central point.[22]

EXPERIMENTAL FINDINGS

Game theory, besides developing theory on its own terms, has given rise to enormous numbers of experiments in the social sciences. Here, the attention shifts from abstract solutions and normative theory to actual behavior, albeit under artificial circumstances. The results of experiments, while on the whole quite interesting, are marked by a particular defect: the inability to go beyond ad hoc explanations. For example, experiments show that people do not behave rationally by cooperating even when the direction of rational behavior is clearly indicated in the payout matrices of the games.[23]

Experimenters variously interpret the results as a response to boredom with the experiment, to the low yield of the payouts, to cognitive failure (the inability to understand the game), and so on. Because of the nature of experimental designs, the data yield little, if any, material on what goes on in the minds of participants. This is not to suggest that experimenters are totally unaware of personality variables as they affect the results. In fact, where personality tests are introduced the results appear to be more intelligible. For example, in experiments involving the choice between cooperating and competing in game situations, cooperative behavior, or the predisposition to cooperate, seems correlated with low authoritarian traits as measured by the F scale.[24] In Fouraker and Siegel's experiments involving potential collaboration and competition, they describe three types of players: maximizers, rivalists, and cooperators.[25] The maximizer is interested primarily in his own profit. The rivalist is mainly concerned with doing better than his partner, and his own payoff is secondary to this consideration. The cooperator is interested in helping both himself and his partner. While these attitudes could be influenced or modified by appropriate incentives, they still suggest a basic orientation attributable to personality although, unfortunately, the studies provide little information to suggest conclusions.

What is so striking to the psychoanalytic observer, and also to those experienced in practical affairs involving negotiation, is the presence of two dominant psychological variables in the experimental studies. The first is the potential for humiliation and the second is the effect of differences (perceived or real) in power among participants. No matter how trivial the game and inconsequential the payoffs, the participants appear sensitive to the possibilities of being bested in a potentially rivalrous situation and wary of their dealings with those who have more power than they. In an experiment using variations of the Prisoner's Dilemma game in which the potential payoff is the same for cooperative and noncooperative strategies, most pairs did not cooperate. In one game the pairs were allowed to communicate at half time, which led to slightly more cooperation, but still the noncooperative strategies significantly exceeded the cooperative. In other games in which communication was not allowed, there was a marked tendency for noncooperative play to increase in the second half of the run. The authors of this study speculate that:

There is a kind of culturally imposed norm (which) leads people who are strangers to each other to act guardedly. It is better to assure one's self of at least equal footing with the other person than to run the risk of being bested by him.[26]

In point of fact, the hidden effect in these experiments appears to be the image of the experimenter, the authority. To be bested by a stranger in a trivial game should not lead to the results found. A better explanation lies in not wanting to be bested in front of an audience, in this case the experimenter. Much of superficial social relations is a problem in maintaining ''face'' and, in conditions of uncertainty, caution prevails. Experienced negotiators recognize this commonplace fact and, interested in aiding the process, they take care to preserve face and avoid humiliations, simply as a matter of practical good sense if not altruistic attitudes.

Following a skirmish on the frontiers of Gaul, a top Roman legion lost its standard to victorious German tribes which took it to a temple in one of the six sacred cities. The Romans faced the costly prospect of having to attack each of these cities in turn to retrieve their standard. Then, in another skirmish, they caught one of the highest German chieftains who surely knew in which city the standard was being kept. The man was tortured extensively to obtain the information, but to no avail. He was finally brought before the Emperor Claudius. At this point, it would seem the chieftain had two strategies from which to choose: either to reveal the truth and escape further torture if not death, or not to reveal the truth. The Emperor, on the other hand, had to overcome one strategy that was doomed to fail: torture the chieftain to death, with the prospect afterward of having to attack six German cities. Instead, he treated the chieftain kindly, asking questions about his country and then asking the names of the larger German cities. The chieftain mentioned the names of five cities only and the Emperor ordered an invasion of the sixth city.[27] Did the Emperor ''trick'' the chieftain, or did he provide him with an honorable way to avoid torture (after all, it may not be dishonorable to be ''tricked'' by an Emperor)? In effect, the recognition of the need to preserve ''face'' and the talents to signal one's intentions increase the options and strategies in solving problems.

The phenomenon of humiliation is an inherent aspect of the psychology of power. The types of decisions in which man faces nature, while apparently individualistic and private, do not escape the dilemmas of face on the interpersonal side and humiliation on the intrapersonal side. When a man who owns a farm prepares to drill a well for water, he may exhaust all the possibilities of science and technology to tell him where to drill. But when it comes time to make a decision, he may also call in a water dowser, who, with his twigs, will walk the terrain and assert, "Drill here," in response to some vibrations he feels.

In the face of uncertainty, it is often perceived wise to share the risks, and to transfer some of the burdens of making a mistake. The major burden, besides the tangible costs, is the loss of esteem in one's own estimation and the arousal of doubt about one's competence in the minds of others. Success and failure in making decisions tend to produce expectations for the future. In this sense, there is always surplus produced in decision situations that do not enter the calculations of game theory and that appear only remotely in the experimental situations of the psychology laboratory. The surplus produced is in the elaboration of meanings attached to decisions and their outcome. Whether it is the sociologist's status hierarchy, as in the case of the Corner Boys in William Whyte's *Street Corner Society* where winning in the bowling matches correlated with rank in the group,[28] or the psychoanalyst's theories of loss and narcissistic injury, the effects of an act or decision cannot be restricted to the consequences of one payout matrix alone. Human beings draw countless, and often incorrect, inferences from decisions and thereby create patterns of expectations of self and others.

In Caplow's studies of coalition formation there is a hint of what occurs through the surplus of meanings that arise out of the simplest and most contrived situations. Investigators set out to compare the actual coalitions that form in three person situations of unequal power among the participants with the predicted coalitions derived from game theory. Vinake and Arkoff[29] devised a game similar to Parcheesi in which the object was to be the first to reach the end of the board and win 100 points. There were three players and each was assigned a weight (his "strength") at the beginning of every trial. The experimenter threw a die and the players moved, simultaneously, the number of squares represented by the number that came up multiplied by their respective weights. Any two players were permitted to combine forces, in which case they would move forward the number of squares equal to the face of the die times the sum of their combined weights. When a coalition was formed, the two members had to announce how they would allocate the 100 points.

Six games were played, each using different weights, corresponding to Caplow's triad types,[30] and results were compared to his original predictions.

Rational analysis of Games 2, 3, and 5 (shown below)—those in which Caplow and game theory disagree—indicates that all coalitions have an equal chance of forming, since any coalition can win: In this respect all players have equal strength and payoffs should, therefore, be evenly split between coalition members. Caplow's predictions, on the other hand, implicitly assume that the weights are significant *beyond* the point when a coalition is formed. In this case, if a player can choose between two others with whom to join, he will prefer to join the weaker of the two, who will presumably demand a smaller share of the winnings. Thus, the weakest player will always be a member of the winning coalition.

Weights		Predicted Coalitions	
Game	*A.B.C.*	*Game Theory*	*Caplow*
1	1.1.1	Any	Any
2	3.2.2	Any	BC
3	1.2.2	Any	AB or AC
4	3.1.1	None	None
5	4.3.2	Any	AC or BC
6	4.2.1	None	None

The results matched Caplow's predictions. The players soon realized that the outcome was determined once a coalition had formed, and did not bother to play the game through to the end; but they apparently *believed* the weights were significant and acted accordingly, both in the coalitions they formed and in the subsequent distribution of points.

Weaker members initiated offers of alliance more often than others, and the weakest member was most often part of the winning coalition. As predicted, strong members tended to demand a larger share in any coalition they might join, and as a result the other players stayed away. Weaker members tended to receive a larger share of the winnings than their strength might seem to warrant, because they were in demand as allies. However, in general the allocation of payoffs took the expected form: symmetry in strength (for example, in Game 1) resulted in 50–50 splits significantly more often than in situations where there was a discrepancy of weights (Games 4 and 6).

In more elaborate terms, the theories of dissonance,[31] consistency,[32] and balanced systems[33] seem to account for the irrational attributions of power that occur in coalitions. A set of expectations about person A held in common in a coalition will be adhered to beyond the situations in which the expectations were fulfilled. If an individual ranks high in the esteem of others on one dimension, the tendency is to rank him high on other dimensions. This effect produces the surplus referred to earlier, or, in simpler terms, the doctrine "nothing succeeds like success."

MOTIVES, MEANINGS, AND FUNCTIONS

The notion of surplus begins to transcend the logic of game theory. The very fact that people form coalitions and establish strategies (note already the subtle shift from "decision" to "strategy," implying a longer time dimension in the latter than the former) indicates a continuity of past, present, and future. Particularly, the projection of a strategy into the future heightens uncertainty and this uncertainty motivates people to theorize, rationalize, simplify, and deny so as to derive meaning out of their experience. The idea of meaning is not an attack on rationality as the dominant assumption in decision theory. Within the assumption of rationality people still operate to maintain the underlying order of their coalition memberships and the dominant world view that governs the methods for formulating strategies. A shift occurs, therefore, in the study of decisions, from the bare-bones analytic techniques of quantitative analysis to the "thick" descriptions of what people do and how they think. In political analysis, this shift inevitably brings into question the models and methods suitable for a new range of questions.

Allison's study of the formation of strategy in the U.S. government in response to the Cuban missile crisis demonstrates how new models prepare investigators for new facts and explanation.[34] Allison compares the types of facts and interpretations that appear in the course of exploiting three models of decision making in complex organizations. The first, the Rational Actor Model, focuses attention on the acts of government as means toward ends. The failure to relate means and ends in some coherent fashion is a lapse in rationality, not the failure of the model and the techniques used in arriving at courses of action. The second, the Organizational Process Model, focuses on decisions as the outputs of complex organizations with differentiated roles and responsibilities. What appears irrational according to the Rational Actor Model becomes rational when viewed as behavior of individuals who follow standard operating procedures designed to order choices and actions in some patterned way. Finally, the third model deals from the frame of reference of organizations as bureaucratic structures, internally differentiated with subgoals and purposes that include enhancing or preserving the power of the subgroups. Organizations compete as well as cooperate, define loyalties to subgroups as well as to the total organization, and view alternatives in the light of their consequences for the stability and strength of the subgroups in which individuals feel committed and with which they identify their careers. This bureaucratic politics model, then, emphasizes decisions as outcomes of internal bargaining among competing coalitions that adopt their survival as a dominant goal.

The sociologist Michel Crozier applied a political model to interpret behavior in a French bureaucratic organization and further expanded the principle of rationality of action to include preserving the power base.[35] In general, the three alternative models have in common a functional point of view. The function of behavior can be interpreted variously as (1) a means to achieve desired ends, (2) to carry out organizational procedures, or (3) to conserve power.

What these alternative models do, in fact, is make intelligible complex behavior by creating a hierarchy of meaning from data about actions. All three models (and the many more that can be contrived to draw out more meaning from complex behavior) address themselves to the motives of key actors, but motives are not assumed to be private and idiosyncratic. Motives for action have to do with the actor's definition of the situation he finds himself in and relates to how he intends to influence allies and opponents toward some desired end. Since decision events involve a dynamic of interaction in which the various sides signal their motives and intention, the problem of decision necessarily calls forth some method or schema for interpreting the communications offered in the course of the event. When the Soviet ships sailing toward Cuba reversed course following the U.S. blockade, it was important to interpet the action accurately as, for example, a first step toward deescalating the conflict or as a shift in tactics with the intention of continuing the conflict.

It is accurate to assert that, on the whole, psychoanalysis has contributed negligibly to the development of methods and theories applicable to action in life situations. This assertion stands in the face of ambitions of psychoanalytic theorists to create a general psychology through the formulation of the adaptive point of view.[36] There is something of a paradox here because psychoanalysis occupies a privileged position in its specialized access to symbolic communication and its framework for interpreting verbal communication. The fact is that the focus of psychoanalysis is psychic reality and the language of unconscious mental life does not logically preclude applications beyond the couch. There are many parallel interests and overlapping tasks in the relation of psychic and external reality for psychoanalysis to bypass the psychology of decision making and coalition formation. The models, of necessity, have to be derived from clinical data, but their applications to other life situations provide tests of validity by exposing new facts and alternative modes of interpreting motives, meanings, and functions in everyday life.

Psychoanalytic theory may offer to the analysis of decisions and their underlying coalition structures new interpretive structures for what Clifford Geertz refers to as "thematic analysis." "The unity (of thematic analysis) is neither of topic nor argument, but of analytical style—of aim and of the methodological issues the pursuit of such an aim entails."[37]

The methodology is the analysis of the particular case in which:

The issues are multiple, involving questions of definition, verification, causality, representativeness, objectivity, measurement, communication. But at the base they all boil down to one question: how to frame an analysis of meaning—the conceptual structures individuals use to construe experience—which will at once be circumstantial enough to carry conviction and abstract enough to forward theory. These are equal necessities; choosing one at the expense of the other yields blank descriptivism or vacant generality. But they also, superficially at least, pull in the opposite directions, for the more one invokes details the more he is bound to the peculiarities of the immediate case, the more one omits them the more he loses touch with the ground on which his arguments rest. Discovering how to escape this paradox—or more exactly how to keep it at bay—is what, methodologically, thematic analysis is all about.[38]

There is a growing debate among psychoanalytic theorists that indirectly reflects on the methodology of thematic analysis. In his recent book proposing revision of the orientation of psychoanalytic theory from a "natural science model" to an "action" model, Schafer[39] presents a critique of metapsychology, in particular the work of Heinz Hertmann who is identified with ego psychology and the adaptive point of view in metapsychology. Schafer is generally critical of psychoanalytic metapsychology because of its attachment to the logic and language of the natural sciences. With this criticism, Schafer allies himself with

Ricoeur[40] who also discusses the limitations of psychoanalysis as a positive science. Ricoeur suggests instead a science of meaning in which the problem is to state the rules for interpreting a text. In the case of a patient, the text is the associative material; in the case of policy and decision situations, the text is the structure and content (both manifest and latent) of relationships that establish and support a particular world view.

The particular constructs of Hartmann which pose the greatest difficulty in interpreting the meaning of verbalization and action, whether in psychoanalytic or other situations, are autonomous function and conflict-free or neutralized energy. Schafer indicates that these constructs fit an overall biological model based on the concept of energy utilization as the primary problem of adaptation to the environment. Since one cannot readily derive meaning from the language of energy flow, it becomes extremely difficult to use this metapsychology either in work with patients or in applied psychoanalysis. Not all critics of psychoanalytic theorizing adopt Schafer's solution to an action framework. Some propose development of a clinical theory, which is presumably different from a deductive scientific theory.[41] Others, however, accept this inherent ambiguity in psychoanalysis and live with the conflicting styles of theorizing as probably necessary for exploratory purposes. Those who live with the ambiguity of competing modes of theorizing do not confuse clinical and scientific activity, but recognize the tension as intrinsic to psychoanalysis almost from its inception.

In Freud's case of "Frau Emmy Von N.," a lady whom he began to treat in 1889, the model of psychic states, excessive excitation and abreaction appeared to dominate the treatment and the language to explain symptom formation. But toward the end of his case report, after acknowledging the weight he attached to "the retention of large sums of excitation" in the formation of hysterical symptoms, Freud continued:

Does this exhaust the aetiology of this case of hysteria? I do not think so. For at the time of her two treatments I had not yet raised in my own mind the questions which must be answered before an exhaustive explanation of such a case is possible. I am now of the opinion that there must have been some added factor to provoke the outbreak of illness precisely in these last years, considering that operative aetiological conditions had been present for many years previously. It has also struck me that amongst all the intimate information given me by the patient there was a complete absence of the sexual element, which is, after all, more liable than any other to provide occasion for traumas. It is impossible that her excitation in this field can have left no traces whatever; what I was allowed to hear was no doubt an *editio in usum delphini* (a bowdlerized edition) of her life story. The patient behaved with the greatest and to all appearances with the utmost unforced sense of propriety, without a trace of prudishness. When, however, I reflect on the reserve with which she told me under hypnosis about her maid's little adventure in the hotel, I cannot help suspecting that this woman who was so passionate and so capable of strong feelings had not won her victory over her sexual needs without severe struggles, and that at times her attempts at suppressing this most powerful of all instincts had exposed her to severe mental exhaustion. She once admitted to me that she had not married again because, in view of her large fortune, she could not credit the disinterestedness of her suitors and because she would have reproached herself for damaging the prospects of her two children by a new marriage.[42]

Freud suspected that he had not exhausted meaning and explanation in this case not because of the information he had, but because of the information he had not heard from the patient, namely, the effects of sexual deprivation following the death of her husband. The imagery Freud used is of powerful forces seeking expression, and exhausting the energies of the individual to prevent their discharge. But the imagery also conveys qualitative impressions of the burdens of responsibility and, by indirection, the reactions of a widowed mother to the budding sexuality of her daughters. The theories of infantile sexuality, which were to come later in the development of psychoanalysis, conveyed further impressions about sexual development. But those who argue that it is only the qualitative images that count in deriving meaning and explanation should ask themselves how it is possible to ignore the power of impulses on the psyche, the kind of power amply available for observation, for example, in the case of adolescent development.

Schafer assumes that biologic and energic concepts such as autonomous ego functions and conflict-free energy distance the interpreter from the experiences to be interpreted. It is, for example, embarrassing to psychoanalysis to pose constructs which the method probably cannot use in interpretation, let alone in observation, because the constructs appear to be tautological. If a patient is able to perform his job well, but has poor relationships with his children, to say that in one sphere he uses neutralized energy and in the other sexual energy simply substitutes one set of words for another in the description of behavioral differences. The new, more abstract words explain nothing unless one is prepared to discover the content of the conflictual experience. Furthermore, the psychoanalytic situation concentrates on the conflictual. Even when observing changes in symptoms or behavior during an analysis, the most conservative explanation of therapeutic change insists on the effect of making conscious what was unconscious. The neurotic response of attributing false and overloaded meanings to desires, objects, and morality changes as a consequence of conscious awareness. The patient's emotional reactions during the course of becoming aware of unconscious material provide the conviction that supports the reversal from neurotic attributions to rational understanding and objectivity. Also, as Schafer points out, the introduction of qualifiers such as "relatively autonomous ego function," serves to add to the embarrassment rather than to enlightenment.

The tradition of thematic analysis provides continuity between theory and observation as well as from situations of patient and analyst to situations of people acting in coalitions to formulate strategies and make decisions. The continuities appear even more impressive if one compares the work of thematic analysis applied to widely differing experiences. For example: A patient in psychoanalysis came to an appointment scheduled at an hour different from the usual time but one the patient preferred. The patient spent a large part of the hour in distress, complaining about poor relationships with co-workers, particularly subordinates. Much of the prior analytic work had uncovered the patient's rage upon the birth of siblings, traumatic experiences that led the patient to build obsessional defenses, to adopt idealized views of work and achievement, and to labor under the pressing need to be worthy and acceptable to parental figures. The interpretations during this hour focused on how the patient had to present to the analyst personal inadequacy, anxiety, and "neurotic" behavior to be deserving of this special hour. This interpretation of what was imminent and directly involved in the patient's images about the analyst took priority over "deeper" interpretations of repressed rage at siblings or sexual feelings toward the analyst, yet these interpretations are connected thematically around conceptions of what one must do to be worthy. The interpretation of the transference prevents anthropomorphizing psychic structure or presenting other detached formulations. The emotional reactions to the analyst propel and channel what the patient experiences as real and what in turn he means to say to the analyst but cannot say easily because of his inhibitions, moral restrictions, and psychological defenses.

A second example of thematic interpretation comes from the observation of a family with a schizophrenic child. The Nussbaums formed a coalition structure with the mother attached to her son and the father to his daughter, obviously creating incestuous collusions, especially in view of the hostile relationship between Mr. and Mrs. Nussbaum.

The Nussbaums' dissension had started shortly after their marriage twenty-five years ago. Mr. Nussbaum had been largely supported by his elder brother, whom he regarded as a father. Mrs. Nussbaum's father had suicided following business reverses, which her family blamed upon his affiliation with Mr. Nussbaum's brother. Mrs. Nussbaum appeared to side with her family in their family's accusation of her husband's brother. Mr. Nussbaum considered her attitude to show utter disloyalty as it furnished the finishing blow to his feelings of being excluded by her close-knit family. There was little or no discussion of the matter, but they drew apart. Mrs. Nussbaum was very sensitive lest her husband dominate her, and stood her ground with the help of a violent temper. She refused to accompany him on social engagements essential to his career and antagonized his friends. Mr. Nussbaum felt unloved and unwanted and constantly deprecated. He stayed away from home much of the time, and fostered the impression that he was having affairs, either to spite his wife or to mask his impotence, or both. Weeks would pass when the couple would not speak to each other. The wife found solace in her relationship to her son, and the husband in his seductive attachment to his daughter [the schizophrenic patient].[43]

When Mr. Nussbaum, the father of the schizophrenic adolescent girl, wanted to entertain the social worker accompanying his daughter on her first visit home by telling sexual jokes, *the worker's dilemma in handling the situation revealed much about the pressures the patient had experienced in her life in this family.* Laughing at the jokes would offend the mother and the patient, who were maintaining a stony silence; not laughing would inflict a painful wound in the father's very tender narcissism. Considering this, together with the patient's propensity for playing off hospital versus family and staff member against staff member, *we can see the total situation with greater clarity.* This was further illuminated in a quarrel between the parents which took place in the interviewing room. They had been informed that their next week's appointment would be canceled because the social worker would be out of town. They assumed that it was to be a vacation, and

Mr. Nussbaum insisted Florida was the place. His wife said Florida was a dreadful spot. Suggestively, he remarked that he was going there soon for professional meetings. She glowered. Suddenly, he proposed the city where they lived and both were in immediate, if brief, agreement. The worker could stay in their apartment and sleep in their daughter's bed. He said she could go to the theatre every night. Mrs. Nussbaum said grimly that he never takes *her* [author's italics] to the theatre, and so it went, giving a clear picture of a scene which must have been re-enacted many times over in their home with their daughter.[44]

In a relatively brief space, the authors of this case vignette convey a picture of a family coalition and the patterns of domination, conflict, and sexual allusion omnipresent in their communications. The creation of delusional scenarios, as in their fantasies about the social worker's absence, their personalizing experience to include every event and person with whom they had contact, demonstrated how the coalition structure formed in the family and what defensive purposes it served. The inclusiveness and sexual allusions dominating all interactions between husband and wife could temporarily channel and buffer their mutual hatred. The delusional scenarios, which centered on the sick daughter, maintained the fragile emotional economy of this family. The vantage point of observation and interpretation in this case vignette is not strikingly different from the position of the analyst. The transference reactions (how the objects of study use the analyst/investigator) become the reference point for integrating the masses of information (both ideas and feelings) that become available as the interaction proceeds.

A third example of thematic interpretation comes from a study of decision making in government. The issue at hand was the decision to deploy the ABM missile system and involved just about every key figure in foreign affairs and national security, including counterparts in the governments of the USSR and China. The central figure in this case example was Lyndon Baines Johnson, President of the United States, but the author of the case study began with Secretary of Defense Robert S. McNamara's speech entitled, "The Dynamics of Nuclear Strategy," that he delivered to a meeting of the United Press International Editors and Publishers in San Francisco on September 18, 1967.

He stressed that neither the United States nor the Soviet Union had increased their security in any way by deploying strategic nuclear weapons, and he suggested that the United States had bought many more weapons than it needed only because of a groundless fear that the Russians would step up their arms production. Having sketched this general background, McNamara turned to a subject which was then in the headlines—namely, the possibility of American deployment of an anti-ballistic missile (ABM) system.

He pointed out that the United States had substantially improved its technological capability. But he emphasized that even an advanced ABM system could easily be defeated if the Soviet Union simply fired more offensive warheads or dummy warheads than there were defensive missiles capable of dealing with them. Proceeding with this line of argument, he asserted:

"Were we to deploy a heavy ABM system through the United States, the Soviets would clearly be strongly motivated so to increase their offensive capability as to cancel out our defensive advantage.

"It is futile for each of us to spend $4 billion, $40 billion, or $400 billion—and at the end of all the spending, and at the end of all deployment, and at the end of all the effort, to be relatively at the same point of balance on the security scale that we are now."

Until then the Johnson administration had been resisting substantial pressure in refusing to deploy an ABM.

The Secretary of Defense, however, did not conclude his statement here. Rather he took another tack. He argued that it was important to distinguish between an anti-Russian ABM and an ABM system designed to defend the United States against emerging Chinese nuclear capability. Reviewing the arguments in favor of a deployment against China, he announced, "We have decided to go forward with this Chinese-oriented ABM deployment; and we will begin actual production of such a system at the end of this year."

Before concluding, McNamara returned to his earlier theme:

"There is a kind of mad momentum intrinsic to the development of all new nuclear weaponry. If a weapon system works—and works well—there is strong pressure from many directions to procure and deploy the weapon out of all proportion to the prudent level required.

"The danger of deploying this relatively light and reliable Chinese-oriented ABM system is going to be that pressures will develop to expand it into a heavy Soviet-oriented ABM system.

"We must resist that temptation firmly, not because we can for a moment afford to relax our vigilance against a possible Soviet first strike, but precisely because our greatest deterrent against such a strike is not a massive, costly, but highly penetrable ABM shield, but rather a fully credible offensive assured destruction capability.

"The so-called heavy ABM shield—at the present state of technology—would in effect be no adequate shield at all against a Soviet attack but rather a strong inducement for the Soviets to vastly increase their own offensive forces. That, as I have pointed out, would make it necessary for us to respond in turn; and so the arms race would rush hopelessly on to no sensible purpose on either side."

Why had Robert McNamara used a speech which was largely anti-ABM in tone and substance to announce an ABM deployment? Some Washington reporters speculated that he had been overruled at the last minute; what was meant by him to be an anti-ABM speech had been converted by others in the administration into a vehicle for announcing an ABM deployment. Others argued that the speech should be taken at face value: the administration had come to the conclusion that an ABM against Russia was not desirable but that one against China was necessary.

Those in the audience and in the country who had followed the issue wondered how the Secretary's speech related to the annual budget message delivered by President Lyndon Johnson in January 1967. The President had asked for funds to deploy an ABM system but had stated that he would defer a decision to start construction pending an effort to begin strategic arms limitation talks with the Russians. At that time the President was vague about the purpose of the ballistic missile defense but stated that the funds might be used to deploy an ABM "for such purposes as defense of our offensive weapons systems." McNamara, in his speech, had briefly mentioned the defense of Minuteman missiles only as a possible add-on to the ABM deployment against China.

The purpose for which the administration was deploying its ABM system was further clouded in the coming weeks. The Joint Chiefs of Staff and leading senators, including Richard Russell, Chairman of the Senate Armed Services Committee, described the ABM deployment as the beginning of a large anti-Russian system, even though McNamara had warned against attempting one. McNamara himself continued to describe the system as a defense against China; the President said nothing.

As the first steps toward deployment were made, it appeared that the initial construction was no different from what it would have been if the purpose were to protect American cities against a large Russian attack.[45]

The problem presented in this case study is an apparent contradiction in the opinions and behavior of the Secretary of Defense. He verbally made the case against deployment of the ABM, but for his "punch line" he proposed a limited deployment that he seemingly opposed. Halperin shows that the behavior of the Secretary was not at all inconsistent but represented his continuing battle to compete with other bureaucracies and to influence the President. Halperin continues:

Each participant, depending on where he sits, will see a somewhat different face of an issue, because his perception of the issue will be heavily shaded by his particular concerns. What is primarily a budget issue to one participant will be an issue of relations with Congress to a third. Those in the Defense Department and the Budget Bureau concerned with limiting military spending tended to view the ABM as a budget issue. Scientists in the Pentagon and in the so-called defense industry felt ABM deployment would maintain the technological superiority of the United States. Officials in the Arms Control and Disarmament Agency viewed the issue in terms of possible arms control agreements with the Soviet Union. Foreign Service Officers in the West European division of the State Department were concerned with the effect of ABM deployment on our relations with European allies and on the cohesion of NATO. Participants sensitive to the President's relations with senior congressional leaders who supported the ABM saw the issue in terms of future dealings with Congress. Secretary of Defense McNamara assessed ABM deployment in terms of decreasing spending for strategic forces and increasing the prospects for arms control arrangements with the Soviet Union. Army officials saw the issue in terms of the size of the Army budget and maintaining an Army role in strategic nuclear deterrence. The President, sitting at the top, saw the issue in terms of his own sense of what national security required, of his relations with McNamara and military and congressional leaders, and of his own desires to keep spending down and to reach agreement with the Soviet Union.

Thus each participant may focus on a different face of the issue and sense different dangers and/or opportunities. For budget officials, preventing large expenditures was most important, and the rationale given for any system or the way decisions were communicated to foreign governments were matters of relative indifference. For State Department officials, the cost of the ABM was not important, for the funds did not come from the State Department budget; but the way the issue was communicated to our allies and to the Soviet Union was a matter of great concern. Where an individual sits in the process determines in large part the faces of the issue that he sees and helps to determine the stakes that he sees involved and hence the stand that he takes.[46]

Behind this interpretation stands a rather simple social-psychological formulation: that individuals perceive and act according to their self-defined interests which are based in part on the roles and positions they occupy. This formulation suggests a psychodynamic interpretation, one which the author only alludes to in his consideration of competitive striving in the bureaucracies.

President Lyndon B. Johnson had the ultimate responsibility for the executive decision. His personality and style of leadership conceivably had a part in causing other individuals, including the Secretary of Defense, to behave ambiguously and competitively.[47] Johnson was a consensus leader, whose experience in the U.S. Senate revealed a man highly tuned to bargaining, persuasion, and other techniques for reconciling conflicting interests. While consensus leadership may be uniquely suited for legislative activity, it may also create problems in exercising executive responsibility.[48] An important requisite of executive leadership is to internalize decision-making activity and the content of final decisions. Even if the chief executive arrives at a compromise among conflicting points of view, the decision is still his and he lives with it. In the case of consensus leadership, the style Johnson used in both the Senate and the Presidency, the decision-making activity remained external to the Chief Executive—it was the Secretary of Defense fighting the Joint Chiefs of Staff rather than members of the President's executive apparatus offering him views, opinions, and ideas for him to assimilate and arrive at a conclusion. In a consensus situation, the atmosphere becomes highly manipulative, the language indirect, all of which feeds on itself and becomes the condition for working within the structure. If this line of reasoning holds, the inquiry of necessity shifts to the personality of the Chief Executive and the personal gains and costs of his style of leadership.

Halperin represents the relationship between personality and decisions as follows:

> President Johnson's behavior in dealing with the question of the ABM suggests the pattern of uncommitted thinking. Secretary of Defense McNamara attempted to get him to see the issue in terms of the danger of stimulating the arms race and of vastly increasing military expenditures. McNamara argued that the ABM was unnecessary and would increase the risk of nuclear war. Senior military officers and leading congressional figures, by contrast, attempted to have Johnson see the issue in terms of the importance of maintaining American strategic nuclear superiority. Since each of these views appeared sensible in its own terms, Johnson moved back and forth between support of the ABM and opposition to it. He probably never made a firm judgment of his own as to which of the two views being presented to him was correct. Rather, he responded to short-run pressures in an effort to keep the participants from breaking out and denouncing the decision that he must make. The President's behavior appeared to be a form of oscillation because his decision was characterized by uncommitted thinking in an effort to find a consensus which would satisfy all of those putting pressure on him.[49]

Students of decision-making and bureaucratic behavior tend to interpret the disposition of a leader to act (in this case by consensus leadership) as a consequence of role pressures. Even when allowing implicitly for variability in what role pressures mean to different individuals, the weight of analysis points toward situational factors and away from the personal forces in interpreting behavior in bureaucracies. Most political scientists avoid personality interpretations not because of a lack of intuitive sense of their importance, but because of a conservative stance with respect to methodology and the logic of interpretation. The solution most commonly followed employs the wisdom of exhausting situational determinants before drawing in personality determinants, especially since reliable data on the inner world of the actors in decision events are limited and fall short of the requirements of clinical interpretation. Personality interpretations also put off decision makers, those who presumably use the theories of decisions in organizations to improve their performance. Since there are few programmed activities to follow as a consequence of personality theory, the tendency is to do what comes easily and usually what comes most easily is working on the decision apparatus rather than on the thought processes of the actors.

PERSONALITY AND DECISIONS

The types of interpretations employed in analyzing decision events depend upon the constructs and models used to elicit and integrate information. Just as the alternative models of decision making in political science point to different events as crucial in determining outcomes, so do alternative ways of looking at personality and decisions affect investigation interpretations.

For clarity, I want to exclude the methodology of psychobiography from consideration. In biographical studies, the focus is on the person as the object of analysis. While biography considers events, the purpose in detailing events and situations is to reveal the character of the individual. Even in Erikson's work, where he explores how change occurs through the simultaneous and interactive effects of personal and public thema, it is through the man that the public issues become meaningful as psychological themes. There are no means, either empirically or empathetically, where the public events can be subjected to interpretation in Erikson's work apart from the play of forces within the charismatic leader and in his developmental history.

In the study of decisions, the structures for collecting, assimilating, and interpreting information and outcomes of interchange among varying interests become the objects of investigation. The individuals are the actors who deal with and filter information, but the purpose of interpretation goes beyond revealing how the minds of the actors function. Strategic problems have a continuity beyond any particular set of actors, and solutions at any given time often set the conditions for later reactions of new actors grappling with the same issues. Thus, the Nixon administration had to deal with the question of ABM deployment but in a context changed by the disillusionment with Vietnam and new doubts about how to use American power and foreign affairs.

There are many reasons to question the direct use of clinical psychoanalytic models in psychobiography. The questions increase in considering the problem of how to interpret decisions. In an earlier paper, I compared two different clinical psychoanalytic models in the traditions of Lasswell's psychopolitics and Erikson's psychohistory.[50] Lasswell adopted a drive-defense model in which he explained behavior as an outcome of the mechanism of displacement. If, for example, a public figure suffered neurotic conflict in the form of unresolved hostile feelings toward his parents, he would tend to displace the hostile feelings onto contemporary figures and seek to impose the same controls on his hostility as he had used in the past. In this sense, the conflict remained alive, current, continuous, and subject to ego defenses as a means of controlling anxiety. The Georges' study of Woodrow Wilson demonstrated how this model worked in solving a problem in political analysis.[51] Since this study is a near classic in political science, it will not be necessary to review it in detail. But beyond the details of the study, it should be emphasized that the Georges examined Wilson's decisions and actions using the classic model of behavior as symptom and displacement of neurotic conflict. The validity of the studies using this model depends upon casting the subject in the role of a patient: The emphasis is on irrationality and the intrusion of primary-process thinking into decision events that called for secondary-process thinking.

Erikson's humanistic approach avoids the problem of treating the subject as a patient by adopting a holistic view of the man and focusing on his self-defined patienthood. The term patienthood refers to the sense the individual has of himself in a condition of change. More precisely, in Erikson's terms, the individual's identity crisis gives rise to this sense of patienthood. The individual's consciousness of himself, therefore, becomes the constant reference point for purposes of analysis, and not his symptoms, conflicts, or defenses. In neither case, however, do the investigators focus on decisions as thematic expressions of the collective activity in coalition structures. Observations of interactions and decisions reveal either the individual's neuroticism or his search for a new identity.

The attempt to get around this problem of shifting the focus from the individual as such to some collective activity poses enormous difficulties. The temptation is to fall back onto some sort of phenomenology, and to avoid an analytic position. Thus, a great deal of the political science literature, particularly studies dealing with events and decisions, remains descriptive. The virtue of description is in appreciating the complexity of the situation; its limitation is in the redundant and often meager interpretations.

How, for example, can the interpreter use the following formulation for analysis?

The power to persuade is the power to bargain. Status and authority yield bargaining advantages. But in a government of "separated institutions sharing powers," they yield them to all sides. With the array of vantage points at his disposal, a President may be far more persuasive than his logic or his charm could make him. But outcomes are not guaranteed by his advantages. There remain the counter pressures those whom he would influence can bring to bear on him from vantage points at their disposal. Command has limited utility: persuasion becomes give-and-take. It is well that the White House holds the vantage points it does. In such a business any President may need them all—and more.[52]

This formulation presents an important orientation of leadership as persuading, bargaining, and trading of advantages rather than exercising command or issuing directions. But what makes it possible to go beyond description of bargaining events, to elicit more general themes in the flow of decisions, circumstances, and the play of personalities? One solution is to compare how different incumbents use their power to make decisions.[53] This comparative approach sets the stage for explanation by sophisticated clarification of questions that can be explained. But comparative studies represent only one level of generalization, somewhat on a par with classifications and typologies, but still distant from a level of explanation that focuses on decisions as reflective of mental activity.

One major attempt to solve this methodological problem appears in Leites's studies of the Bolshevik elite.[54] By analyzing writings and contextual literature, Leites presents the underlying schemata through which the Russian leaders individually and collectively organized their decision activity. In suggesting the concept of the "operational code," Leites moved analytic studies of decision making beyond events into the beliefs and attitudes of the elite that guide how it approaches problems and arrives at strategies. Leites defines the operational code as the conceptions of political strategy that dominate the thinking of the elite, a "metaprogram" for processing information. The nature of the themes is extremely suggestive of that region of mental life, the preconscious, that lies between the conscious and unconscious thinking. Here we move closer to an intrapsychic study of adaptation that takes account of political structure and events as external reality. Clinicians know about themes such as the fear of annihilation, of death and dying, and of being controlled. But in Leites's hands, these themes appear in the structure of dominant beliefs of a political decision-making coalition. The beliefs control how information is taken in, sorted, and interpreted.

Leites's psychoanalytic interpretation of the "operational code" uses a conflict-defense model in which the inner and outer worlds come together through the mechanisms of introjection and projection. At the time Leites conducted his studies, the fear of an enemy without and within dominated the thinking and reactions of the men in the Politburo and gave the studies a sound empirical foundation. For example:

Against the dangers within oneself the major defense is a ruthless and incessant fight which aims at the utter eradication in the soul of all the manifestations of "spontaneity," and their replacement by their opposites, the various aspects of "consciousness." Instead of a romantic, sentimental, moralizing adoration of Revolution, there must be maximization of power by any means; instead of vagueness and wordiness, precision and realism; instead of being overwhelmed by feelings or by distress about the lack of them, there must be restraint of soul and muscles; instead of procrastination or precipitation, incessant but well-prepared action; instead of vacillation or doctrinaire rigidity, persistence and flexibility; instead of taking the line of least resistance, one must go to the limits of one's strength and skill; instead of dispersion of effort, there must be concentration.[55]

The theme of destruction from within fits with the revolutionary ardor of the Bolsheviks, the contempt for prerevolutionary man, and the ideal of creating a "new man." The harshness of these beliefs about the enemy within, the need for constant self-scrutiny and vigilance against the dominance of an older psyche, defines the requirements of membership in the Politburo. While alert, vigilant, and harsh toward the enemy within (the psyche and society), parallel hostile expectations appear toward the enemies without.

Ideally, the destruction of the enemies within one's soul must be accomplished instantaneously; but the Party must allow for the existing strength of outside enemies which makes their liquidation possible only over long periods. (The penalty for not taking account of any aspect of reality is to be dominated—and hence annihilated—by it.) The Party must deter the enemy's annihilatory attempts by maximizing its power and vigilance, and by resisting the very beginnings of attacks, preferably by counter-attacks. However, if the "relationship of forces" is too unfavorable, the Party must take account of this by retreating; as penalty for not doing so there threatens, again, annihilation.[56]

An interpreter of Leites's work, Alexander George, indicates that the operational code acts as a defense against unconscious impulses.[57] George, however, does not pursue the questions of how the defense works or what unconscious impulses have to be suppressed, and what consequences the defense or the eruption of impulse have for decision making. In fact, George turns his attention to the operational code as conscious beliefs and attempts thereby to bring it into line with cognitive psychology rather than psychoanalytic theory. But even the suggestion that the operational code acts within the defensive structure of the elite group and the individual narrows the concept and reduces its leverage in understanding the formulation of policies and decisions. George, however, hints at the broader use of the operational code as a concept in thematic interpretation of decision making:

Whether it be from the standpoint of philosophy, history, psychology, sociology, economics, or political science, students of human behavior have long agreed that the individual must necessarily simplify the structure and complexity of his world in order to cope with it. In everyday life as in the laboratory, problem-solving often requires deliberate or unwitting simplification of a more complex reality. This applies also to the political actor, for he too must somehow decide how best to deal with them. In doing so, the actor typically engages in a "definition of the situation," i.e., a cognitive structuring of the situation that will clarify for him the nature of the problem, relate it to his previous experience, and make it amenable to appropriate problem-solving activities. The political actor perceives and simplifies reality partly through the prism of his "cognitive map" of politics. This includes the belief system that has been referred to in the past as the "operational code" of a political actor.[58]

If beliefs about politics (the operational code of the decision maker and the coalition structure within which decisions emerge) simplify reality to make action possible, how do ideas perceived, relationships structured, and actions taken maintain balance, a steady state within the psyche? Attention now turns to stabilization of internal mental activity and external relations in the face of complex problems, competitive pressures, and above all the pressure to make decisions under uncertainty. The concept of defense deals with the mechanisms of the ego that respond to signal anxiety. The question of stabilization goes beyond signal anxiety to the problem of constancy, both internal and external.

The operational code of an executive group acts as the metaprogram for strategic thinking and decision making. The problem of stability (or equilibrium of the self and the coalition) moves from the actors' responses in a role to issues of continuity and self-definition within a political apparatus over time.

THE ECONOMY OF THE SELF

As with all aspects of psychoanalytic theory, it is best to anchor discussion of applications to the area from which its body of knowledge developed. Psychoanalysis is a science of the pathologies of the mind. The conceptions of pathology, however, are neither static, nor do they lend themselves to simple differentiation of what is normal and abnormal. For example, the mental activity of dreaming involves certain pathological structures in which the perceptual apparatus cannot readily distinguish between the inner and outer world. Yet dreaming is an integral part of normal mental function. The fact that dreaming illuminates or models hallucinatory activity, which is associated with the most severe pathologies, neither detracts from its value in understanding the ordinary regressions of everyday life, nor does a theory of dreaming provide clean connections to the problem of thinking and adaptation.

Psychoanalysis has recently turned attention to alternative conceptions of the mind, partially as a result of renewed clinical interest in the more severe pathologies, and partially as a result of dissatisfaction with prevailing modes of explanation.[59] The arousal of interest in adolescent "identity" disturbances, and renewed reflections on the nature of psychoses, raise questions about the ego and the self and erect a new bridge to the psychology of thinking and problem solving. All of the pathologies referred to above involve some disturbed relationship between self-perception and experience in the object world. As to the theoretical problems alluded to above, the major move seems to be related to overworking the structural theory of the mental apparatus: the tripartite division of the mind into id, ego, and superego. Analysts admit freely that in making interpretations to patients they never frame their comments to patients using such theoretical constructs, yet they do often refer to feelings of emptiness, worthlessness, the sense of being dead, detached, incapable of loving or being loved. The experience of despair centers on a diminished sense of self and impoverished relations to the outside world. This language of despair involves the uses of thematic interpretation.

The best way to illustrate thematic interpretation in connection with ideas about the self is to turn to a brief but highly interesting case report of a severely disturbed adolescent boy:

I shall conclude with a brief case report on a brilliant boy who suffered his first psychotic paranoid break at the age of fifteen. His case illuminates the pathological processes to which I have referred. The boy's first acute episode developed after an infatuation with a beautiful girl who rejected him in favor of another boy friend. It is characteristic that the boy never seriously tried to approach her. His parents did not really notice that anything was amiss until they found a revolver in his bed. He had another break after entering college and had to quit school for a year. Although he never fully recovered, he was then able to re-enter college, to finish it at the age of twenty-three, and to go into his father's business. From then on he seemed to have made a fairly good adjustment, though on a lower level.

I observed and treated the boy between his eighteenth and twenty-third year. During this period he was unable to relate to his peers, either boys or girls, and vacillated between paranoid rages at his parents and other authorities and extreme submission, submersion in, and dependency on them. For years he maintained the paranoid conviction that all wives, including his mother, a school principal, tried to kill their husbands. His relations to the object world during these years were limited to homosexual or heterosexual sadomaso-chistic fantasies, in which he would alternately identify himself with sadistic dictators or with their victims. He frequently felt the urge either to rape and strangle girls on the street or to castrate himself. Outwardly he was extremely polite and formal, though he tried to imitate the behavior of admired schoolmates, mostly of the bully type. He was extremely self-conscious, felt continuously observed, and was afraid of being exposed as a homo-ual or a killer. Consequently he avoided social activities of any kind. His pathological pseudo relations to the object world interacted with severe identity conflicts. He com-plained bitterly that he did not know who he was and what he wanted, that he had no goals, no directions, no beliefs, and no ideals; that he was nobody and different from everybody else; that he never felt the same from one day to the next.

The boy's identity conflicts reflected those characteristic parental attitudes to which I have repeatedly referred. The parents were elderly people who had married at the end of their thirties. He was the only child. They were indeed both uniquely narcissistic; they had been dutiful parents but unloving and completely unaware of their child's needs, and exceptionally contradictory in their educational attitudes toward him. To give an example: the parents told me that when they caught their boy masturbating at the age of nine, they threatened him with future insanity and wept in front of him about their poor child's sexual precocity. From then on they constantly watched over him, accompanying him to the toilet; at the same time the mother put ointment on his "sore" penis every night, thus causing erections which led to obsessional masturbation with incestuous fantasies.

The mother admitted that she had never allowed the boy to play with other children outside their own home. But after another mother told her that she was "over-protec-tive," he was sent alone from Westchester to New York on the following day, got lost, was frightened out of his wits, and was almost run over by a car. These parents reported to me with great satisfaction, how, from earliest childhood on, he had been "precisely the way we wanted him to be, precisely the way we are ourselves." This was true. Whereas he had never built up consistent and selective ego and superego identifications with his parents, he had so completely imitated and emulated his parents, and later his teachers, that he had never known the pleasure of spontaneous, free, ego activity. Until the age of fifteen, when he broke down, he had been a mixture of an overly dependent baby and a highly intelligent but rigidly compulsive-depressive character. The reasons for the instability and fragility of his ego and superego structure, which caused the psychotic illness, was the overpowering hostility provoked, early in childhood, by the premature smothering of his ego autonomy, and the complete interference with a normal process of identity formation. This boy remembered fantasies, even at the age of seven, in which he saw himself strapped to his mother's breast, flying straight to hell. "I hated her so much that I wanted her to go to hell," he said, "but being chained to her, I had to go to hell with her." This sounded like a premonition. His psychotic episode in adolescence ensued from frantic efforts to rebel and to free himself by shaking off the intolerable burden of his enslavement, his inhibitions, his rigid reaction formations and compulsions, and by sending the over-powerful superego-ego-mother to hell. The result was chaos, and his breakdown did drive his mother to despair.[60]

The problem this patient experiences is a lack of constancy in self-perception and in relation to objects. The two problems are, however, as one because the self as experienced cannot be detached from the fragments of object representations that constitute his self-image. The hated mother lives within as representations of stern, ungiving, and seductive figures. The instability of object relationships is the reverse of the diffusion and fragmentation of the self.

Attention to the theory of the self arises out of a concern for the problem of continuity, sameness, and self-recognition throughout development. The notion of ego as functions, including defense, fails to capture the significance of continuity.[61] Erikson's term "identity," because it is so closely linked to social perception and social roles, deflects attention away from the idea of self in the evolution of unconscious mental life.[62] The identity crisis of adolescence and adulthood, in which the individual fails to be recognized in social roles, may be a symptom of the failure in self-experience and self-worth. The latter problems can be conceived of in intrapsychic terms as the consequences of failing to integrate object representations, and the aggressive-destructive presence of internal images which are incorporated through experience with, and reaction to, parents.

The problems of constancy and continuity call special attention to the pregenital stages of development. The stages of life preceding the oedipus complex become more significant in understanding the failures in self-experience since from a clinical perspective it is apparent that the presence of malevolent, grandiose, and devalued self-images persist from these early stages of development.

The pregenital stages also establish basic vulnerabilities, as well as strengths, in the exhibitionistic aspects of achievement and work. The sensitivity to humiliation and shame, affects which bear directly on the integrity of the self, measure the risk of regression when confronting disappointment and loss.

Positions of power expose individuals to potentially humiliating experiences in the difficult task of making decisions and confronting power in bargaining and negotiating. Coalitions sometimes take on latent purposes, to protect against the risks of humiliation and to avoid being shamed in the uses of power. Sociologists and political scientists are aware of these problems and give them considerable weight under the rubric of "face, status, and the 'presentation of self.' "[63] From a sociological perspective, the problems of face require an acuity to role demands. In meeting expectations, one preserves face in the present, but also credibility for possible future transactions. The concern for future regard, for example, appears to dominate thinking in foreign relations. Representatives think nothing of exaggerating the importance of immediate issues on the grounds that actions today create the expectations for the future.

The psychological counterpart of face is the need to maintain self-esteem where the measure of fulfilling standards does not exist in social expectations but in the ego ideal. There is evidence to suggest that individuals create social relations in the service of preserving continuity in the self. The Georges' study of Woodrow Wilson and Colonel House[64] lends itself to reinterpretation based on the way House served as a narcissistic object choice for President Wilson. These two men appeared, on the surface, to complement each other with Wilson's idealizing tendencies and House's general practical approach to making decisions. The extent to which House openly aggrandized Wilson's self-image enabled House to act in his sponsor's name. The relationship fell apart when another aggrandizing figure, Wilson's second wife, became openly jealous of the influence House exerted on her husband. In reaction to this rivalrous feeling, Mrs. Wilson began to sow the seeds of suspicion in the President's mind. When House sought an open and formal power position instead of being content with indirect influence, Wilson's new-found suspicions found some substance. The two men ended their collaboration, leaving Mrs. Wilson in the dominant role of the aggrandizer.

The presence of coalitions in part to gratify the leader's narcissistic needs may account for some of the mystique surrounding John F. Kennedy.[65] The Camelot legend created an aura around his person and office and served the obvious purpose of enhancing Kennedy's image in the eyes of the electorate. But it served other purposes as well, including supporting the leader's self-esteem as well as his subordinates' feelings of self-worth. What is less clear-cut from descriptions of his presidency, and the mystique surrounding his person, is the regulative effects legends had in warding off depressive reactions. The vulnerability to depression, while difficult to document, would seem to depend on the presence of conflicting self-images that predate oedipal rivalries. Some suggestion of depressive vulnerability comes from Theodore Sorenson's reflections on the President's investment in decisions that he made or that were made in his name:

A President knows that his name will be the label for a whole era. Textbooks yet unwritten and school children yet unborn will hold him responsible for all that happens. His program, his power, his prestige, his place in history, perhaps his re-election, will all be affected by every decision. His appointees, however distinguished they may be in their right, will rise or fall as he rises or falls. Even his White House aides, who see him constantly, cannot fully perceive his personal stakes and isolation. And no amount of tinkering with the presidential machinery, or establishment of new executive offices, can give anyone else *his* perspective.[66]

If presidential aides believe in the awesomeness of the Chief Executive's job, as suggested in Sorenson's reflections, the desire to protect him, to support his self-esteem, becomes a paramount objective in their role. It is no wonder, therefore, that objectivity may be difficult to preserve in the face of unspoken priorities given to protecting the Chief Executive.

The need to preserve self-esteem can account for some of the acting out that occurs in organizations. The head of a medium-sized corporation instigated a reorganization for the ostensible purpose of delegating operating responsibilities. He appointed one of his key executives to the President's job and became Chairman of the Board. He announced that he intended to devote himself to long-range planning in this new position. Not long after the change, it became apparent that the business was facing major reverses. When the troubles surfaced, the Chairman announced he was taking over once again, but he left unstated the implication that he was not responsible for the troubles. Further investigation showed that he had created a scapegoat in the form of his new appointee, and thereby preserved his self-image as a successful executive.

The particular means by which individuals regulate self-esteem depends on the degree of their vulnerability to narcissistic injury. Distorting reality suggests a high degree of vulnerability best explained by early experience. The particular forms of acting out, however, may be laid down in the actual experiences with siblings and peer groups during the latency stage of development.

Psychoanalytic investigations of sibling and peer relations tend to emphasize the displacement effect: that unresolved conflicts with parents, maintained in self-representations, tend to be acted out in relationships with siblings. A young boy's masculine anxieties, for example, may originate in ambivalent attachments to parents. But the conflicts are then displaced onto a sibling and are acted out. A patient described how he rejected a younger brother who represented to him all of the qualities which he imagined his father would scorn if discovered in himself. The antagonistic relationship provoked massive guilt feelings (the patient felt he had ruined his brother) and limited his ability to compete and use aggression in his work life. The sexual activity with this younger brother gave substance to feelings of shame that further complicated his relationship with men because of the ever-present fear that his fantasies would be uncovered and he would be humiliated.

While it is undoubtedly correct to ascribe primary significance to parental attachments in considering the origins of shame, guilt, and the fear of humiliation, from the point of view of the means selected for regulating self-esteem, weight should be given to the forms of acting out that occur in sibling and peer relations. The forms in actual behavior presumably establish patterns and vulnerabilities which are bound to reappear in many relationships in adult life. The structure of coalitions would presumably be determined by the patterns of action that appear in latency relationships.

CONCLUSION

The search for the origins of self-regulating activity in personal history points up one of the dilemmas in applied psychoanalysis. Clinical investigations, as well as theories of explanation, attach considerable weight to the hypothesis that the past determines the present in human behavior. Yet it is difficult to reproduce in applied psychoanalysis what is central to clinical psychoanalysis: the uncovering of the past through the lever of the transference. In the case of psychobiographical studies, genetic interpretations are often made, but the basis for these interpretations is far removed from the authentic material that becomes accessible in clinical work. This problem becomes even more severe in the case of applied studies where the focus is on decision-making and organizational structures.

The progression of studies in decision making, from the logic of game theory, which ostensibly abstracts the actor from the decision, to organizational models that interpret decision making as the interaction of interests, leads inevitably to constructs that originate in psychoanalytic theory. In particular, the model of decision making that includes as a variable the continuity and stability of the self directs investigation to the economy of the self. While understanding the evolution of self-esteem is essential to such studies, the access to historical data is not essential. Thematic interpretation provides the methodology for empirical work. The development of this methodology will undoubtedly raise new questions for psychoanalytic theory since its principal interest is in meaning and interpretation, issues of enduring concern in psychoanalytic explanation.

NOTES

1. O. Henry, "The Gift of the Magi," *The Complete Works of O. Henry* (New York: Doubleday and Company, Inc., 1953), p. 11.

2. R. Duncan Luce and Howard Raiffa, *Games and Decisions* (New York: John Wiley and Sons, Inc., 1957), p. 90.

3. A foray in the application of psychoanalysis to decision making appears in Leo Rangell, "The Decision-Making Process: A Contribution from Psychoanalysis," *The Psychoanalytic Study of the Child* (New York: Quadrangle Books, 1971), Vol. 26, pp. 425–52.

4. Sigmund Freud, "The Psychopathology of Everyday Life," in *The Complete Psychological Works of Sigmund Freud,* standard ed. (London: Hogarth Press, 1960), Vol. VI.

5. John Dewey, *How We Think* (New York: D.C. Heath, 1933).

6. Kenneth E. Boulding, *Economic Analysis* (New York: Harper & Brothers, 1941), Chapters 29 and 30.

7. Robert Waelder, "The Principle of Multiple Function." *Psychoanalytic Quarterly* 1 (1936).

8. James G. March and Herbert A. Simon, *Organizations* (New York: John Wiley and Sons, Inc., 1958), pp. 140–41.

9. Edward H. Chamberlin, *The Theory of Monopolistic Competition* (Cambridge, MA: Harvard University Press, 1946).

10. John Von Neumann and Oskar Morgenstern, *The Theory of Games and Economic Behavior* (Princeton, NJ: Princeton University Press, 1953), p. 40.

11. Morton D. Davis, *Game Theory: A Nontechnical Introduction* (New York: Basic Books, Inc., 1970), pp. 19–24.

12. Sudhir Kakar, *Frederick Taylor: A Study in Personality and Innovation* (Cambridge, MA: The MIT Press, 1970).

13. Luce R. Duncan and Howard Raiffa, *Games and Decisions,* p. 91.

14. Luce R. Duncan and Howard Raiffa, *Games and Decisions,* p. 91.

15. Georg Simmel, *The Sociology of Georg Simmel.* Translated by Kurt Wolff (Glencoe, Ill.: The Free Press, 1950), p. 163.

16. Von Neumann and Morgenstern, *The Theory of Games and Economic Behavior,* p. 221.

17. Ibid., p. 222.

18. Ibid., p. 274.

19. Thomas C. Schelling, *The Strategy of Conflict* (New York: Oxford University Press, 1963), p. 163.

20. *The Strategy of Conflict,* p. 163.

21. *The Strategy of Conflict,* p. 111.

22. *The Strategy of Conflict,* pp. 54–55.

23. G. Scodel et al., "Some Descriptive Aspects of Two-Person, Non-Zero-Sum Games." *The Journal of Conflict Resolution* III (1959): 114–19.

24. M. Deutsch, "Trust, Trustworthiness, and the F-Scale." *The Journal of Abnormal and Social Psychology* LXI (1960): 366–78.

25. Lawrence E. Fouraker and Sidney Siegel, *Bargaining Behavior* (New York: McGraw-Hill, 1963), pp. 66–69.

26. Scodel, Minas, Ratoosh, and Lipetz, op. cit.

27. Graves, Robert, *Claudius the God* (London: Methuen, 1969).

28. William F. Whyte, *Street Corner Society* (Chicago: The University of Chicago Press, 1955), pp. 16–25.

29. W. E. Vinake and A. Arkoff, "An Experimental Study of Coalitions in the Triad." *American Sociology Review* (1957): 406–14.

30. T. Caplow, "Further Development of a Theory of Coalition in the Triad." *American Journal of Sociology* (1959): 488–93.

31. Leon Festinger, *A Theory of Cognitive Dissonance* (Evanston, IL: Row, Peterson, and Company, 1957).

32. Robert P. Adelson, et al., eds., *Theories of Cognitive Consistency: A Sourcebook* (Chicago: Rand McNally and Company, 1968).

33. Fritz Heider, *The Psychology of Interpersonal Relations* (New York: John Wiley and Sons, Inc., 1967), p. 201.

34. Graham Allison, *The Essence of Decisions* (Boston: Little, Brown & Co., 1971).

35. Michel Crozier, *The Bureaucratic Phenomenon* (Chicago: The University of Chicago Press, 1964).

36. Heinz Hartmann, *Ego Psychology and the Problem of Adaptation* (New York: International Universities Press, 1953).

37. Clifford Geertz, *The Interpretation of Cultures* (New York: Basic Books, 1973), p. 313.

38. Geertz, *The Interpretation of Cultures,* p. 213.

39. Roy Schafer, *A New Language for Psychoanalysis* (New Haven, CT: Yale University Press, 1976).

40. Paul Ricoeur, *Freud and Philosophy, An Essay on Interpretation* (New Haven, CT: Yale University Press, 1970).

41. John Gedo and Arnold Goldberg, *Models of the Mind, A Psychoanalytic Theory* (Chicago: The University of Chicago Press, 1973).

42. Josef Breuer and Sigmund Freud, *Studies on Hysteria. The Standard Edition of the Complete Psychological Works of Sigmund Freud* (London: Hogarth Press, 1955), Vol. 11, pp. 102–103.

43. Theodore Lidz; Stephen Fleck; and Alice R. Cornelison, *Schizophrenia and the Family* (New York: International Universities Press, 1965), pp. 140–41.

44. *Schizophrenia and the Family,* pp. 91–92. Italics added except where noted.

45. Morton H. Halperin, *Bureaucratic Politics and Foreign Policy* (Washington, DC: The Brookings Institution, 1974), pp. 1–3.

46. *Bureaucratic Politics,* pp. 16–17.

47. Tom Wicker, *JFK and LBJ: The Influence of Personality upon Politics* (New York: William Morrow & Company, 1968). See also Philip Geyelin, *Lyndon B. Johnson and the World* (New York: Praeger, 1966).

48. Abraham Zaleznik and Manfred F. R. Kets de Vries, *Power and the Corporate Mind* (Boston: Houghton-Mifflin, 1975), pp. 230–56. See also Abraham Zaleznik, "Charismatic and Consensus Leaders: A Psychological Comparison." *Bulletin of the Menninger Clinic* 39 (May 1974).

49. Halperin, *Bureaucratic Politics,* pp. 24–25.

50. Abraham Zaleznik, "Psychopathology and Politics Reconsidered." *Bulletin of the Menninger Clinic* 39, no. 2 (March 1975).

51. Alexander George and Juliette George, *Woodrow Wilson and Colonel House: A Personality Study* (New York: Dover Publications, 1964).

52. Richard Neustadt, *Presidential Power* (New York: John Wiley and Sons, Inc., 1960), pp. 36–37.

53. *Presidential Power,* pp. 36–37.

54. Nathan Leites, *A Study of Bolshevism* (Glencoe, IL: The Free Press, 1953).

55. *A Study of Bolshevism,* p. 25.

56. *A Study of Bolshevism,* p. 25.

57. Alexander George, "The Operational Code: A Neglected Approach to the Study of Political Leaders and Decision-Making" (Santa Monica, CA: The Rand Corporation, 1967), Memorandum RM-3427-PR.

58. Ibid., p. 16.

59. Heinz Hartmann, "Comments on the Psychoanalytic Theory of the Ego," *The Psychoanalytic Study of the Child* (New York: International Universities Press, 1964); Heinz Kohut, *The Analysis of the Self* (New York: International Universities Press, 1971); Otto Kernberg, *Borderline Conditions and Pathological Narcissism* (New York: J. Aronson, 1975); Arnold Modell, *Object Love and Reality* (New York: International Universities Press, 1968); John Gedo and Arnold Goldberg, *Models of the Mind* (New York,

International Universities Press, 1973); Erik H. Erikson, "The Problem of Ego Identity: Identity and the Life Cycle." *Psychological Issues* (New York: International Universities Press, 1959), 1, no. 1; Edith Jacobsen, *The Self and the Object World* (New York: International Universities Press, 1964).

60. Edith Jacobsen, *The Self and the Object World,* pp. 214–16.

61. Heinz Hartmann, "Comments on the Psychoanalytic Theory of the Ego," *Psychoanalytic Study of the Child.*

62. Erik H. Erikson, "The Problem of Ego Identity."

63. Erving Goffman, *The Presentation of Self in Everyday Life* (Garden City, NY: Doubleday, 1959).

64. Alexander George and Juliette George, *Woodrow Wilson and Colonel House.*

65. Abraham Zaleznik, "Friends, Lovers, and Enemies: Reflections on Coalition Politics." *Journal of the Philadelphia Association for Psychoanalysis* (Autumn 1975).

66. Theodore C. Sorenson, *Decision Making in the White House* (New York: Columbia University Press, 1963), pp. 83–84. Noted in Joseph H. deRivera, *The Psychological Dimension of Foreign Policy* (Columbus, OH: Charles E. Merrill Publishing Company, 1968), p. 131.

REFERENCES

Adelson, Robert P. et al. (eds). *Theories of Cognitive Consistency: A Sourcebook.* Chicago: Rand McNally and Company, 1968.

Allison, Graham. *The Essence of Decisions.* Boston: Little, Brown & Co., 1971.

Boulding, Kenneth E. *Economic Analysis.* New York: Harper & Brothers, 1941.

Breuer, Josef and Freud, Sigmund. *Studies on Hysteria. The Standard Edition of the Complete Psychological Works of Sigmund Freud.* Vol. II. London: The Hogarth Press, 1955.

Caplow, T. "Further Development of a Theory of Coalition in the Triad." *American Journal of Sociology* (1959).

Chamberlin, Edward H. *The Theory of Monopolistic Competition.* Cambridge: Harvard University Press, 1946.

Crozier, Michel. *The Bureaucratic Phenomenon.* Chicago: The University of Chicago Press, 1964.

Davis, Morton D. *Game Theory: A Nontechnical Introduction.* New York: Basic Books, Inc., 1970.

deRivera, Joseph H. *The Psychological Dimension of Foreign Policy.* Columbus, OH: Charles E. Merrill Publishing Company, 1968.

Deutsch, M. "Trust, Trustworthiness, and the F-Scale." *The Journal of Abnormal and Social Psychology* 61 (1960).

Dewey, John. *How We Think.* New York: D.C. Heath, 1933.

Erikson, Erik H. "The Problem of Ego Identity: Identity and the Life Cycle." *Psychological Issues* 1, no. 1. New York: International Universities Press, 1959.

Festinger, Leon. *A Theory of Cognitive Dissonance.* Evanston, IL: Row, Peterson, and Company, 1957.

Fouraker, Lawrence E. and Siegel, Sidney. *Bargaining Behavior.* New York: McGraw-Hill, 1963.

Freud, Sigmund. "The Psychotherapy of Everyday Life," in *The Complete Psychological Works of Sigmund Freud*, Vol. VI. London: Hogarth Press, 1960.

Gedo, John and Goldberg, Arnold. *Models of the Mind, A Psychoanalytic Theory*. Chicago: The University of Chicago Press, 1973.

Geertz, Clifford. *The Interpretation of Cultures*. New York: Basic Books, 1973.

George, Alexander. "The Organizational Code: A Neglected Approach to the Study of Political Leaders and Decision-Making." Memorandum RM-3427-PR. Santa Monica, CA: The Rand Corporation, 1967.

George, Alexander and George, Juliette. *Woodrow Wilson and Colonel House: A Personality Study*. New York: Dover Publications, 1964.

Geyelin, Philip. *Lyndon B. Johnson and the World*. New York: Praeger, 1966.

Goffman, Erving. *The Presentation of Self in Everyday Life*. Garden City, NY: Doubleday, 1959.

Graves, Robert. *Claudius the God*. London: Methuen, 1969.

Halperin, Morton H. *Bureaucratic Politics and Foreign Policy*. Washington, DC: The Brookings Institution, 1974.

Hartmann, Heinz. "Comments on the Psychoanalytic Theory of the Ego." *The Psychoanalytic Study of the Child*. New York: International Universities Press, 1964.
———. *Ego Psychology and the Problem of Adaptation*. New York International Universities Press, 1953.

Heider, Fritz. *The Psychology of Interpersonal Relations*. New York: John Wiley and Sons, Inc., 1967.

Henry, O. "The Gift of the Magi." *The Complete Works of O. Henry*. New York: Doubleday and Company, Inc., 1953.

Jacobsen, Edith. *The Self and the Object World*. New York: International Universities Press, 1964.

Kakar, Suhir. *Frederick Taylor: A Study in Personality and Innovation*. Cambridge: The MIT Press, 1970.

Kernberg, Otto. *Borderline Conditions and Pathological Narcissism*. New York: J. Aronson, 1975.

Kohut, Heinz. *The Analysis of the Self*. New York: International Universities Press, 1971.

Leites, Nathan. *A Study of Bolshevism*. Glencoe, IL: The Free Press, 1953.

Lidz, Theodore; Fleck, Stephen; and Cornelison, Alice R. *Schizophrenia and the Family*. New York: International Universities Press, 1965.

Luce, R. Duncan and Raiffa, Howard. *Games and Decisions*. New York: John Wiley and Sons, Inc., 1957.

March, James G. and Simon, Herbert A. *Organizations*. New York: John Wiley and Sons, Inc., 1958.

Modell, Arnold. *Object Love and Reality*. New York: International Universities Press, 1968.

Neustadt, Richard. *Presidential Power*. New York: John Wiley and Sons, Inc., 1960.

Rangell, Leo. "The Decision-Making Process: A Contribution from Psychoanalysis." In *The Psychoanalytic Study of the Child*, Vol. 26, pp. 425–452. New York: Quadrangle Books, 1971.

Ricoeur, Paul. *Freud and Philosophy, An Essay on Interpretation*. New Haven: Yale University Press, 1970.

Schafer, Roy. *A New Language for Psychoanalysis*. New Haven: Yale University Press, 1976.

Schelling, Thomas C. *The Strategy of Conflict.* New York: Oxford University Press, 1963.

Scodel, G., et al. "Some Descriptive Aspects of Two-Person, Non-Zero-Sum Games." *The Journal of Conflict Resolution* 3 (1959).

Simmel, Georg. *The Sociology of Georg Simmel.* Translated by Kurt Wolff. Glencoe, IL: The Free Press, 1950.

Sorenson, Theodore C. *Decision Making in the White House.* New York: Columbia University Press, 1963.

Vinake, W. E. and Arkoff, A. "An Experimental Study of Coalitions in the Triad." *American Journal of Sociology* (1957).

Von Neumann, John and Morgenstern, Oscar. *The Theory of Games and Economic Behavior.* Princeton: Princeton University Press, 1953.

Waelder, Robert. "The Principle of Multiple Function." *Psychoanalytic Quarterly* 1 (1936).

Whyte, William F. *Street Corner Society.* Chicago: The University of Chicago Press, 1955.

Wicker, Tom. *JFK and LBJ: The Influence of Personality upon Politics.* New York: William Morrow & Company, 1968.

Zaleznik, Abraham. "Psychopathology and Politics Reconsidered." *Bulletin of the Menninger Clinic* 39 no. 2 (March 1975).

———. "Friends, Lovers, and Enemies: Reflections on Coalition Politics." *Journal of the Philadelphia Association for Psychoanalysis* (Autumn 1975b).

———. "Charismatic and Consensus Leaders: A Psychological Comparison." *Bulletin of the Menninger Clinic* 37 (May 1974).

Zaleznik, Abraham and Kets de Vries, Manfred F. R. *Power and the Corporate Mind.* Boston: Houghton-Mifflin, 1975.

7

THE ENTREPRENEUR AND SOCIETY

Joshua Ronen

THE NATURE OF ENTREPRENEURSHIP

Entrepreneurship must be predicated on the concept of change. Static equilibrium theories of the economy will never have a place for the entrepreneur. And yet it is not the entrepreneur that one wishes to model but the entrepreneurial act which may inhere in even those who would be regarded by most as non-entrepreneurial. Economists have focused on the modeling of a "rational" man, the attribution to him of basic, primitive characteristics thought to lead to useful predictions of his behavior individually and, more importantly, as member of a society, a subsystem. Some ascribe to the entrepreneurial force the loving of risk, the taking of chances, and so the on-setting of destructive capitalism, innovation, challenge of what exists, the venturing beyond into new realms that would make existing modes of production and transaction obsolete.

Creative thinking and change generally originate with people who are not happy with their lot. The economist's view of man has always presented an individual who maximizes the utility from his consumption over his lifetime. A variant of that is one who maximizes wealth at any point in his life, including the very last moments before his death; then he would be bequeathing property to his descendants. But would a man who has become very wealthy ever be so content that he would no longer embark on adventurous paths or lose the quest for novelty? In a static world this seems to be the verdict: neither palatable nor realistic. Throughout history, men, poor or rich, have striven to change their lots, not only financially, but also emotionally and intellectually.

Reviewing the history of entrepreneurial activities, bursts of creativity, and the kind of risk taking that throughout time has made for great discoveries and revolutions reveals a pattern that is consistent with continuous quests for novelty regardless of man's social status, occupational position, or monetary wealth. The need for change may perform a rehearsal function in the face of an ultimate and final change: death. Oblivion may be prevented and a measure of immortality gained by constant change, constant growth, and, perhaps most importantly, standing out, growing beyond one's own reference group.

Thus the entrepreneur tends to seek novel ventures in the context of an environment of uncertainty. Because of his passion for novelty he may be willing to give up a measure of the low-risk return he might possibly secure elsewhere. But, more importantly, he must bear the risk of bankruptcy which tends to be high from the very novelty of his undertaking. He would proceed innovatively and resourcefully to devise the kind of complex financing arrangements that would lure capital. Thus the entrepreneur's "Knightian" risk-bearing observed to accompany his "Schumpeterian" zeal for the new triggers with its urgent immediacy yet another outburst of innovativeness, now in the area of financing arrangements that seek creative ways to avoid bankruptcy.

IMPEDIMENTS TO THE EXERCISE OF ENTREPRENEURSHIP

So far, we have speculated that the quest for change or novelty would be a source of satisfaction (whether in the securing of a measure of immortality or a measure of prevention against anticipated oblivion). In economic parlance, this would mean that change would enter separately as an argument into the utility function. However, novelty can play an additional role: Change from the customary often involves greater uncertainty (less information is available about the nonroutine) and also greater chance of large gains, as some time elapses before profit is eroded by competitors (who are yet to enter the new field). But this desire for change can be blunted by psychological and real constraints. Unawareness of the possibility of change is an impediment. The poor who have never seen and thus never been made aware of, the wealthy, would not be and perhaps never will be, cognizant of the possibility of enjoying higher standards of living. But even if the poor man were aware of the possibility of being rich, his path to such riches may be blocked by a stifling regulatory environment that constricts his actions and limits his freedom to choose or to act; any attempt to better his lot would be unsuccessful, futile, and therefore unrealistic. Moreover, the passion for novelty itself seems to decay over time with the accumulation of wealth or accomplishments.

Our view of the entrepreneur, therefore, is that of a man characterized by one argument in his utility function, wealth. At low wealth levels, the desire to achieve a satisfactory standard of well-being combines with the inherent passion for change to draw the individual on to seeking novel ventures with the promise of large rewards, but inevitably with a greater burden of risk. Hence, this novelty-seeking activity will be perceived, at low levels of wealth, as indicating risk loving, whereas the decaying quest for novelty, after satiation, will be seen as risk aversion. However, the individual entrepreneur is subjected to environmental, natural, and man-made constraints. The poor farmer born in a remote, isolated village with a poor population, who had never left the village, would not be aware of the opportunity of gain. On the other hand, the poor man living in a community with a highly unequal distribution of wealth but shackled by a strict code of prescribed behavior and regulations would not be able to better his lot even though he recognizes the potential for doing so in the absence of constraints.

THE CONCEPT OF WEALTH

Wealth is another potent factor. However, it seems that the utility functions of the entrepreneurial individuals are better specified throughout the life cycle with wealth as an argument in addition to or in lieu of the consumption vector. For some, the appetite for wealth seems to grow with its accumulation, thus implying a positive second derivative of utility in wealth. But how can a marginal utility that increases with wealth be reconciled with the observation that the entrepreneurially oriented are no greater risk takers than those less entrepreneurially oriented? One explanation is that in the game of making money, winning (money gain) and losing (money loss) enter separately into the utility function with positive and negative signs, respectively.

In their recent review of decision making, Tversky and Kahneman (1981) cite findings consistent with their prospect theory (1979). This theory predicts, among other things, that the value (utility) function is S-shaped, concave above the reference point (assigned a value of zero), and convex below it. Moreover, the response to losses is more extreme than the response to gains. If the reference point is continually adjusted to reflect the status quo, so that the decision maker views each choice incrementally in terms of a "minimal account" (Tversky and Kahneman, 1981), the departure from the expected utility model embedded in this aspect of prospect theory would reconcile the entrepreneur's exhibited risk-taking behavior with a marginal utility that increases with wealth below the reference point.

Wealth here is defined as encompassing not only money, but also prestige, power, sense of independence, respect, recognition, and so on. Substitutions among these may be possible. A measure of monetary wealth may be willingly sacrificed for prestige and recognition; respect of peers can be given up somewhat to attain power. Assuming that the most optimal substitutions have been made, the maximum wealth attained after such substitutions is the wealth entering into this utility function.

If the present wealth of the individual is below his aspiration level or expectation, he will behave like a risk lover and gamble entrepreneurially, artistically, religiously, or physically. He may commit crimes or become a creative artist or enterprising businessman. Which direction he will take depends on personality and sociological characteristics as well as constraints, opportunities, and endowments. Very high penalties attached to crime will deter his turning to that resource. (If crime is committed nonetheless, monetary wealth must be a very salient contributor to utility.) He may turn to entrepreneurial gambles but only if the regulatory environment is not too stifling; he may become a poet or artist but only if he would not be burned on charges of witchcraft; he may become a guru of a new religion if the community he lives in is tolerant of such "deviation," and yet he may become a violent revolutionary if all other avenues have been blocked.

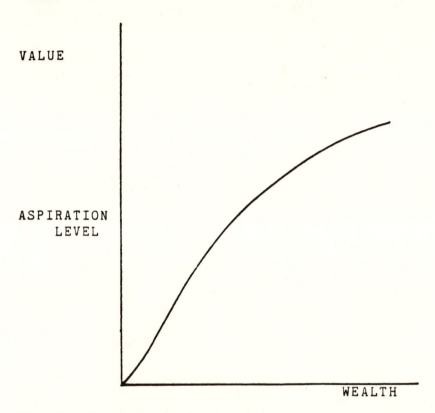

Figure 7.1.   The value function of the entrepreneur.

Even after the individual accomplished his expected wealth, he would still look beyond for change, for his thirst for novelty is never quenched. But here his utility function would typically become concave, thus exhibiting decreasing marginal utility in wealth. Some individuals may continue to have increasing marginal utility (these may be typical, eternal entrepreneurs), but most would exhibit risk aversion after this point. (See Figure 7.1 for a stylized value function). With the accumulation of accomplishments, success, and monetary wealth, the appetite for additional wealth will abate slightly. Nonetheless, this individual still seeks change and novelty (whether in the field of art, crime, or drugs (for kicks); violent or perverse pleasures; or a continued entrepreneurial accumulation of wealth). He certainly would operate under fewer constraints than his poor counterpart: He has the wealth to invest entrepreneurially, or the prestige and power to gain easy access into financing. But while he has greater ability to engage in entrepreneurial acts, his willingness to do so is mitigated by his increased risk aversion.

This is in contrast to his poorer counterpart, who eagerly seeks the entrepreneurial gamble and who does not have the financial means to engage or the credible track record or power of prestige to persuade others to provide him with the necessary wherewithal. Thus, constraints of capital availability binding when the entrepreneurial individual is relatively poor, inhibit creativity (in the entrepreneurial sense) when it is most sought, whereas the lesser willingness to gamble entrepreneurially depresses creativity on the part of the wealthier, even though they are not bound by capital or financing constraints. This reality points to lucrative social policy implications if entrepreneurship is to be encouraged: schemes of risk sharing that channel capital of the wealthy to the relatively poorer exhibiting more eagerness to engage in novelty.

SUBSTITUTIONS AMONG COMPONENTS OF WEALTH WITHIN A CONSTRAINED ENVIRONMENT

Our view of the entrepreneur thus admits the possibility of substitution among the components constituting total wealth: money, prestige, power, independence, and so on. If the level of one of the components is uncontrollably reduced by some exogenous factors, the individual will strive to compensate for it by seeking more of the other components. Whether other components can, in fact, be increased to substitute for the loss in monetary wealth or any of the other ingredients and which components would be selected for such substitution will depend on individual factors: the characterization of the marginal substitution rate among the components for that given individual, and the environmental constraints (since, after all, some components may not be within the ability of the individual to increase in the given environment). For example, independence cannot be increased in an environment that does not allow for freedom. In certain communities, prestige may be closely related to the level of education which, in turn, can be obtained only by wealth, the very ingredient which had been diminished. Thus, it is interaction of the characteristics of the individual's rate of substitution among the ingredients and the constraints (and opportunities) available in the environment that dictate who would commit an entrepreneurial act, a crime, ignite a revolutionary fervor, or compose or recite poetry.

This "model" of the entrepreneur is consistent with existing speculations and evidence. Ronen (1983), reporting on a series of interviews, described how the feeling of "displacement" or the state of being in dire need pushed toward entrepreneurship. In such a state of low "wealth," marginal utility in wealth would be increasing and, further, societal and other constraints deter amelioration of position through other means (such as governmental, political, or other civic or private-sector positions). Almost the only choice left for the individual is to act entrepreneurially.

Existence of such constraints implies low opportunity cost, which can act as a powerful inducement for exploring entrepreneurial ventures; thus, the higher incidence of entrepreneurs among immigrants and other "outsiders" whose relatively restricted economic opportunities spell lower cost of opportunity than for established "insiders." Whether restriction of economic opportunity for "outsiders" stems from discrimination or the naturally high cost of gaining knowledge about new communities to which the individual immigrated, or learning how to communicate effectively with established members of the population and of inspiring trust and credibility among potential financiers, the outcome is a push toward an entrepreneurial gamble.

Indeed, a sociological tradition endows the displaced outsider with the perspective of cultural deviance or social marginality. Note Simmel's concept of the stranger and Park's (1928) notion of the marginal man, Veblen's interpretation of the Jew's contribution to economic and intellectual progress, and Weber's emphasis on the impact of Protestantism's "worldly asceticism" on the rise of capitalism. (Of course, the emergence of the Protestant ethic itself needs to be endogenously explained. Creation of the ethos could compensate the poor for the discomforting absence of worldly wealth in a manner consistent with our view of the entrepreneur.) Collins, Moore, and Unwalla (1964) suggest that ". . . the carriers of the basic entrepreneurial values of our society tend, paradoxically enough, to be those who are marginal to the established social networks" (p. 145).

CHANGING REALITIES

The thesis here is that "marginal" men, regardless of whether they used to be wealthy or wealthier, *tend* to be more entrepreneurial on two counts: (1) being fairly low on the wealth scale, they tend to have an increasing marginal utility in wealth (note again that wealth is defined to include other dimensions such as prestige, power, independence, peer recognition) and (2) sets of constraints imposed on such men (refugees, immigrants, minorities) make entrepreneurial endeavors almost the only feasible route.

But one would also predict that entrepreneurial sparks will tend to be observed more frequently during periods of change in the political, economic, demographic context, and when the natural environment introduces different, novel realities. New realities can take on fundamental forms of natural evolution (in a very long perspective) or they might appear in the form of new technological and social configurations (including, for example, changes resulting from wars and migrations). These constitute new opportunities for profit and for betterment of wealth (of all kinds). The "marginal" men of our society, aware of their constrained path to prosperity in other endeavors, will make it their business to be alert to newly unfolding realities; the supply of creativity will increase, a burst of innovative activity. Consider, however, that some of these changing realities, such as demographic shifts (migrations or other instances of vast increases in population) must be treated as endogenous in a global analysis.

Brenner (1983) cites various studies in anthropology, sociology, and history to support his view that only changes in the distribution of wealth that make the individual impoverished (increase the percentage of the wealthier) induce creativity and entrepreneurial acts. Our contention here, however, is that people do not have to become impoverished. Given any existing genetical distribution of skills and creativity, the actual supply of creative works and entrepreneurial acts (as well as crime and drug addiction) will increase at all wealth levels once the opportunities for these acts increase as a result of changing realities (opportunities) or, when a shift in the constraints "pushes" more into the ranks of the creative (in all manners) and the entrepreneurial. One always would expect, however, a greater percentage of the increase in entrepreneurial activity and other forms of creativity to come from the ranks of the poor simply because of the hypothesized increasing marginal utility in wealth below the reference wealth point.

For example, we believe that Brenner's attribution of the development of Holland, England, France, and other European countries—as contrasted with the relative stagnation of Spain—to the relative increase of wealth of Spain (shift in distribution of wealth) does not tell the whole story. Our contention is that the increased demand brought about by a richer Spain, along with changing opportunities inducing the residents of the poorer European countries to commit entrepreneurial acts, better explains the phenomenon described in Brenner's quotation of C. Cipolla (1976, pp. 233–35):

The decline of Spain in the 17th Century is not difficult to understand. . . . Spain, as a whole . . . became considerably richer than . . . during the 16th century. . . . The riches of the Americas provided Spain with purchasing power but ultimately they stimulated the development of Holland, England, France, and other European countries. . . . At the end of the 16th century, Spain was much richer than a century earlier, but she was not more developed—"like an heir endowed by the accident of an eccentric will". . . . In the meanwhile . . . a century of artificial prosperity had induced many to abandon the land, schools had multiplied, but they had served mostly to produce a half-educated intellectual proletariat who scorned productive industry and manual labor and found positions in the bloated state bureaucracy which served above all to disguise unemployment. Spain in the 17th Century lacked entrepreneurs and artisans.

Also, we believe that it is the substitution between monetary wealth and spiritual elatedness suggested by our model of entrepreneurship that contributed to the poetic fervor described in the passage from Toynbee (1966) in his *Change and Habit* quoted by Brenner, rather than changes in distribution of wealth:

The classical Persian poetry had been written in the course of the half millenium between the breakup of the Abbaud Empire and the political reunification of Iran in the Safari

Empire. During this period, . . . in spite of the consequent insecurity of life and destruction of wealth, a fractured Iran, like a fractured Italy or Greece, excelled in the arts. (p. 93).

The same elements we used to portray entrepreneurship are consistent with yet another quotation by Brenner related to seventeenth- and eighteenth-century economic innovation in France, which Brenner observes was correlated with the Huguenots who were barred from membership and close association with the King's court:

Although the Edict of Nantes gave the Protestants theoretically equal rights in government service, they were actually discriminated against and were only reluctantly, and often with difficulty, admitted to government positions. Moreover, after 1661 they were formally excluded from admission to public service. Thus, the large families in the Protestant centers had no incentive to invest their capital in public posts. For this reason Protestants rather than Catholic families tended to build family businesses, to train their sons for business careers, and to expand their business interests by prudent intermarriage. Since the Huguenots formed the leading elite in French business, it can easily be understood what a terrible blow was dealt to French economic growth and French entrepreneurship by the revocation of the Edict of Nantes and the accompanying mass emigration of French Protestants. (Houselitz, 1968, p. 101).

The list goes on and on (see Hagen's study of the Antioquenos, Kulke's (1974) and Karaka's (1884) documentation of how the Parsees fared in Bombay and again Hagen's (1975) evidence on the incidence of entrepreneurship among those who in 1667 seceded from the Roman Catholic Church and were condemned as schismatics who, while persecuted, were prominent in the accelerating economic growth that occurred in Russia during the last half of the nineteenth century). Sowell's (1975) reports on the coming into prosperity of the Scots before the nineteenth century (who were discriminated against) is also noteworthy.

In more recent times, stories about supply of entrepreneurial activities by immigrant groups have been abundant. Note Barry Chiswick's (1978) evidence on the performance of immigrants in the United States and the more numerous evidence focusing on the performance of the Jews (see, for example, Kuznets, 1972 and Engelman, 1962). We find it instructive to elaborate on the latter.

THE EXAMPLE OF THE JEWS

The fate of the Jews as a minority is a vivid illustration of how a combination of constraints, opportunities, and the type of discrimination that decrease wealth (as construed above) would produce entrepreneurial venturesomeness. Since the fourteenth century, Jews have been associated with a "capitalist" image. A unique history facilitated disproportionate representation of the Jews in "capitalistic" endeavors. They were forced by Christian regulations to specialize in commerce and banking (then called "usury") and to avoid agriculture. These scorned industries revealed themselves as a great opportunity for the Jews: They offered novelty which promised high returns. The particular combination of constraints and opportunities, the Jewish "literacy" inherited from Moses' inscribed commandments, and risks of confiscation, "pushed" the Jews to invest in education and jewelry. The Jews' relatively higher endowment in literacy and education spurred on the process.

It has been insinuated that trade-offs are continuously effected between various ingredients entering into the broad "wealth" concept which had been introduced. One of these ingredients we had contended was a measure of immortality. It is not inconceivable, therefore, that the poor (those who have always been or became poor) gamble on the idea of the hereafter as substituting a measure of eternal bliss for worldly wealth. This possibility would explain the emergence of "religious fervor" at various points in time when famine and death struck suddenly and unexpectedly. Having acquired the idea of a blissful afterworld, it becomes entrenched and ingrained and passes on from generation to generation. Even if circumstances change, it is difficult to extinguish the idea inherited from older generations. As a result, bliss in heaven becomes an established ingredient of wealth that substitutes for and thus attenuates the drive for attainment of worldly matter. Thus, one would expect those whose ethos is manifest in notions of reincarnation (therefore, in due time infinite wealth) to exhibit, ceteris paribus, much less passion for the entrepreneurial attainment of wealth. Consider that for such as the Hindus (as perhaps contrasted with the Jews) the future state of infinite bliss (self-believed) must render far less urgent any entrepreneurial accumulation of worldly wealth.

When wealth drastically diminished throughout history, people variously searched for and adopted comforting ideologies that substituted for worldly poverty and misery. Brenner suggests that the rats and fleas that induced the Black Death which in 1346 killed a third of Europe's population, were attributed to the Almighty as punishment for human sins so that those spared must be designated for the eternal bliss in the hereafter. Thus, desolation in the world of the tangible for those still alive must be rewarded by the paradise of the world of the intangible. Nemesis is thus manifest; the substitution between the ingredients of wealth has been accomplished. Brenner quotes McNeill (1976) who wrote:

Popular and respectable was an upsurge of mysticism, aimed at achieving encounter with God in inexplicable, unpredictable, intense and purely personal ways. Hesychasm among the orthodox, and more variegated movements among Latin Christians—e.g., the practices of the so called Rhineland mystics, of the Brethren of the Common Life and of heretical groups like the Lollards of England—all give expression to the need for a more personal, antinomian access to God. (p. 163).

The above exemplifies religious ideas that people sought to adopt during the period of the Black Death.

Evidence on the impact of the "constraints" through discrimination on entrepreneurial activity by minority groups, notably Jews, has been amply quoted by Brenner. The theme recurs with great convincing force: Groups can be pushed into entrepreneurial activities (as well as into crime and revolution) simply by directing their behavior toward entrepreneurship (mostly because of actions taken to solidify stability and power of the majority group) by allowing these groups to do almost nothing else. Brenner suggests that, if for lack of other choices, Jews were made to gamble more frequently on novel ideas and if the percentage of lucky hits stayed constant, they would have been disproportionately represented among successful entrepreneurs and they would have built up their reputation for "speculative thinking." This could imply that the Jews' average monetary income may become higher than that of the rest of the population; importantly, this also would be the fate of other minority groups subjected to similar circumstances.

Brenner notes the entrepreneurially successful Jewish families of eighteenth-century Europe (Zeligman, Oppenheimer, Rothschild, and others) as well as famous Italian merchant families of the late Middle Ages and Chinese minorities in contemporary Singapore and West Malaysia. Also reported by Brenner are the similar adaptations made by the Parsees and the Palestinians. The seventeenth-century Parsees were reported by European travelers as traders who have "mental characteristics" similar to those of Jews (Brenner, p. 297); they served as brokers in Portuguese, French, Dutch, and English factories. Similarly to Jews, 89 percent of the men and 73 percent of the women are literate, in contrast with the average for the rest of the population of 15 percent and 2 percent, respectively. As to Palestinian refugees, the percentage of elementary and secondary students rose gradually from the prerefugee status of 9 percent in 1948 Palestine (roughly similar to that prevailing in neighboring Arab countries during the same time) to 21.8 percent in 1977. Also in Jordan, which granted citizenship to all Palestinian refugees in 1948, even though retaining the opportunity to continue the previous occupation (agriculture) there was a significant jump in the level of education.

What would determine the choice between entrepreneurship or crime for a displaced group whose opportunity cost is low for either? It follows from the thesis developed above that the choice would be determined by the set of relative constraints and opportunities. For the blacks and the Irish in the United States (see Sowell, 1975), political mechanisms coupled with egalitarian ideas could be used to increase relative wealth at minimal costs (because of number of people and political structure), whereas this route was not open for the Japanese and the Jews, who thus directed their effort into individual entrepreneurial strategies. Notice, however, the vastly different implications for society: The first set of activities (crime or political mechanisms) only redistributes societal wealth, whereas the latter set (entrepreneurial strategies) increases relative wealth of the minorities as well as wealth of the society as a whole.

RECONSTRUCTION AND POLICY IMPLICATIONS: THE SOCIETAL VIEWPOINT

So far our crude model of the entrepreneur depicts an individual seeking novelty and change, as well as wealth that includes money, power, prestige, and other like ingredients that contribute to utility. Appetite for wealth increases with its accumulation up to and until a reference point, after which marginal utility in wealth starts to decrease. At any point, the individual mixes the ingredients of wealth (the monetary and the psychic varieties) in a way that maximizes his utility. Throughout this process of wealth accumulation, the quest for change is constant; it is aided by emerging opportunities, but hampered by natural or man (or society)-made constraints. The genetically received distribution of skill, interest, et cetera, and the prevailing and evolving configuration of constraints and new realities combine to determine the equilibrium amount of entrepreneurial activity in a given society.

How does this model of the individual entrepreneur reconcile with the systemic societywide framework?

Reconciliation is attained once we recognize that the individual himself is a subsystem, needing to both self-stabilize and self-organize. The individual needs to self-organize because of being subjected to threats, among which is the possibility of being rejected by the large system and thus having his survival threatened. The point at which this threat is eliminated appears to be the reference point above which marginal utility in wealth (broadly construed) starts decreasing and below which marginal utility in this wealth is increasing. Since the larger system is always subjected to environmental shocks and new randomly appearing realities, the individual (as a subsystem) needs to adapt in an ongoing fashion. Thus, because the larger system itself changes to adapt to the larger environment of the universe, the quest for novelty of the individual as a subsystem is also ongoing.

Now we address ourselves to policy implications: Suppose we wish to encourage entrepreneurial activities, new technologies, the break-out into new frontiers, but within the framework of existing institutional arrangements, including the government. What should be done?

What follows from our analysis of the entrepreneur within a well-defined social setting is that, to encourage novel explorations, the central authority needs to rechannel savings and incentives from ongoing industries into the exploration of new ideas. As noted previously, those who have greater drive to search for and implement new concepts and ideas are typically those who lack the wealth to do so on their own; they need financing. On the other hand, those who have the resources are less likely to engage in the process of entrepreneurial innovation as eagerly as their poorer counterparts. Incentives to take risks by providing capital to the poorer entrepreneurs must be provided. Paradoxically, we observe at present that the government subsidizes (and provides incentives for) precisely those who have made it for mere expansion and investment in the type of equipment that produces existing products, rather than providing incentives for those who seek highly uncertain new projects. The implication of all this analysis is, therefore, that rather than devoting societal resources as an incentive for existing products, the government must divert these resources to induce the creation of new ventures. Risk sharing (the wealthy providing capital and the entrepreneurially driven poor, effort and time) must be secured. Can the free market do the job effectively on its own?

Insurance policies and common stock eliminate inefficiences in resource allocation in that they allow risk to be shared in an optimal way among individuals. With enough markets for risk, such as exist whenever a new security is introduced into the capital market, uncertainty can be allocated in accordance with each individual's attitudes toward risk. If an individual is uncertain as to which of several different states of the world will obtain, he can then make contracts contingent on the occurrence of possible states. With such markets for contingent contracts, a competitive equilibrium can arise under the same general conditions as in the absence of uncertainty. It is not even necessary then that individuals agree on the probability distribution for the unknown states of the world. Each can have his own subjective probability distribution.

Thus, in theory, entrepreneurial activities should go on unimpeded as long as there are enough developed capital markets and insurance markets that allocate risk efficiently. However, there is more to the story; it is evident that markets for risk can break down. Whenever we have uncertainty we also have the possibility of the existence or the absence of information. For example, no contingent contract can be made if, at the time of execution, either of the contracting parties does not know whether the specified contingency has occurred or not. This fact eliminates a large number of opportunities for mutually favorable exchanges.

The problem of adverse selection is well known. And, indeed, entrepreneurial supply exhibits precisely the potential for such a phenomenon. Our potentially entrepreneurial but poor individuals, who lack the capital to embark on their creative ideas and who have not accumulated a track record, would possibly possess information about their skills, abilities, and drive. However, this information is not shared by the would-be financiers who have the greater wealth and who look for lucrative investments. Under these circumstances, and assuming a distribution of would-be entrepreneurs who differ in their abilities, skills, or drives (or integrity), the market for claims on prospects that might be initiated by entrepreneurial ideas can indeed become very thin or nonexistent.

For a simple illustration through analogy to the insurance world, consider the existence of two types of individuals, A and B, with different life expectancies. The insurance company cannot distinguish between the two (it has no information); in other words, it cannot identify the present circumstances in all their relevant aspects (see Arrow, 1971). An optimal risk allocation would require separate insurance policies for the two types, but in the absence of information this would be impossible. Now suppose that each individual knows which type he belongs to (compare with each entrepreneur knowing his abilities and potential). The company may charge a rate based on the probability of death for the two types together, but then A would buy less insurance than B (other things being equal). With time, the insurance company would experience unfavorable results and would have to raise its rate. Some equilibrium rate would emerge, in the absence of information; it would not be the most-efficient allocation. In this case, as Arrow argues, it would not be clear that this free market would be superior to compulsory insurance even though the latter is not efficient because it typically disregards individual differences in risk aversion. To complete the analogy with the entrepreneurial market, it is not clear that a mandatory system of risk allocation that deliberately channels resources from nonentrepreneurial into entrepreneurial activities would not be superior to the absence of such an arrangement.

In fact, rechanneling in the direction of encouragement of entrepreneurial activity is needed precisely because there are forces in our society that are averse and hostile to entrepreneurship. Moreover, these forces are most prevalent among the ranks of past entrepreneurs or the business giants who wish to protect their wealth and their inefficiencies from the invasion of new entrepreneurs by means of inviting regulatory, governmental protection. In our day many businessmen talk about opposing government interference but they in fact oppose it in practice only when their interests are adversely affected. Indeed, as Baumol (1983b) suggests:

. . . . These proponents of free enterprise have regularly undertaken legal actions to curb entrepreneurial activities by others, particularly when those activities threaten to become too successful. And, incidentally, they have unintentionally fueled the activities of the utopian left by joining in the verbiage proclaiming the business community's dedication to its social responsibilities, while systematically and determinately opposing each and every attempt to provide effective measures to bring the associated goals into realization.

The argument Baumol presents is convincing in its simplicity: Once uncertain activities are undertaken, the entrepreneur attempts to keep the risk as low as practicable by hedging, insurance, and diversification. But there is yet another universal, systematic risk which is not easy to diversify against. This is:

the risk that competitors will prove too successful. That alert entrepreneurs will find an opportunity to enter with a better product, a cheaper production technique, a more effective marketing approach, or some other improvements which enable them to take business away from the incumbent. This is a risk for the incumbent but not for society, which will benefit as a result by obtaining a cheaper or a better product.

In seeking to protect themselves from entrants and for inefficient entrants to protect themselves from competent incumbents, propaganda is launched, language is resourcefully manipulated, and terms are invented: "cream skimming," "predatory pricing," "dumping," and "unfair competition." These labels are used to extract tariffs, import quotas, antitrust actions of central authorities, or to launch new private antitrust suits. And again, in Baumol's words:

> from the viewpoint of the public welfare it is simply intolerable. "Cream skimming" often simply refers to a case in which an entrant offers to sell certain products or to certain customers more cheaply than the incumbent can. Similarly, "predatory pricing" often refers to a case in which the shoe is on the other foot. "Dumping" often labels a case in which a foreign seller offers a disturbingly better or cheaper product. In each such case what is a loss to the aggrieved party constitutes a net benefit to the community.

The point we are trying to emphasize here is that we reward the incumbents for expanding old product lines and/or replacing old equipment; one can transfer wealth only from those who are taxed into those appropriating the incentives. One should reverse the direction of those incentives, especially given the observations above that the incumbents enlist all the power at hand to use the sociopolitical process for setting obstacles in the path of entrepreneurial competition.

The kind of uncertainty the entrepreneur faces is one that is extremely difficult to diversify or to share with would-be financiers. In contrast to conventional inventions, the discovery of the entrepreneur relates, according to Fellner (1983), in its pure form exclusively to ". . . how other people will react to specific market opportunities and incentives in circumstances that are new in some essential respects" (p. 40). This assessment of how other people react involves entrepreneurial judgment on which one can rarely find a consensus. Herein lies the difficulty in persuading financiers to invest in this new insight. The entrepreneur's foresight cannot be made noncontroversial among intelligent, well-informed individuals as would be activities involving the manufacturing of routine products and the offering of recurring services. Fellner's analysis of the entrepreneurial function reinforces the views presented above regarding the distinction to be made between entrepreneurship and inventions and innovations. Fellner lists the first element of the entrepreneurial function as the making of judgments that are legitimately controversial among well-informed individuals about the prospective results of using inputs in specific ways which have new characteristics. The second equally important element is achieving the acceptance of those judgments by economic agents so that the inputs are used in accordance with the entrepreneurial judgment. "The 'new' modes of resource application may, but need not, depend on technological inventions of the recent past."

For the entrepreneur who invested his own capital—as used to be the case in earlier times (eighteenth-century)—these judgments and implementation involved considerable risk in that he paid a "certain" price for the goods and services which he acquired for the sake of selling those goods and services for an "uncertain" price. But in those times the entrepreneur was both fulfilling the entrepreneurial function and providing the resources to implement it. In our time, with the separation between owners and entrepreneurs, or more precisely between residual claimants (claimants of residual income) and entrepreneurs, the stockholders or residual claimants must be guided in their investment decisions by confidence in the risk and uncertain entrepreneurial judgment of the agents managing the resources for them. The confidence of the stockholders in the entrepreneurial judgments is essential for their agreement to finance the entrepreneur's novel venture. The entrepreneurs, therefore, must face up to the immense difficulty of convincing the stockholders on the basis of the entrepreneurs' own track records (which are sometimes nonexistent since they have just embarked on their entrepreneurial careers) or their personality characteristics of the soundness of their "controversial" entrepreneurial judgments.

It takes considerable time to develop new products or new processes and to gain the market's acceptance for them. Thus, considerable financial resources are needed to ensure survival of a new business. Indeed, of the new companies organized each year, a significant number fail because of inadequate financing. The kinship and trust relations of antiquity that allowed members of extended families to gain help for their trading and other business activities are no longer available; if they existed, they would be inadequate today. Thus, new market mechanisms must arise to fill the need. Ad hoc venture capital groups will provide initial financing, particularly for products developed from exciting technological breakthroughs. An investment banker assembles a group of private investors to provide the necessary funds. The phenomenon of corporate venturing has emerged in recent years. Some large companies, including Exxon, General Electric, and Citicorp, have set up large venture capital funds which they use to finance promising new ventures. The Small Business Investment Corporation (SBIC) is yet another source. Yet there are still many resources now devoted to incentives to existing businesses in the form of investment tax credit, accelerated depreciation, and the like which instead could move into encouragement of new ventures.

Shapiro, Chairman of the Executive Committee of General Instruments Corporation (1983), reinforced our modeling of the locus of entrepreneurial activities: Those who have accumulated wealth (broadly construed to include all ingredients aforementioned) would not be as eager to embark on the new:

In my experience and in the experience of others, large corporations are not really centered on a vision of the future but rather on the success of the past and the present, their public statements to the contrary notwithstanding. Indeed, the function of a large corporation is typically to preserve (and, if possible, to enlarge) the position already obtained and to administer an empire already conquered. These tasks are best accomplished by professional managers working in teams. In such an environment, it is natural that change works best when it comes slowly.

If one can argue that a major corporation that has matured with managerial executive personnel at the top has all pertinent decisions made by such personnel and that, therefore, it can be likened to a wealthy entrepreneur who has accumulated wealth, then one can understand and "explain" perhaps the decline in basic research which, by necessity, is linked to high uncertainty in major U.S. corporations. Indeed, according to Edwin Mansfield (1983):

The composition of R&D expenditures in many major U.S. industries changed considerably during the late 1960's and 1970's. In practically all industries, the percentage of R&D expenditures devoted to basic research declined. In the aerospace, metals, electrical equipment, office equipment and computer, chemical drug, and rubber industries, this percentage dropped substantially. In some industries, like aerospace, chemicals, metals, and rubber, there was a substantial reduction in the proportion of R&D expenditures devoted to relatively long-term projects (specifically ones lasting five or more years). (p. 104).

One of the reasons offered for this is, according to Mansfield: ". . . there is more emphasis on detailed control, formality in R&D projects selection, and short-term effects on profit. This shift in emphasis has tended to reduce the proportion of R&D expenditure going for basic and long-term projects." All this implies that risk aversion sets in in large corporations. But Mansfield does attribute much of the fault to the environment and to the lack of proper incentives: ". . . The regulatory policies of the government have sometimes resulted in managerial behaviors that do not promote innovation. Also, despite good intentions, the government has not provided a macroeconomic climate that is conducive to many kinds of innovation." (p. 106).

Indeed, Ronen (1983) has commented on the isomorphism between the managerial-type individual and the large corporation and the process of self-selection that virtually excludes the entrepreneurial type from bureaucracies:

The entrepreneur rarely resides in a large, bureaucratic organization. The innovative ideas the entrepreneur seeks to implement (characteristically with high uncertain prospects) sometimes require long periods of incubation. They are thus difficult to defend to those internal-capital allocators who are not so bold, who are less entrepreneurially inclined. This kind of innovative idea can run into a grim fate in a large organization given to incentive schemes that emphasize the short-run, visible-performance measures of management, militating against investment in innovative research. The uncertain results can be visible only in the longer run.

So we see the novelty seeking entrepreneur shy away from the large, little changing organization; conversely, the less entrepreneurial, the managerial type individual seeks association with (and is sought by) the large organization and, when there, discourages entrepreneur adventurers from joining its work force or staying in it. This mutual self-selection can induce a notable incidence of innovative research in small, entrepreneurial firms, while erecting within the large firm an internal capital allocation mechanism of a bureaucratic and relatively non-flexible nature. It is the non-entrepreneurial, managerial type of individual who seems inevitably destined to house the executive suite.

The analysis of the entrepreneur presented in this paper points to the direction that policies should take to encourage entrepreneurship if so desired by society.

If indeed after a certain stage risk aversion increases with wealth accumulation, then the greater ability of the wealthy entrepreneur to give "satisfactory guarantees" in Frank Knight's words (1940) is offset by the higher risk aversion. Indeed, Kihlstrom and Lefont (1979) demonstrate how inefficiencies in the risk allocation caused by institutional constraint on risk trading can arise when individuals are risk-averse. Introduction of any institutional mechanism that facilitates risk trading would eliminate some inefficiencies. The stock market is one such institution, but it does not appear to be sufficient to facilitate the financing of the entrepreneurial risk lovers who do not have sufficient wealth or the track record of success that can easily lure capital. Venture capital firms that pool resources for investment in entrepreneurial ideas are a possible solution. Tax incentives that are reallocated from replacement of what exists into the novel are another.

PERSONALITIES OR SOCIETAL CIRCUMSTANCES: A REVISIT AND CONCLUDING REMARKS

The discussion so far points to an important conclusion: economic and societal circumstances create and shape the entrepreneur and, ultimately, spell his or her success or demise. The entrepreneur's personality and his or her individual traits and idiosyncrasies are not relevant dimensions of analysis when the objective is to focus on regularities in the stimuli that prompt entrepreneurial action.

It was hypothesized above that *any* individual would be characterized by any S-shaped value function in wealth, convex below a reference point which represents the aspiration level of the individual, and concave above it. Economic and social circumstances that "pull down" the individual into lower wealth (broadly construed) will encourage bold entrepreneurial moves, provided the individual is *free* to act on his acquired taste for novelty, unfettered by rules or regulations. And conversely, when good luck, skill, talent, or hard work, as well as exogenous social and economic forces "push" the individual beyond his or her aspiration level into the concave region of the S-shaped value function, entrepreneurial decay is witnessed as the rate of innovating declines. Personal traits ascribed to entrepreneurs may well have developed as a result of entrepreneurial experiences (success or failure) rather than having induced entrepreneurial action. And in any case, personal characteristics would not play as salient a role as economic, social, and cultural circumstances.

Emphasis on the "entrepreneurial act" rather than on the entrepreneur will thus offer analytical enrichment. An individual can be seen as entrepreneurial at certain phases of his life, wealth, and status, and nonentrepreneurial at other phases. If it is desired to encourage entrepreneurial acts, policies must be directed at shaping circumstances that incite the entrepreneurial impulse, that is, manipulate the determinants of innovative engagements.

How is an entrepreneurial act defined? Definitions of entrepreneurship abound in the literature: Countless numbers of transactions have been considered entrepreneurial, but they had no agreed-upon rule of definition and exclusion; that is, without consensus as to whether or not manifesting entrepreneurship.[1] In this paper, I focused on the view of the individual who undertakes a novel venture, where novelty is characterized by the remoteness of the venture from past or existing business engagements: The venture has little in common with familiar product lines or services; hence, it is associated with a higher degree of uncertainty which inevitably results from the lack of experience with similar activities and the relative ignorance concerning potential consequences.

My selection of this definition for discussion and emphasis is not merely a reflection of personal taste (although personal preferences cannot be totally ruled out): The interviews I conducted with representative entrepreneurs reinforced this characterization (Ronen 1983). The above definition is appropriately based on the actions observed to be taken by the individual considered to be entrepreneurial. Indeed, as I have concluded from my interviews (1983) and asserted above, circumstances can affect the degree to which a given individual exhibits entrepreneurial character at different times; hence, it is more fruitful to concentrate on the characterization of the "entrepreneurial act" and the "entrepreneurial events" that preceded the act (see pages 151–54 in my 1983 paper).[2] Concentrating on the entrepreneurial act can perhaps lead to closer identification of factors that encourage sparks of entrepreneurship among individuals hitherto not identifiable as entrepreneurial in any way.

The primary impetus for venturing beyond the routine (existing products and services) is, thus, the quest for novelty (Ronen 1983). Accidentally stumbling on a new market while engaging in routine improvements in, say, a manufacturing process does not exhibit the *purposefulness* of innovation that constitutes the essential entrepreneurial element. But the degree of innovativeness counts and it most likely differs along a continuum of entrepreneurship. Altering a sequence of sewing machines in an apparel factory is not as entrepreneurial as a new method of transport from railroad to airplane. Clearly the latter is more significant. A continuum of entrepreneurship can also be found within the corporation. Common to the continuum is the Knightian "exercise of responsible control," that is, the function of business decision making under uncertainty. But the entrepreneurial function is not restricted to top management, as decision making under uncertainty is faced by a continuum of ranks and positions within an organization. The extreme of the continuum is the simple laborer, placed by Knight in contrast to the entrepreneur.

Among individual businessmen, the vast majority of those who own their own businesses are not entrepreneurial to a significant extent. Most duplicate existing products or services. While there always exists a measure of newness in the start of any engagement, as duplicative as it might be, only a very few ventures are entrepreneurial to a significant degree, if indeed it is the engagement in novelty that characterizes the entrepreneurial act along the continuum. The organizational locus of an individual along that continuum, whether within a corporation or outside it, that is, owning his or her own business, should be of concern only to the *extent that the organizational context (or lack thereof) affects the extent of his or her novel moves*. In large organizations, one can risk human capital as much as owners of businesses might risk financially bold, venturesome novelties. Distinguishing between owners of business whose entrepreneurial output must be marked low from those who exercise novelty at a higher level might contribute to a more lucid discourse on the subject of entrepreneurship. Elsewhere (1985) I suggested that we refer to the former group as "enterprisers" and to the act of launching a new "nonentrepreneurial" business as "enterprising."

The contribution of enterprisers to growth of the economy can be very large indeed. Enterprising, as well as entrepreneurship, needs to be explained and clarified. Leibenstein (1985) ably shows how even the relatively more mundane enterprising activities have eluded standard economic analysis. In his focus on enterprisers, Leibenstein argues for demystification and deromanticization of the entrepreneur. But by defining every business entry as entrepreneurial, might we not lose sight of the more impressive breakthroughs of the Schumpeterian "creative destruction" variety? Unless both acts, the mundane and the novel, can be illuminated by the same intellectual paradigm, we ought to make certain that by addressing the demystified "entrepreneur"—the enterpriser—we do not overlook those who are still shrouded in mystique.

The implications of this distinction are likely to be nontrivial. While, along with Leibenstein, I am comfortable with the notion that an entrepreneur can be both diagnosed and trained, I seriously doubt that individuals about to commit an entrepreneurial act can systematically be identified or trained. In this regard, I am in agreement with Baumol (1983) that, once entrepreneurial ingredients are systematized, they become transformed into a component of management so that elements that remain entrepreneurial elude us. The discussion in this paper has focused on a conceptualization of determinants of entrepreneurial acts. Thus the emphasis is not on an entrepreneur who is distinguishable from nonentrepreneurs, but rather on those circumstances that activate in individuals the entrepreneurial impulse.

NOTES

1. Webster's *Third International Dictionary* (1961) defines the entrepreneur as "the organizer of an economic venture, especially one who organizes, owns, manages and assumes the risk of the business." The Funk and Wagnalls *Standard Dictionary* (1958) similarly defines him as "one who undertakes to start and conduct an enterprise or business, assuming full control and risks." Mill (1909) emphasized as entrepreneurial functions direction, control, superintendence, and risk bearing. To him, risk bearing most sharply distinguished an entrepreneur from a manager. For Schumpeter, the distinguishing factor was innovation; risk taking, he believed, characterized both the entrepreneur and the manager. McClelland (1961) did not even require an entrepreneur to own the business: Any innovative manager could assume decision-making responsibilities. Weber (1930) considered the entrepreneur the ultimate source of formal authority within the

organization, in that character distinguished from the manager. Today, many writers regard any owner-manager of a business to be an entrepreneur.

2. This is in accord with Schumpeter's statement that "we maintain that someone is only then by definition entrepreneur if he implements new combinations—after which he loses this characteristic, where he then continues to manage the founded enterprise systematically." (Schumpeter, 1931, p. 166, as translated by M. DeVries, 1977).

REFERENCES

Arrow, K. J. *Essays in the Theory of Risk-Bearing.* Markham: Chicago, 1971.

Baumol, W. J. "Entrepreneurship and the Sociopolitical Climate." In *Entrepreneurship and the Outlook for America,* edited by J. Backman. New York: The Free Press, 1983a.

Baumol, W. J. "Towards Operational Models of Entrepreneurship." In *Entrepreneurship,* edited by J. Ronen. Lexington: Lexington Books, 1983b.

Brenner, R. *History—the Human Gamble.* Chicago: University of Chicago Press, 1983.

Chiswick, B. R. "Effect of Americanization on the Earnings of Foreign-born Men." *Journal of Political Economy* (October 1978).

Cipolla, Carlo M. *Before the Industrial Revolution: European Society and Economy, 1000–1700.* New York: W. W. Norton, 1976.

Collins, D. F.; Moore, D. G.; and Unwalla, D. B. *The Enterprising Man.* East Lansing: Michigan State University Bureau of Business and Economic Research, 1964.

De Vries, M. F. R., "The Entrepreneurial Personality: A Person at the Crossroads." *Journal of Management Studies* (February 1977): 34–57.

Engelman, U. Z. *The Rise of the Jew in the Western World.* New York: Berman's Jewish Book House, 1962.

Fellner, W. "Entrepreneurship in Economic Theory: The 'Scientific Method' and Vicarious Introspection." In *Entrepreneurship and Outlook for America,* edited by J. Backman. New York: The Free Press, 1983.

Hagen, E. E. *The Economic Development.* Homewood, IL: Richard D. Irwin, 1975.

Houselitz, Bert F. "Entrepreneurship and Capital Formation in France and Britain Since 1700." In M. E. Falkus, *Readings in the History of Economic Growth.* London: Oxford University Press, 1968.

Kahneman, D. and Tversky, A. "Prospect Theory: An Analysis of Decision Under Risk." *Econometrica* (March 1979).

Karaka, D. F. *History of Parsees.* London: Edler Smith, 1884.

Kihlstorm, R. E. and Laffont, J. J. "A General Equilibrium Entrepreneurial Theory: A Front Formulation Based on Risk Aversion." *Journal of Political Economy* 4 (1979).

Knight, F. H. *Risk, Uncertainty, and Profit,* 5th ed. Boston: Houghton Mifflin, 1940.

Kulke, E. *The Parsees in India.* Munich: Welforum Verlag, 1974.

Kuznets, S. *Economic Structure of U.S. Jewry: Recent Trends.* Jerusalem: Hebrew University Press (in Hebrew), 1972.

Leibenstein, Harvey. "Entrepreneurship, Motivation and X-Efficiency Theory." Presented at the meetings of the American Economic Association, New York, December 1985.

Mansfield, E. "Entrepreneurship and Management of Innovation." In *Entrepreneurship and Outlook for America,* edited by J. Backman. New York: The Free Press, 1983.

McClelland, D. C. *The Achieving Society.* Princeton, NJ: Van Nostrand, 1961.

McNeill, W. H. *Plagues and People.* New York: Anchor Books, 1976.

Mill, J. S. *Principles of Political Economy,* edited with an introduction by Siv. W. J. Ashley. New York: Longmans, Green and Co. 1909, as reprinted 1926.

Park, R. E. "Human Migration and Marginal Man." *The American Journal of Sociology* (May 1928).

Ronen, J. A Discussion of Papers Presented at a Session Entitled "Enterprise, Entrepreneurship and Innovation: A Behavioral Approach" at the Annual Meeting of the American Economic Association in New York City, December 30, 1985.

Ronen, J., "Some Insights into the Entrepreneurial Process." In *Entrepreneurship,* edited by J. Ronen. Lexington MA: Lexington Books, 1983.

Shapiro, M. "The Entrepreneurial Individual in the Large Organization." In *Entrepreneurship and Outlook for America,* edited by J. Backman. New York: The Free Press, 1983.

Schumpeter, J. A. *Theorie der Wirtschaftlichen Entwicklung, e Aufl.,* Munchen and Leibzig: Duncker und Humlat, 1931.

Sowell, T. *Race and Economics.* New York: David McKay, 1975.

Toynbee, A. J. *Change and Habit: The Challenge of Our Time.* London: Oxford University Press, 1966.

Tversky, A. and Kahneman, D. "The Framing of Decisions and the Psychology of Choice." *Science* (January 1981).

Veblen, T. "The Intellectual Pre-eminence of Jews in Modern Europe." In *The Portable Veblen,* edited by M. Lerner. New York: Viking Press, 1948.

Weber, M. *The Protestant Ethic and Spirit of Capitalism.* Translated by T. Parsons. New York: Scribner, 1930.

8

TOWARD A NEW PARADIGM

Amitai Etzioni

An often-suggested cure for the considerable difficulties encountered by neoclassical economics is to draw on sister social sciences to provide more "realistic" assumptions about human motivation and institutions (for example, Shultz, 1974; Thurow, 1983; Streeten, 1976; Dunlop, 1977). This approach might be referred to as an attempt to resurrect the traditional field of political economy or institutional economics. However, these terms have acquired over the years specialized meanings not intended by those who call for injection of new psychological and sociological assumptions into the study of economic behavior. Hence the reference to the suggested approach as "socioeconomics" ("neither Samuelson, nor Marx" as one wit put it). I explore here four areas in which progress is being made in fashioning such an alternate paradigm and the difficulties that are being encountered: opening up the preferences; modifying the assumption of rationality (again!); the societal nestling of the market (a matter of institutions and political power); and increasing the empirical, inductive elements of the study of economic behavior.

OPENING UP THE PREFERENCES

If one could register bets on the future developments of social sciences, I would register a bet that the study of the factors that shape preferences will prove to be the most productive staging ground for socioeconomics. Neoclassical economists typically assume that the preferences are stable. Hence, if behavior has changed between two points in time it is typically assumed that the change

This article is based on a concluding presentation by the author to the Middlebury Conference. A previous version was published in *Challenge* (Etzioni, 1986).

"must be" due to changes in "constraints," not in preferences. Thus, observing that in year X Americans consumed less liquor than five years earlier, a neoclassical economist will ask if the price of liquor has increased, the drinking age has been raised, bar hours have been shortened, and so on. Other social scientists will suggest that the rise of a fitness-and-health movement and of a neotemperance movement may explain why the "taste" for liquor has declined. (By the way, the latter is a rather parsimonious interpretation because the same factor may also explain, in part, whatever changes have occurred in constraints; for example, the imposition of higher taxes on "sinful" consumption.)

A neoclassical economist may say that such explanations are "too easy"; one may always assume that tastes have changed. However reference here is to (*a*) empirical evidence that preferences actually have changed in the period specified and (*b*) to spelling out the factors that account for these changes and demonstrating that they have been at work. The first step can be undertaken when one analyzes several movements in the level of consumption of liquor and collects both data about changes in prices (and other constraints) and evidence concerning changes in the social valuation of liquor. Regression analysis can then determine how much of the variance in consumption of liquor is attributed to changes in preferences versus constraints.

Concerning the factors that cause changes in preferences, numerous hypotheses are found in psychological, sociological, anthropological, and political science literature; for instance, in the parts that deal with the dynamics of social movements (Douglas, 1979; Thompson, 1979). However, attempts to demonstrate that these factors are at work have run into three difficulties. First, the social sciences involved are very overdetermined and contested. There are too many factors to be considered and not an agreed list. The list includes, but is not limited to, attributes of leaders, psychic and social attributes of the members, the substance of the values at issue and their internal dynamics, the level of legitimation of established social institutions, the effects of cross-cutting groups, and many others. Significant progress can be expected only after social scientists will agree, as a first approximation, to focus on a shorter and agreed-upon list of factors.

Second, many of the factors involved are difficult to operationalize (for example, emotions) and the correlations of inner mental states of the subjects and their behavior have often been found to be quite low. Recently, though, these difficulties have been reduced and progress has been made in developing various measurements. (Re emotions, see Izard, 1977; Izard, Kagel, and Zajonc, 1977; Zajonc, 1980. Re values, see England, 1967; and Watson and Barone, 1976.)

Without going into detail, a masterful example of such a socioeconomic study well grounded in evidence is the analysis of the causes of crime by Wilson and Herrnstein (1985). The study encompasses neoclassical economic findings, the findings that crime rates reflect "costs" (size, certainty of penalty) and "profits" (size of loot) (Ehrlich, 1973). Wilson and Herrnstein recognize that these factors account for a significant chunk of the variance. However, they also show that another considerable amount is accounted for by differences in preferences, due to such factors as moral socialization (differences in family structures and values) and personality (ability to defer gratification). Similarly, Lewis (1982) showed that both kinds of factors affect the extent of compliance with tax laws, and Stern and Aronson (1984), the conservation of energy.

Possibly the greatest opposition to such an approach is a hidden normative "hang up." Neoclassical economists seem to adhere to the notion that the preferences are fixed, in part, because they fear that if preferences are changeable they also can be manipulated. This would fly in the face of the notion of consumer sovereignty and their cherished assumption of individual autonomy. As Michael S. McPherson pointed out, they are committed to a fallacy by assuming that, if their theory will be free from manipulation, the real world will also be free from it. Possibly once the impossibility of tailoring the world to a theory is brought into the open, resistance to opening up the preferences, a main barrier in the way of more collaboration between economics and other social sciences, will be removed (for additional discussion, see Etzioni, 1985a).

RATIONALITY: HOW MUCH LESS IS ENOUGH

The major second front—and a front it is—between neoclassical economics and the sister social sciences concerns the assumption of rationality. Hardcore neoclassical economists still argue that (*a*) individuals are, or it is productive to assume that they are, rational utility maximizers and (*b*) that if people act nonrationally their behavior is lawless and hence cannot be studied. Ergo, you either assume rationality or leave the realm of science. Sociologists, since the 1840s, have shown that nonrational behavior by subjects of scientific study, the behavior of individuals, can be understood and systematically explained by scientific observers. If a lemming runs off the cliff, all his followers may do so; we, though, will remain standing on the top, observing the effect of the lead lemming.

Attempts to reduce the distance between neoclassical economics and other social sciences on this crucial issue have followed mainly two approaches: relaxing the definition of rationality, and arguing that individual behavior may approximate rationality even if it does not quite qualify. Neither approach seems sufficient.

The first line is illustrated by the notion of "intended rationality," according to which the actor is rational when he/she uses all the information available, in a logical manner based on the actors' assumptions, as distinct from collecting all the information necessary, and using it in line with established rules of reasoning, that is, logically. The trouble with "intended rationality" is that anything goes; it is a concept that does not differentiate and does not help our thinking, explanations, or predictions. Thus, one author argued that a preliterate tribe that maintains a cargo cult (they believe that if they worship a plane that crashed in their woods, more white-man goods will be delivered) act rationally, because according to the information available to them and their logic this makes sense (Shweder, 1986). Such an approach may save the label "rational" but deprives it of content. If the concept does not allow us to distinguish between what a cargo worshiper does and a scientist, between soothsayers and modern management, between rain making and irrigation, between magicians and economists, what is it good for?

The moderating approach, launched by Herbert Simon's "satisficing" and much expanded by recent psychological work, which uncovered various systematic biases in human inferences (Kahneman, Slovic, and Tversky, 1982; Nisbett 1980), is pointing in the right direction for socioeconomics. The main question is whether it goes far enough. These approaches do not deal with the intrusion of emotions and values into inferences and decision making; indeed they explicitly reject these factors (see Nisbett and Ross, 1980, ch. 10) and focus instead strictly on intracognitive limitations. However, as Katona (1975), and a whole stream of psychologists have demonstrated since then (Houthakker and Taylor, 1970; Hansen, 1972; Engel and Blackwell, 1982), people's economic behavior is determined largely by impulse and habits. Neoclassical economists respond that these acts are rational because they reduce transaction costs. For instance, a person who keeps buying at the same supermarket rather than engage in comparative shopping, "must have established" that the savings to be gained that way are smaller than the costs involved (Baumol and Quandt, 1964, make the same point about rules-of-thumb). However, it seems individuals adhere to their habits, especially addictions, long after this point has been passed. And, to apply Winter's well-taken point: Most people are unable to know or calculate the cost and benefits of less versus additional searching. The suggestion that evolution sees to it that only societies (or economies or organizations) with rational rules survive, ignores the fact that very few societies ever cease to survive and that highly inefficient organizations exist right next to more efficient ones.

What is needed is a theory of decision making that assumes a rather low ability to know and to infer logically, and one that recognizes that the selection of means, not just goals, is deeply affected by emotions and values. For important contributions see Janis and Mann (1977) who examine the role of stress in decision making (stress leads most people to over- or undersearch or some other form of pathological behavior) and Schwartz's (1970) model of moral decision making (which shows the significance of feeling responsible. For example, a mother may rush into a fire for her children but not for those of others).

ECONOMIC NESTLING

The role of preference changes, emotions, and values, discussed so far, concerns either the meta assumptions and core concepts of socioeconomics or micro (individual) behavior. Progress is also being made on the macro, collective, institutional level. This is well illustrated by the way markets are conceptualized.

Neoclassical economists tend to assume that the market is basically self-regulating. This notion is deeply rooted, going as far back as Adam Smith's famous point that, following division of labor, people engage in exchanges out of self-interest, not out of benevolence. It finds formal technical expression in works such as those of Walras (1954) and Debreu (1959), who specified the conditions of perfect competition without reference to any exogenous factors. A typical list is: The largest firm in any given industry is to make no more than a small fraction of the industry's sales (or purchases). The firms are to act independently of one another. Actors have complete knowledge of offers to buy or sell. The commodity (sold and bought in the market) is divisible, and the resources are movable among users (Stigler, 1968, pp. 181–82). A neoclassical economist may acknowledge that the values of a society and its government are necessary for the working of a market, but they naturally do not study the specific conditions under which the ethical and political system protect the market.

A core assumption of socioeconomics is that all economies are nestled within a society, which in turn contains specific ethical and political institutions. Their specific attributes determine both whether the market forces are accorded sufficient range for the economy to be able to flourish (for instance, via legitimation of commerce and of entrepreneurship) and whether antimarket forces are contained. These forces emanate not only from the societal-political realm but are also generated by powerful economic actors using both intraeconomic means (for example, predatory pricing to block the entry of new competitors) and political means (for example, lobbying for tariffs, quotas, tax exemptions), and unethical means, violating the trust which lies at the root of all transactions. The ability of the market to function "autonomously" is hence shown, in effect, to be largely affected by the ability of the societal capsule to protect the market from such forces.

Two simple socioeconomic propositions illustrate this approach. *The higher the ethical commitments of individuals who transact with each other, and the stronger the shared norms of proper conduct, all other things being equal, the lower the production costs, the higher the productivity* (Phelps, 1970, pp. 1–9). The reason basically is that, when ethical bonds are low, large amounts of reasoning must be dedicated to lawyers to draft and execute written contracts, to retaining inspectors, accountants, and so on, while when the level of ethics and trust are high, these costs—which add nothing to production, are significantly lower. The high level of theft by employees is found to be a major factor effecting productivity in the United States (Denison, 1979). The low rate of crime in Japan is a major factor in its favor.

Second, the level of industrial concentration is not due merely to changes in intraeconomic strategies (for example, greater use of advertising) but also reflects changes in the regulatory environment (for example, in the enforcement of antitrust laws), and in the political activities of the powerful economic actors (for example, a change from the Republican to the Democratic Party may enhance the ability of auto and steel workers' unions to gain protections; favors Coke over Pepsi; and affects the distribution of routes among American airlines. For additional discussion, see Etzioni, 1985). In short, the level of industrial concentration is determined in part by the extent to which the economic realm is isolated from the political one. This isolation is higher the more private power cannot be converted into political power; for example, when the costs of campaigning for political office are paid by the public (as is the case in U.S. presidential elections) and not by private power wielders (as in the case, in part, for Congress).

Attempts to model such political factors in neoclassical economic terms, that is, as themselves subject to the competition, say among these corporations who organize political action committees (PACs), have not proven quite successful. The need for more traditional political science analyses, especially of coalition formation among interest groups, seems called for. For example, the success of the 1981 American Economic Recovery Act is often attributed only to President Reagan's great communicative powers. When Congress balked, it is said, the President appealed to the country, which flooded Congress with mail. However, the bill was also supported by an unusually wide array of business lobbies which were often in conflict in the past, and since. And the bill was greatly redrafted and much expanded to, in effect, pay off a large variety of special interests. (For details, see Etzioni, 1983, pp. 75–76).

MORE INDUCTION

Neoclassical economics has become increasingly, many believe excessively, deductive (Leontief, 1976). The other social sciences tend to be more inductive. A combined socioeconomic approach may hence serve to restore a balance to the study of economic behavior. Already psychologists, who conduct laboratory experiments and field experiments, and sociologists, using attitude surveys, have enhanced the inductive elements of the study of economic behavior. For instance, survey studies have shown the effect of attitudes on consumer choice (Bearden and Woodside, 1976) and on economic achievement (Maital, Maital, and Schwartz, 1983), and the effects of personal characteristics of the owner/ manager on firm performance (Judd and Powell, 1985).

A "MARKET" FOR SOCIOECONOMICS

In principle there should be no difficulty in adding another interstitial discipline to the academic scene, the way, say, biochemistry was added to those two disciplines. However, there are some reasons to believe that the interest in socioeconomics ranges farther. First, in the private sector there is considerable disappointment with the way MBAs are trained and a growing demand to train future business executives in a broader manner. True, the curricula of business schools already include some classes in psychology and a few in organizational sociology or in political science. However, many business schools are still dominated by neoclassical economics, by formalistic, highly quantitative approaches, and lack an integrated conceptual scheme of the work of firms, markets, and economies. They may teach a course on management by the numbers and one on human relations, but they leave it to the student to integrate these often-conflicting perspectives. The same holds for classes that focus on the firm as a profit-maximizing "black box" versus those that see it as a small subpolity, part and parcel of an encompassing society. Socioeconomics ought to do well here once its conceptual scheme is evolved so that it is able to provide the much-needed balanced and integrating framework.

The public sector, which regularly deals with the "political economy," whether it is economic development in the Third World or reindustrialization of the West, education vouchers, or changes in the institutions that provide health services, requires policy analysts and evaluators who can combine the examination of economic forces with those of other aspects of society, in short, for socioeconomics. To put it in another way, the demand for socioeconomics is quite evident; could the supply be far behind?

REFERENCES

Baumol, William J and Quandt, Richard E. "Rules of Thumb and Optimally Imperfect Decisions." *American Economic Review,* 54 (1964): 23–46.
Bearden, William O. and Woodside, Arh G. "Interactions of Consumption Situations and Brand Attitudes." *Journal of Applied Psychology* 61, no. 1 (1976): 764–69.
Debreu, Gerard. *Theory of Value: An Axiomatic Analysis of Economic Equilibrium.* New York: Wiley & Sons, 1959.
Denison, Edward F. *Accounting for Slower Economic Growth in the United States in the 1970's.* Washington, DC: Brookings Institution, 1979.
Douglas, Mary. *The World of Goods.* New York: Basic Books, 1979.
Dunlop, John T. "Policy Decision and Research in Economics and Industrial Relations." *Industrial and Labor Relations Review* 30, no. 3 (1977): 275–82.
Ehrlich, Isaac. "Participation in Illegitimate Activities: A Theoretical and Empirical Investigation." *Journal of Political Economy* 81 (May/June 1973): 521–65.
Engel, J. F. and Blackwell, R. D. *Consumer Behavior,* 4th ed. New York: Dryden Press, 1982.
England, G. W. "Personal Value Systems of American Managers." *American Management Journal* 10, no. 1 (March 1967): 53–68.
Etzioni, Amitai. *An Immodest Agenda: Rebuilding America Before the 21st Century.* New York: McGraw-Hill, 1983.
Etzioni, Amitai. "The Political Economy of Imperfect Competition." *Journal of Public Policy* 5, part 2 (1985b): 169–86.
Etzioni, Amitai. "Opening the Preferences: A Socio-Economic Research Agenda." *The Journal of Behavioral Economics.* XIV (Winter 1985a): 183–205.
Etzioni, Amitai. "Founding A New Socioeconomics." *Challenge,* Nov.-Dec. 1986: 13–25.
Hansen, F. *Consumer Choice Behavior: A Cognitive Theory.* New York: Free Press, 1972.
Houthakker, H. S. and Taylor, I. D. *Consumer Demand in the United States, 1929–70,* 2d ed. Cambridge, MA: Harvard University Press, 1970.

Izard, Carrol E. *Human Emotions.* New York: Plenum Press, 1977.

Izard, Carrol E., Jerome Kagel, and Robert B. Zajonc (eds.) *Emotions, Cognition and Behavior.* New York: Cambridge University Press, 1984.

Janis, Irving and Mann, Leon. *Decision Making: A Psychological Analysis of Conflict, Choice and Commitment.* New York: The Free Press, 1977.

Judd, Taylor and L. Powell. "The Personal Characteristics of the Small Business Retailer: Do They Affect Store Profits and Retail Strategies?" *Journal of Behavioral Economics* 14, no. 2 (Summer 1985): 59–75.

Kahneman, Daniel; Slovic, Paul; and Tversky, Amos. *Judgment Under Uncertainty: Heuristics and Biases.* Cambridge: Cambridge University Press, 1982.

Katona, George. *Psychological Economics.* New York: Elsevier, 1975.

Leontief, Wassily W. *Essays in Economics: Theories and Theorizing.* White Plains, NY: International Arts and Sciences Press, 1976.

Lewis, Alan. *The Psychology of Taxation.* New York: St Martin's Press, 1982.

Nisbett, Richard E. and Ross, Lee. *Human Inference: Strategies and Shortcomings of Social Judgment.* Englewood Cliffs, NJ: Prentice-Hall, 1980.

Phelps, Edmund S. *Microeconomic Foundations of Employment and Inflation Theory.* New York: W. W. Norton, 1970.

Schwartz, Shalom H. "Moral Decision Making and Behavior." In *Altruism and Helping Behavior: Social Psychological Studies of Some Antecedents and Consequences,* edited by J. Macaulay and L. Berkowitz, pp. 127–41. New York: Academic Press, 1970.

Schultz, George. "Reflection on Political Economics." *Challenge* (March/April 1974): 6–11.

Shweder, Richard A. "Divergent Rationalities." In *Meta Theory in Social Science: Pluralisms and Subjectivities,* edited by R. W. Fiske and R. A. Shweder. Chicago: University of Chicago Press, 1986.

Stern, Paul C.; Aronson, Elliot; et al. *Energy Use: The Human Dimension.* New York: W. H. Freeman and Co, 1984.

Stigler, George J. "Competition." *International Encyclopedia of Social Science.* Vol. 3, pp. 181–86. New York: Macmillan, 1968.

Streeten, Paul. "The Meaning and Purpose of Interdisciplinary Studies: As Applied to Development Economics." *Interdisciplinary Science Reviews* 1, no. 2 (1976): 144–48.

Thompson, Michael. *Rubbish Theory: The Creation and Destruction of Value.* Oxford: Oxford University Press, 1979.

Thurow, Lester C. *Dangerous Currents.* New York: Random House, 1983.

Walras, Leon. *Elements of Pure Economics: Or, the Theory of Social Wealth.* Translated by William Jaffe. Homewood, IL: Richard D. Irwin, 1954.

Watson, J. G. and Barone, Sam. "The Self Concept, Personal Values, and Motivational Orientations of Black and White Managers." *Academy of Management Journal* 19, no. 1 (March 1976): 442–51.

Wilson, James Q. and Herrnstein, Richard T. *Crime and Human Nature.* New York: Simon and Schuster, 1985.

Zajonc, R. B. "Feeling and Thinking: Preferences Need No Inferences." *American Psychologist* 35, no. 2 (February 1980): 151–75.

INDEX

ABOUT THE EDITOR
AND CONTRIBUTORS

Paul J. Albanese is an assistant professor of marketing at the School of Business Administration, University of Michigan, Ann Arbor, and was an assistant professor of economics at Middlebury College from 1983 to 1988.

Amitai Etzioni is university professor and director of the Center for Policy Research at the George Washington University.

Manfred F. R. Kets de Vries is professor of organizational behavior and management policy at the European Institute of Business Administration (INSEAD) and a practicing psychoanalyst.

Shlomo Maital is professor of economics at Technion—Israel Institute of Technology, Israel.

Danny Miller is on the faculty of management at McGill University and the Ećole des Hautes Études Commerciales, Montreal.

Joshua Ronen is professor of accounting at the College of Business and Public Administration, New York University.

Tibor Scitovsky is emeritus professor of economics at Stanford University.

Richard L. Solomon is university professor of psychology at the University of Pennsylvania.

Lester D. Taylor is professor of economics at the University of Arizona, Tucson.

Abraham Zaleznik is Konosuke Matsushita professor of leadership at the Graduate School of Business Administration, Harvard University.